Internationalizing Teaching and Teacher Education for Equity

A volume in
Research for Social Justice: Personal~Passionate~Participatory Inquiry
Ming Fang He and JoAnn Phillion, *Series Editors*

Internationalizing Teaching and Teacher Education for Equity

Engaging Alternative Knowledges Across Ideological Borders

edited by

Jubin Rahatzad
Purdue University

Hannah Dockrill
Purdue University

Suniti Sharma
Saint Joseph's University

JoAnn Phillion
Purdue University

INFORMATION AGE PUBLISHING, INC.
Charlotte, NC • www.infoagepub.com

Library of Congress Cataloging-in-Publication Data

A CIP record for this book is available from the Library of Congress
http://www.loc.gov

ISBN: 978-1-68123-660-5 (Paperback)
        978-1-68123-661-2 (Hardcover)
        978-1-68123-662-9 (ebook)

Printed in the United States of America

CONTENTS

RESEARCH FOR SOCIAL JUSTICE

Personal~Passionate~Participatory Inquiry

Ming Fang He and JoAnn Phillion

Research for Social Justice: Personal~Passionate~Participatory Inquiry is a book series that features social justice research on life in schools, families, and communities. This work connects the personal with the political, the theoretical with the practical, and research with social and educational change. The inquiries demonstrate three distinct and interconnected qualities. Each is personal, compelled by values and experiences researchers bring to the work. Each is passionate, grounded in a commitment to social justice concerns of people and places under consideration. Each is participatory, built on long-term, heart-felt engagement, and shared efforts. The principle aspects of the inquiries that distinguish them from others are that researchers are not detached observers, nor putatively objective recorders, but active participants in schools, families, and communities. Researchers engaged in this form of inquiry have explicit research agendas that focus on equity, equality, and social justice. Rather than aiming solely at traditional

Internationalizing Teaching and Teacher Education for Equity, pages vii–xi

educational research outcomes, positive social and educational change is the focal outcome of inquiry.

Researchers engaged in personal~passionate~participatory inquiry in this series are diverse and their inquiries are far ranging in terms of content, people, and geographic locations studied. Their studies reflect new and exciting ways of researching and representing experiences of disenfranchised, underrepresented, and invisible groups and challenge stereotypical or deficit perspectives on these groups. It is our hope that this book series will inspire preservice and inservice teachers, educators, educational researchers, administrators, and educational policymakers to commit to the enactment of educational and social change that fosters equity, equality, and social justice.

The work in this book series draws on diverse research traditions that promote social justice (Ayers, Quinn, & Stovall, 2008) and the "Democratic Ideal" (Dewey, 1916, pp. 86–88) in education and life. The work of Du Bois (1903/1994), Cooper (1892/1988), Woodson (1933/1977), Freire (1970), and Ayers (2006) has also influenced social justice work in terms of its emphasis on the emancipatory, participatory, and social activist aspects of research. This work builds upon narrative inquiry (Clandinin & Connelly, 2000; Schubert & Ayers, 1999), particularly cross-cultural and multicultural narrative inquiry (He, 2003; He & Phillion, 2008; Phillion, 2002; Phillion & He, 2008) in response to recognition of the complexity of human experience in increasingly diversified societies. These researchers incorporate narrative, story, autobiography, memoir, fiction, oral history, documentary film, painting, and poetry into inquiries. One special quality of their inquiries that distinguishes them from other forms of educational research lies in understanding experience in its own terms rather than categorizing experience according to predetermined structures and theories (Phillion, 1999). Their inquiries are "peopled" with characters, rather than filled with categories and labels. In some forms of traditional educational research, experience is seen, shaped, and written about by the researcher using theoretically derived forms; in effect the experience is determined by the theory. Experience is the starting point of these inquiries and is in the forefront at every stage of research. Their inquiries arise from experiences of researchers and participants, rather than being formulated as abstract research questions, and they proceed by continual reference to experience as field texts are collected, analyzed, and interpreted, and as meanings are crafted.

Researchers engaged in this form of inquiry also draw on critical race theory (Gutierrez-Jones, 2001; hooks, 1991; Ladson-Billings, 1998, 2003; Parker, Deyhle, & Villenas, 1999; Stovall, 2005) and use stories to disclose hidden and silenced narratives of suppressed and underrepresented groups to counter metanarratives that portray these groups as deficient and inferior.

They ask themselves questions about what is missing from the *official story* that will make the problems of the oppressed more understandable. By telling counterstories, researchers recognize the importance of commitment to equity and social justice and their obligation to link inquiry to social and educational change. The explicit aim of democratic and social justice work is to engage with oppressed groups and individuals and empower them to take effective action toward more just and humane conditions.

Three distinct and interconnected qualities, *personal~passionate~participa tory*, permeate the process of these social justice inquiries. Researchers not only collect, but often live in the stories of people with whom they engage in inquiry. They position stories collected in historical, sociopolitical, economic, linguistic, and cultural contexts, and they contextualize their inquiries within struggles of underrepresented individuals and groups. Stories are presented in lifelike ways; readers vicariously experience complexities, contradictions, and dilemmas of people's lives. There is a sense of "being there" and a sense of urgency for change. The stories told challenge orthodoxy, awaken critical consciousness, and create possibilities for change.

The work featured in this book series, embedded in life in schools, communities, and societies on the one hand, and powerful ideas of being human with strong commitment to a just society on the other, are at the heart of social justice work. Researchers begin with conscious reflection on experience to challenge assumptions, "to raise embarrassing questions," and "to confront orthodoxy and dogma" (Ayers, 2006, p. 85). They listen to "issues that marginalized or disadvantaged people speak of with excitement, anger, fear, or hope" (Ayers, 2006, p. 88). They learn directly from individuals and communities about problems and obstacles they face and explore possible solutions by drawing upon the experience and knowledge of participants. Researchers demonstrate strong commitment to the plight of their participants and the injustice embedded in the larger society. This commitment permeates every aspect of life, begins with small changes, and expands to larger contexts.

Personal~passionate~participatory inquiry thrives on the researcher's passionate involvement, strong commitment, and unfaltering advocacy for disenfranchised, underrepresented, and invisible individuals and groups. This passion, commitment, and advocacy can not be cultivated in isolation. Rather, it calls for researchers to work with allies in schools and communities, to take to heart the shared concerns of individuals and groups, to build a community to develop strategies for the enactment of educational and social change that fosters equity, equality, social justice, freedom, and human possibility. Such a community can only flourish when the efforts of researchers join with the efforts of all educational stakeholders—preservice and inservice teachers, educators, administrators, educational policymakers, students, parents, and community members. We hope that the inquiries featured in this series will help social justice researchers and workers of this community move beyond boundaries, transgress orthodoxies, and build a participatory movement to promote a more balanced, fair, and equitable human condition. An expanded community, such as this, embodies possibilities and creates hope for more fulfilling, more equitable, more humane lives in an increasingly diversifying world.

REFERENCES

Ayers, W. C. (2006). Trudge toward freedom: Educational research in the public interest. In G. Ladson-Billings, & W. F. Tate (Eds.), *Education research in the public interest: Social justice, action and policy* (pp. 81–97). New York, NY: Teachers College Press.

Ayers, W. C., Quinn, T., & Stovall, D. (Eds.). (2008). *Handbook of social justice in education.* New York, NY: Routledge.

Clandinin, D. J., & Connelly, F. M. (2000). *Narrative inquiry.* San Francisco, CA: Jossey-Bass.

Cooper, A. (1988). *A voice form the South.* New York, NY: Oxford University Press. (Original work published 1892)

Dewey, J. (1916). *Democracy and education: An introduction to the philosophy of education.* New York, NY: Free Press.

Du Bois, W. E. B. (1994). *The souls of Black folks.* New York, NY: Fine Creative Media. (Original work published in 1903)

Freire, P. (1970). *A pedagogy of the oppressed.* New York, NY: Seabury.

Gutierrez-Jones, C. (2001). *Critical race narratives: A study of race, rhetoric, and injury.* New York, NY: New York University Press.

He, M. F. (2003). *A river forever flowing: Cross-cultural lives and identities in the multicultural landscape.* Greenwich, CT: Information Age.

He, M. F., & Phillion, J. (2008). *Personal~passionate~participatory inquiry into social justice in education.* Greenwich, CT: Information Age Publishing.

hooks, b. (1991). Narratives of struggle. In P. Mariani (Ed.), *Critical fictions: The politics of imaginative writing* (pp. 53–61). Seattle, WA: Bay.

Ladson-Billings, G. (1998). Just what is critical race theory and what's it doing in a nice field like education? *International Journal of Qualitative Studies in Education, 11*(1), 7–24.

Ladson-Billings, G. (Eds.). (2003). *Critical race theory perspectives on the social studies: The profession, policies, and curriculum.* Greenwich, CT: IAP.

Parker, L., Deyhle, D., & Villenas, S. (1999). *Critical race theory and qualitative studies in education.* Boulder, CO: Westview.

Phillion, J. (1999). Narrative and formalistic approaches to the study of multiculturalism. *Curriculum Inquiry, 29*(1), 129–141.

Phillion, J. (2002). *Narrative inquiry in a multicultural landscape: Multicultural teaching and learning.* Westport, CN: Ablex.

Phillion, J., & He, M. F. (2008). *Multicultural and cross-cultural narrative inquiry in educational research.* DeKalb, IL: Thresholds in Education.

Schubert, W. H., & Ayers, W. C. (Eds.). (1999). *Teacher lore: Learning from our own experience.* Troy, NY: Educators International Press.

Stovall, D. (2005). A challenge to traditional theory: Critical race theory, African-American community organizers, and education. *Discourse: Studies in the Cultural Politics of Education, 26*(1), 95–108.

Woodson, C. G. (1977). *The mis-education of the Negro.* Trenton, NJ: Africa World Press. (Original work published in 1933)

PREFACE

Since the year 2000, the internationalist turn in curriculum studies has promised a paradigmatic shift—presumably more inclusive, transnational, and with the potential of transcending the ethnocentric trends of curriculum studies in the United States altogether. The study of curriculum is a broad field that examines questions around the theory and practice of teaching and learning. It is also a field that looks into the intersection between power and politics in the formation of teacher educators and the stated objectives of education. To internationalize the field, from a U.S. perspective, suggests an opening towards other contexts, histories, and ideas as we (educators) reflect on our practice and challenge the institutional structures and forces that have deepened antiintellectualism among educators and established a highly business-oriented model in education.

In Bill Pinar's terms, internationalization was partly developed to "contest the narcissism of the U.S. curriculum studies" (2000, p. 3). Internationalization is defined as an effort that "supports transnational communication," might "produce more defensible metanarratives of curriculum work than nationalism," and "promises deepened understanding of the local and individual through an encounter with the global and collective" (Pinar, 2000, p. 3). As opposed to globalization, in which cultural artifacts, representations, and meanings enter into circulation in the global marketplace, internationalization is not so much about consuming or appropriating other cultural forms, but rather, engaging in dialogue with other ways of knowing, assessing, and/or understanding educational practices in localized contexts.

Internationalizing Teaching and Teacher Education for Equity, pages xiii–xvi
Copyright © 2016 by Information Age Publishing
xiii

Some may argue that globalization is the first step in internationalization, as the capacity to engage in dialogue with "others" depends upon the ability to gain an awareness of other places, ideas, traditions, and worldviews. Globalization, to a certain extent, allows internationalization to happen. In theory, internationalization promotes an opening of the field of curriculum studies, presumably breaking away from the binary codes of core and periphery when it comes to understanding the impacts of geographical borders in relationship to knowledge production (i.e., the power dynamics between knowledge produced in the "West" and the "rest"). Yet, in practice, internationalization requires a profound understanding of the material and social relations that establish local frames of experience in relationship to global systems of social differentiation. It is not enough to think about the benefits of traveling across borders and engaging with others as a form of developing an understanding of difference. The point is to recognize the mutuality between self and other, acknowledge that privilege and disadvantage are co-dependent, and see that localized experiences generate meaning through a historical, cultural, political, and economic exegesis of our globalized social order.

> *"Columbus sailed the ocean blue. He had three ships and left from Spain;*
> *He sailed through sunshine, wind and rain . . . "*

It was not too long ago that the above lyrics were sung in nearly every classroom across the United States. The story of conquest and the "founding" of the Americas has upheld the noble and heroic image of the colonizer, established the foundation for U.S. exceptionalism, and in so doing, expatriated First Nations peoples not to another country, but to the status of permanent outsiders in their native lands. The legacy of conquest and colonization is not unique to the Americas. Conquest, war, and genocide have afflicted every continent, and their legacy continues to be felt in the very fabric of our collective social being. From a decolonial point of view, the soul-wounds of conquest and colonization are actively reproduced in the structural organization of society. That is, our institutions and related economic and social practices reinforce Eurocentric ideas over knowledge and being, racial and gendered hierarchies of difference, the elimination of indigenous languages and ways of life, and attendant acts of inclusion and exclusion in a global system of differentiation. The point here is to reconcile the past with the present. While we cannot undo the acts that have led to wide-scale devastation and historical trauma, we can acknowledge their continued impact on the ways we relate to one another, our lands and all life forms, and to knowledge itself. Internationalization is about deepening our understanding of society as well as creating spaces to generate new thinking about the social, political, ethical, and epistemic considerations of everyday life. In linking knowledge with the history, perspectives, worldview, and logic of the historically oppressed social subjects, dominant knowledge is transformed. Put simply, this should be one of the goals of engaging in transnational dialogue.

With respect to education, the impetus for internationalizing teacher education is clear. Since its inception, formal schooling has been impacted and informed by the social context of the era. Schooling has played a pivotal role in establishing hierarchies of knowledge production, supporting the development of those deemed capable to pursue higher forms of learning, and conditioning those deemed incapable into the lower strata of the social order. Schooling has been assimilative, disciplining, and contributory to a collective experience of subjugation for those whose identities, languages, and knowledge(s) have been silenced in the construction of curriculum and teaching practices. On the other hand, schooling has also shown its potential to be transformative and empowering.

Critical philosophies and pedagogies in education have challenged the legacy of formal schooling and its accompanying disciplinary practices in an attempt to facilitate the full development of teacher and student alike. And in so doing, critical education attempts to resolve the discord between the learning that takes place inside a school's walls and the necessities of our collective community. On this point, teachers are encouraged to remember the contributions of critical thinkers such as Paulo Freire, who in his noteworthy text *Letters to those who Dare Teach* (1998), discussed the importance of attributes such as lovingness and humility among teachers, as well as the necessity for teachers to understand that education is neither a neutral endeavour nor a preoccupation with the technocratic transfer of subject matter from one person to another. And there is also the late philosopher Maxine Greene, who wrote extensively and tirelessly about the importance of the *social imagination,* "the capacity to invent vision of what should be and what might be in our deficient society, on the streets where we live, in our schools" (2000, p. 5). The social imagination encourages teachers to create and recreate themselves, in an effort to develop a vision of schooling as the practice of generating new possibilities for students. The idea is that the principles of care, concern, and equity can incite the imagination and propel teachers to address with courage the need for youth to develop their full potential in education.

In this edited collection, *Internationalizing Teaching and Teacher Education for Equity: Engaging Alternative Knowledges across Ideological Borders*, the contributors have imagined the possibilities of education to address society's ills for a better collective future. From Canada, Honduras, South Korea, Hong Kong, Russia, and the United States, the authors have reflected upon their own practices as teachers with various communities. Together, the authors challenge traditional views of schooling and reorient the reader's gaze to the lived experiences of communities as the source to generate transformative teaching and learning. They demonstrate that teacher education is not an easy task. It requires commitment, creativity, and self-reflection. The hope, however, is that education can serve a broader mission to support our collective wellbeing. And to accomplish that, teachers need to listen to the unfamiliar voices that reside in distant places. Teachers can learn from one another, be empathetic towards the conditions of others who seemingly have less, and challenge themselves to recognize their own biases and dispositions. In the end, education should be about improving ourselves *with* others. It is a dialectical relationship, one that can open our minds to histories untold and radicalize our imagination and skills for a more humane society, one in which many worlds fit.

—Nathalia Jaramillo
Atlanta, Georgia, U.S.A.
Kennesaw State University

REFERENCES

Freire, P. (1998). *Teachers as cultural workers: Letters to those who dare teach.* Boulder, CO: Westview Press.

Greene, M. (2000). *Releasing the imagination: Essays on education, the arts, and social change.* San Francisco, CA: Jossey-Bass.

Pinar, W. F. (2000, November). *The internationalization of curriculum studies.* Paper presented at the biannual meeting of the Mexican Council of Educations' National Conference on Education Research, Guadalajara, Mexico. Retrieved from   http://www.riic.unam.mx/doc/Internationalizaton_Curriculum_W_PINAR_(MEXICO).pdf

INTRODUCTION

TEACHER EDUCATION, HISTORICAL AMNESIA, AND THINKING OTHERWISE

Jubin Rahatzad and Hannah Dockrill

The aim of this edited volume is to represent multiple perspectives the work towards imagining alter-globalizations as a form of resistance and alterity to the hegemonic designs of neoliberal ideology. While taking up internationalization as a North American/Western-based concept, the collection of research presented in this book seeks to disrupt ethnocentric and ideological norms through questioning normalized constructions of knowledge and through building knowledges from various lived experiences that influence teaching and teacher education. In addition to geographical travel, and perhaps in place of political and physical borders, the ideological borders that delineate international teacher education research are challenged by many of the authors herein. Alternatives to neoliberal economic globalization exist and flourish beyond the ideological confines of neoliberalism and, when globalization "stumbles," break through the veneer of teleological "progress" (López, 2007). The viewpoints presented by scholars in this book think through many of the assumed benefits of internationalization from various vantage points and remind us that other ways of being and

Internationalizing Teaching and Teacher Education for Equity, pages xvii–xxviii
Copyright © 2016 by Information Age Publishing
All rights of reproduction in any form reserved.

thinking have not been erased. We hope that the contributions within this book, taken together, open discussions about the ways that colonial social relations continue to define the project of education, and critique the ideals of modernity. Our desire is that scholars within teaching and teacher education will strengthen their challenge to hegemonic designs.

To imagine equitable social relations necessitates an ontoepistemological decolonization on the part of all educators. This is a demanding task for educational scholars as the commercialization, privatization, and wholesale dismantling of public education impose an ideology that seeks to influence educators' minds (e.g., Watkins, 2012). The process of ontoepistemological decolonization on the horizon of research in education challenges the status quo of neoliberal ideology, which flourished after nation-states underwent legalistic, political decolonization but remained within a system still maintained by the original colonizers. Spivak (2012) has stressed the need for a different approach to education (research and practice) in an era of globalization; thus, alternatives must come from multiple, and often dissenting, voices based on a multiplicity of backgrounds. Baker (2009) provides an additional call for new forms of engagement in the process of internationalization: "Transnational educational research has convincingly shown . . . that former theoretical constructs, such as self and nation-state, no longer remain adequate to the task of describing or understanding current issues in schools" (p. 25). The issues within international teaching and teacher education are rooted in historical and systemic patterns of reproduction of inequalities that are most often acknowledged and addressed outside of educational research. Within the process of the internationalization of teacher education, there is a need to consider different perspectives to address the significant issues of social inequities.

COLONIALITY

This identity of the men of the "New World" was to be put on trial and judged by the jury of its conquerors. So it was to be the dominators who ultimately decided this supposed humanity.
—Zea, 1988–1989, p. 36

Zea's astute description of the initial interactions between peoples of the "New World" and the Western European conquerors still applies to the relationship between episteme that have been ranked by supposed value and the constricting processes of Enlightenment rationality over the last 500 years. Coloniality developed in parallel to modernity. Planetary social relations have been shaped by Eurocentric mindsets based on a hierarchical system of valuing people, places, traditions, and, ultimately, knowledges.

European knowledges have been set as standards, through the processes of colonization and the maintenance of colonial social relations, by which other ways of knowing, whole systems of knowledge, are judged. Educational research should move toward understanding othered knowledges on their own accord, by their own standard. The ontoepistemological process of decolonization is the horizon from which transformative educational research jumps. It is not a "working from within," but just *working*, whether from outside or across or within a dominant Eurocentric viewpoint. Attempting to construct more equitable social relations within the project of education requires the inclusion of other ways of knowing on equitable terms, not just in comparison to the contemporary dominant understandings.

The conquerors determined a system in which political liberation (legal, political decolonization) limited the possibilities of how groups of humans can self-define. The contemporary case of Kosovo demonstrates the complex issues of self-definition by people. The original colonizers and the inheritors of power (e.g., the United States) direct and determine cases, such as self-determination of groups in the Balkans before and after the end of the Cold War. The case of Kosovo and Serbia, for example, is complex and nuanced; however, powerful nation-states continue to determine what is possible within a system of nation-states based on colonial social relations. The façade of human rights and the identification of a tyrannical enemy (Slobodan Milošević) seem to override any historical understandings of a region of the world that has intermixed histories of various groups of people. The case of Kosovo is illustrative because it demonstrates the catastrophe of finalized understandings as the focus of global news before the media moves onto another topic. One contemporary propagandistic catastrophe we find ourselves glossing over instead of deeply interrogating is the United States' "War on Terror."

At the time of writing this introduction, the release of Shaker Aamer, a British resident who was detained by the United States for 14 years without charge, is attracting media attention. We choose to employ this example because we hope that readers in the future look to the case of Shaker Aamer to recognize how such injustices often fall away from our understandings of our social world. The case of Shaker Aamer can be placed within a larger pattern of injustice created by those seeking to maintain power, despite claims of serving the greater good. Aamer's wrongful detention and torture (Norton-Taylor, 2015; Walker, 2015) flout any human rights sensibilities that the majority of United Staters and Britons claim to hold. Yet, most United Staters and Britons seem to have reached a place of daily normality that ignores the premise of the "War on Terror" (Lipstiz, 2014).

In fact, U.S. President Barack Obama announced in May 2013 that the "Global War on Terror" was over (Shinkman, 2013). This announcement is laughable for several reasons. If the "War on Terror" is indeed a "global" (international) effort, as the rhetoric implies, then why is it the president of the United States who declares whether it is ongoing or has ended? Why must the "Global War on Terror" be transitioned to specific conflicts that defend U.S. national interests, with the assumption that U.S. national interests should be defended by all? Indeed, why the assumption that the United States *has* national interests that deviate from a portfolio of profit-seeking, corporate interests? Also absurd about Obama's statement is the lived reality of Muslims in the United States and other Christian-majority societies. Islamophobia was so extended through the "War on Terror" that it is now firmly entrenched as a normalized viewpoint in the psyche of many U.S. residents. Propagandists have successfully fulfilled their function, carried out through the rhetoric of fearing unknown Others.

A direct, material manifestation of such a mindset toward an Other that has been Orientalized (Said, 1978), while the United States has been Occidentalized (Mignolo, 2000), is the Obama administration's decision to militarily intervene in Syria (with the stated goal of countering the Islamic State, without acknowledging the reality that U.S. and Russian troops will be on the ground in Syria in a "post" Cold War world). As one columnist described the U.S. government's decision to intervene militarily in Syria, "This is the latest in a series of U-turns and broken promises that further cements our Forever War" (Timm, 2015, para. 1). The words of government officials and powerful elites are not empty, but tactical and strategic in their unfounded nature. The world in which we currently exist has our leaders stating that the "Global War on Terror" is over because we do not want to be engaged in an endless war, yet the Forever War continues. Anything goes to maintain power. Anything can be said by those in power. We continue living beyond the absurd and tragic.

Colonialism is often viewed as a contained occurrence that exists in the past. Educational researchers seldom understands planetary social relations as being imbued not only with the legacy of colonialism, but actually structured by the concept of coloniality (Mignolo, 2000; Rizvi, 2007). The cases of Kosovo and the "War on Terror" provide examples of the hegemony of Eurocentric epistemologies in framing and understanding social and material realities. The ontological understanding of non-Europeans—Others, from a Eurocentric worldview—does not influence the epistemological construction of the globe. The globe itself has been constructed with such an "ignore-ance"—with particular divisions, cartographies, layouts, spatial recognitions, myths, delineations, carvings, and imaginations that exclude other possibilities for understanding the earth. A spinning globe sitting on a table epitomizes specific ways of knowing. The presumed inevitability of the nation-state system has masked planetary social relations in a shroud of sophistication, despite the lived reality of clan allegiances at various levels. The rhetoric of inevitable progress and increased interconnectedness privilege a world that has never been before, yet we are from the past and continue the past into the present and future. We have constructed social relations that have supposedly never been before, but that must have been in various trading leagues, social systems, and planetary interactions prior to the past 500 years of the colonial world system.

The alternatives we seek have always and do exist. The postcolonial is not a temporal understanding, but rather one of resistance and existence from the initial moment of interaction between Indigenous populations and Western European colonizers. The "advancements" of modernity would not have been possible without the hierarchical setup of colonial social relations. Educational researchers have an ethical responsibility to strive for social equity through an understanding of coloniality as a normalized atmosphere.

INTERNATIONALIZATION NORMALIZED

If we, as educational scholars and members of local and global communities, are to seriously undertake a process of ontoepistemological decolonization, we must reconsider what we experience as normalized environments of being. Shahjahan (2015) discusses how "taken-for-granted" concepts like time and temporality represent a colonial logic that normalizes social contexts and reifies colonial binaries:

> Linear Eurocentric notions of time were used to sort individuals into opposing categories such as intelligent/slow, lazy/industrious, saved/unsaved, believer/heathen, developed/undeveloped, and civilized/primitive; in the process, most of the world's people and their knowledge came to stand outside of history. (p. 490)

The curricular and pedagogical implications of altering our sense of time, for example, are important because they illustrate interpolated beliefs about how we should live our lives.

The internal colonization of temporal understandings relates to questions at the personal and the systemic level. As we engage in educational research we ask, what is at stake? For whom, and why? Why is action taken? What is considered "action"? How are social relations conceived?

As education scholars endeavor to push forward the internationalization of teaching and teacher education, a pragmatic pause may be in order. Our research suggests the need to reflect on the internationalization of teaching and teacher education as the acquisitive model of study abroad sells cultural capital to U.S. university study abroad participants (e.g., Dockrill, Rahatzad, & Phillion, 2015; Phillion, Malewski, Rodriguez, Shirley, Kulago, & Bulington, 2008). What of the host communities in which U.S. university students study abroad? What is the nature of that relationship? Much as Wilson (1982) questioned the nature of certain international cross-cultural experiences over 30 years ago, scholars in the field of education must demonstrate a commitment to asking difficult questions.

Self-reflexivity is paramount in the examination of the internationalization of teaching and teacher education. While the self-reports from study abroad participants about their transformation and newly formed (rarely defined) "global competence" are plentiful, it is productive to consider how "uncritical and celebratory articulations of global citizenship potentially legitimize, enact and expand, rather than mitigate the unfettered international power of the U.S." (Zemach-Bersin, 2011, p. 89). Coloniality must be named as the past *and* the present source of global injustice (Mignolo, 2012). Martin and Griffiths (2012) highlight the importance of naming coloniality *if* our objective is to expand and challenge study abroad participants' worldviews: "Participants' attention is naturally drawn to the most obvious difference, that of inequality in the world *today*, without necessarily understanding the influence of the *past*... which potentially denies an understanding of how that inequality came about" (p. 909). Similarly, Kinginger (2010) suggests:

> As researchers, we should move beyond our focus on American students and their perceptions, and design studies including the students' host families, teachers, and program administrators. We need studies moving beyond description and into analysis of student experience in relation to sociocultural contexts, including the local settings frequented by the students and the students' own histories of engagement in language learning. (p. 225)

International cross-cultural interactions can also maintain certainties of modernity and coloniality insidiously through, for example, Ogden's (2007–2008) metaphor of the "colonial veranda," wherein study abroad participants "remain within the comfortable environs of the veranda while observing their host community from a safe and unchallenging distance" (p. 36). The re-entry home from international cross-cultural experiences is a significant, if not the most important, aspect of educational programs that aim to broaden the perspectives of participants. Program leaders and educational scholars have the ethical responsibility to understand systemic inequalities in participants' home societies (which, in the case of much of the research published on this topic, is usually the U.S.), and work with participants to identify and focus on injustice at *home* instead of looking "over there" with a deficit view. Bartolome (2004) attributes some of the undesired and unintended outcomes of study abroad, such as reinforcements of negative stereotypes, to the fact that students are often left to make sense of their experiences alone, without facilitation. Working to combat these outcomes, Bartolome suggests:

A well-conceptualized teacher education program would foresee and plan for this type of student reaction. At the very minimum, debriefing sessions designed to deal with dominant ideologies and resulting social hierarchies in Mexico and in the U.S. would serve to increase students' understanding of oppression. This would also require an in-depth analysis of the devastating effects that international trade "agreements" like NAFTA have on the people, economics, and politics of both nations. Unfortunately, educators are rarely encouraged to explore how nations, like the U.S. and Mexico, via a long history of foreign and economic policies, are intertwined socially, politically, and culturally. (pp. 117–118)

The ideas of Bartolome (2004), Zemach-Bersin (2011), Mignolo (2012), Martin and Griffiths (2012), Kinginger (2010), and many other scholars doing critical work in this area provide direct points for all educational researchers doing international work to consideration. Superficial multicultural aims are not sufficient in the internationalization of teaching and teacher education (Rahatzad, Ware, & Haugen, 2013). Conceptualizations like "global citizen" must be complexified through nuanced understandings that consider multiple vantage points. Each chapter offers a consideration of what is possible in the pursuit of more equitably constructed social relations.

BRIEF OVERVIEW OF THE BOOK

The book chapters have been placed to speak to neighboring chapters. Diane Watt provides a possible ethical reconceptualization of education with her chapter "Toward the Internationalization of Teacher Education for Social Justice: Interrogating our Relation to Difference in between *Here* and *There*," suggesting the need to understand how a Eurocentric standard can be decentered as an ethical imperative to understanding Others on their own terms. Encouraging the negotiation of difference within teacher education programs is one way of decentering Eurocentric epistemologies that influence our well-intentioned humanist actions.

Watt focuses on the colonial social relations that inform our lived experiences and suggests critical self-reflection as a strategy within the internationalization of teacher education to take a step back from the neoliberal project of global homogenization. Watt shares a personal narrative based on her experiences as a White, non-Muslim woman living in Muslim societies, and in doing so demonstrates an academic honesty that is seldom found in educational research. A nuanced reflection of intermixed histories demonstrates the benefits of avoiding static certainties when engaged in education at all levels.

Helen Marx's chapter, "Preparing Culturally Responsive Teachers: An Intercultural Developmental Approach," provides grounding in the definitions of culturally responsive teaching and intercultural competence, exploring specific ideals related to providing equitable opportunities in schools to all students. Marx illustrates a strategy for pushing preservice teachers to become relationally adept at "getting" students. She proposes international cross-cultural experiences as one way of challenging preservice teachers' preconceptions about Others. Anatoli Rapoport contributes to this discussion with the chapter "In Search of Framework for Teaching Global Citizenship and Social Justice." Rapoport presents some of the challenges and benefits of defining and enacting a global citizenship model for teacher education, suggesting that social justice is at the heart of the debate for what defines global citizenship. The definition of social justice is explored with the goal of critical self-reflection in teacher education. Rapoport examines the prospects of social media, electronic communication, and international cross-cultural experiences as means to develop a new form of socializing preservice teachers as active global citizens.

Sandro Barros critically examines some of the oft-assumed benefits of study abroad in his chapter, "Power, Privilege, and Study Abroad as 'Spectacle.'" Using Guy Debord's concept of "spectacle" and Augusto Boal's theorization of the social dimension of Western drama, Barros explores the ways in which power and privilege shape the discourse around study abroad programs.

Kadriye El-Atwani's chapter, "Teaching Social Justice within Other Communities: Study Abroad Coordinators' Perspectives on the Impacts of Community Practices in Honduras, India, and Tanzania," discusses how study abroad program leaders construct interactions for preservice teacher program participants with members of the host communities they are visiting. El-Atwani ties together program leader experiences from three different contexts in the examination of how preservice teachers actively participate in their own learning. Connections between schooling and society made by preservice teachers illustrate how international cross-cultural experiences are utilized from a programmatic perspective to focus on social inequities. El-Atwani emphasizes the aim of social justice and the importance of host communities' roles as educators as an intentional design to directly challenge preservice teachers' prior conceptions about Others.

Eloisa Rodriguez, Suniti Sharma, and JoAnn Phillion focus on the conceptual implications from the examination of a rural Honduran community school in their chapter "Community Schooling in Honduras: A Simulated Dialogue with Freire, Dewey, and Pinar." From teacher educator perspectives, the social justice aims of the rural Honduran community school are outlined as examples to draw on for rethinking educational priorities in other contexts. Rodriguez, Sharma, and Phillion acknowledge the limitations of the Honduran context but demonstrate how more equitable social relations can be pursued despite institutional challenges. The understandings of place-based and contextual examinations are imperative to conceptualizing alternatives to dominant trends of predetermined curriculum.

Sunnie Lee Watson's chapter, "Rethinking Teachnology—'Technology as a Public Good': Examining the Korean Government's Policy for Bridging Digital Inequality," critically examines the assumption that information technology and access to electronic communication would reduce social inequity. Watson addresses the uneven distribution of information access in South Korea, one of the most "connected" nation-states in the world. The digital divide is of concern to the national Korean government and has implications for formal and informal educational opportunities. Approaches to equitable access can be adapted to other contexts from Watson's analysis of the Korean case.

Nastaran Karimi, Reiko Akiyama, and Yuwen Deng examine concepts around equity from the perspective of international students in the U.S. in their chapter "Sociocultural Alienation of Female International Students at a Predominantly White University." As doctoral students in the U.S. from different countries, Karimi, Akiyama, and Deng provide testimonies of international cross-cultural experiences through their navigations of novel higher education norms. Their work as teacher educators has direct connections to their personal experiences, and implications for all educators to explore social equity at the personal level. Karimi, Akiyama, and Deng depict various challenges in adapting to U.S. society.

Betty Eng's chapter, "Ethnic Minority Students in Hong Kong," relates to the concept of cultural outsiders with specific focus on students. The marginalization of ethnic minorities throughout the social context of Hong Kong accentuates the experience of ethnic minority students in the school system. Eng outlines the disparity in opportunities experienced by minority groups in Hong Kong and explores curricular, policy, and social changes. Eng seeks to recognize the difficulties of being a cultural outsider when dominant social perceptions limit access to opportunities. The need for rethinking what it means to include all students is evident in Eng's proposals for change.

In the chapter "Professional Development for 'Professional Pedagogues': Contradictions and Tensions in Reprofessionalizing Teachers in Cyprus" by Stavroula Philippou, Stavroula Kontovourki, and Eleni Theodorou, tensions around retraining elementary teachers are embraced as a productive space of new understanding. Practicing teachers' needs must be met with the cultivation of learning communities so that any professional development is not just forced upon them. Philippou, Kontovourki, and Theodorou emphasize the ethical responsibility to practice democratic ideals within a critical reorientation of teachers' dispositions. If the goal is to foster pedagogical independence through professional development, then in this case the means belie the goal. Philippou, Kontovourki, and Theodorou suggest seeking a balance between guidance and autonomy in the discussion of how professional development should engage practicing teachers.

Inna Abramova's, chapter "Across Cultural Boundaries: Immigrant Teachers as Potential for Dialoguing," explores the potential of Russian immigrant teachers' experience teaching in the U.S. for the purpose of recognizing teachers as professional intellectuals. The link between emotional, sociocultural, and professional experiences and development highlight the ability of immigrant teachers to practice across differences with beneficial outcomes for all. Abramova keenly demonstrates a rethinking by immigrant teachers and domestic students alike as part of the learning process of teachers. The importance of understanding learning across differences is paramount to a social justice aim in education as the U.S. populace becomes increasingly diverse.

It is our aim that all readers, but perhaps especially graduate students, teacher educators, educational researchers, policymakers, and cultural workers, will find motivation to contemplate the seemingly impossible in rethinking social norms toward a socially equitable planet. The social project of education, inside and outside of schooling, is ontoepistemological in nature. The intimate knowledges of various local communities can translate into new hybrid understandings through border thinking (Mignolo, 2000). Border thinking is reflection, imagining, and contemplating between, across, and along the border(s) of two or more knowledge systems. The intermixed histories of the past 500 years of the colonial world system are valuable through recognition that pluralistic approaches are possible to understanding the social world. The collection of chapters will hopefully ignite and challenge readers to engage in the process of ontoepistemological decolonization for the enrichment of all involved in the social project of education.

REFERENCES

Baker, B. (2009). Western world-forming? Animal magnetism, curriculum history, and the social projects of modernity. In B. Baker (Ed.), *New curriculum history* (pp. 25–68). Rotterdam, NL: Sense Publishers.

Bartolome, L. I. (2004). Critical pedagogy and teacher education: Radicalizing prospective teachers. *Teacher Education Quarterly, 31*(1), 97–122.

Dockrill, H., Rahatzad, J., & Phillion, J. (2015). The benefits and challenges of study abroad in teacher education in a neoliberal context. In J. A. Rhodes & T. M. Milby (Eds.), *Advancing teacher education and curriculum development through study abroad programs* (pp. 290–305). Hershey, PA: IGI Global.

Kinginger, C. (2010). American students abroad: Negotiation of difference? *Language Teaching, 43*(2), 216–227.

Lipstiz, G. (2014). Teaching in a time of war and the metaphor of two worlds. In B. Ngo & K. K.

Kumashiro (Eds.), *Six lenses for anti-oppressive education: Partial stories, improbable conversations* (2nd ed., pp. 283–290). New York, NY: Peter Lang.

López, A. J. (2007). Introduction: The (post)global south. *The Global South, 1*(1), 1–11.

Martin, F., & Griffiths, H. (2012). Power and representation: A postcolonial reading of global partnerships and teacher development through North-South study visits. *British Educational Research Journal, 38*(6), 907–927.

Mignolo, W. D. (2000). *Local histories/global designs: Coloniality, subaltern knowledges, and border thinking.* Princeton, NJ: Princeton University Press.

Mignolo, W. (2012). Coloniality: The past and present of global unjustice. Retrieved from http://waltermignolo.com/coloniality-the-past-and-present -of-global-unjustice/

Norton-Taylor, R. (2015, October 31). Shaker Aamer's Guantánamo detention is a shameful episode for Britain. *The Guardian.* Retrieved from http:// www.theguardian.com/world/2015/oct/31/shaker-aamers-guantanamo -detention-is-a-shameful-episode-for-britain

Ogden, A. (2007-2008). The view from the veranda: Understanding today's colonial student. *Frontiers: The Interdisciplinary Journal of Study Abroad, 15*, 35–55.

Phillion, J., Malewski, E., Rodriguez, E., Shirley, V., Kulago, H., & Bulington, J. (2008).

Promise and perils of study abroad: White privilege revival. In T. Huber-Warring (Ed.), *Growing a soul for social change: Building the knowledge base for social justice* (pp. 365–382). Greenwich, CT: Information Age.

Rahatzad, J., Ware, J., & Haugen, M. (2013). Chocolate-covered Twinkies: Social justice and superficial aims in teacher education. In L. C. de Oliveira (Ed.), *Teacher education for social justice: Perspectives and lessons learned* (pp. 35–52). Charlotte, NC: Information Age.

Rizvi, F. (2007). Postcolonialism and globalization in education. *Cultural Studies— Critical Methodologies, 7*(3), 256–263.

Said, E. W. (1978). *Orientalism.* New York, NY: Pantheon.

Shahjahan, R. A. (2015). Being 'lazy' and slowing down: Toward decolonizing time, our body, and pedagogy. *Educational Philosophy and Theory, 47*(5), 488–501.

Shinkman, P. D. (2013, May 23). Obama: 'Global War on Terror' is over. *U.S. News and World Report.* Retrieved from http://www.usnews.com/news/ articles/2013/05/23/obama-global-war-on-terror-is-over

Spivak, G. C. (2012). *An aesthetic education in the era of globalization.* Cambridge, MA: Harvard University Press.

Timm, T. (2015, October 30). US special forces in Syria are Obama's latest broken foreign policy promise. *The Guardian.* Retrieved from http://www.theguardian.com/commentisfree/2015/oct/30/us-special-forces-syria-obamas -latest-broken-foreign-policy-promise

Walker, P. (2015, November 1). Shaker Aamer feared US would spike his food on flight home. *The Guardian.* Retrieved from http://www.theguardian.com/world/2015/nov/01/shaker-aamer-eat-drink-flight-us-authorities-spike-food

Watkins, W. H. (Ed.). (2012). *The assault on public education: Confronting the politics of corporate school reform.* New York, NY: Teachers College Press.

Wilson, A. (1982). Cross-cultural experiential learning for teachers. *Theory into Practice, 21*(3), 184–192.

Zea, L. (1988–1989). Identity: A Latin American philosophical problem. *The Philosophical Forum, XX*(1–2), 33–42.

Zemach-Bersin, T. (2011). Entitled to the world: The rhetoric of U.S. global citizenship education and study abroad. In V. de Oliveira Andreotti & L. M. T. M. de Souza (Eds.), *Postcolonial perspectives on global citizenship education* (pp. 87–104). New York, NY: Routledge.

CHAPTER 1

TOWARD THE INTERNATIONALIZATION OF TEACHER EDUCATION FOR SOCIAL JUSTICE

Interrogating Our Relation to Difference in Between Here and There

Diane Watt

My story, no doubt, is me, but it is also, no doubt, older than me.
—Trinh, 1989, p. 123

ABSTRACT

I often see myself in the teacher candidates I meet in my Bachelor of Education courses. Entangled in the humanist language of Canadian multiculturalism, for years I imagined school and society as benevolent sites open to the Other. Similarly caught up in humanist discourses, students from dominant "White" cultures often find it difficult to believe that systemic racism and oth-

Internationalizing Teaching and Teacher Education for Equity, pages 1–19
Copyright © 2016 by Information Age Publishing
All rights of reproduction in any form reserved.

er forms of exclusion continue to exist in our schools and in broader societal contexts. They arrive in the program with an understanding of colonialism as a historical period rather than a worldview that continues to live on in our minds and bodies through binaries that hierarchically divide up the world and our place in it. My own assumptions began to unravel during the years I lived in Islamabad, Damascus, and Tehran. However, it was not until I had the critical language to re/read my own encounters with difference that I could appreciate the enormity of the personal and public tasks we face as educators in this era of globalization. To engage the question of how we might further the project of decolonization in teacher education, I turn to life writing as curriculum inquiry. By juxtaposing theory with stories of lived experience in between *here* (working with teacher candidates at a large Canadian university), and *there* (living and traveling abroad), I write decolonizing perspectives into the internationalization of teacher education for social justice.

INTRODUCTION

Preparing teachers to negotiate difference is critical to the internationalization of teacher education for social justice given the global transformations of the past two decades, such as advances in technology, increased student and faculty mobility, and economic factors. How we read difference matters—whether it is students in our classrooms, or portrayals of Otherness in the mass media.[1] There has recently been a great deal of attention focused on Muslims in Western nations due to terrorist attacks, overseas conflicts, global migration, and the ongoing war on terror. Although the estimated 1.6 billion Muslims worldwide (Pew Research Center, 2011) represent an extremely diverse population, in Western societies there is a tendency to view Muslims through a reductive lens. Kincheloe (2004) reminded us that "there is no essentialized, unified Islamic world about which we can make uncomplicated generalizations" (p. 20), and yet fixed meanings proliferate in the discursive contexts of schooling, society, and mainstream media. For this reason, teacher candidates need to be attentive to othering processes, which potentially have material effects in between individual, national, and international contexts.

Traditional approaches to multicultural education place the emphasis on learning *about* the other without taking the *self* into account. This is a critical omission given our entanglement in language and the relational nature of identities and cultures (Aoki, 2005a, 2005b; Bhabha, 1994; Todd, 2003). As Willinsky (1998) pointed out, the enormity of imperialism's educational project lives on for many as an unconscious aspect of our eduction. The binary oppositions of humanism—self/other, us/them, East/West, center/margin—represent the "violent hierarchy on which imperialism is based and which it actively perpetuates" (Ashcroft, Griffiths, & Tiffon, 1998, p. 24). Teacher candidates who are able to deconstruct their relation to difference through the interrogation of binaries may be more likely to understand "why differences of color and culture, gender and nationality, continue to have such profound consequences" (Willinsky, 1998, p. 1). In this chapter, I share my efforts to decolonize my own relation to difference as an example of what such processes might look like for teacher education. This involves deconstructing my encounters with difference while living abroad in predominantly Islamic countries, upon return home to Canada, and in the mass media, with a focus on my relation to Muslim women.

I work as a teacher educator at two large Canadian universities in the areas of curriculum studies, critical literacies, and cultural studies. My doctoral research juxtaposed the following three interrelated strands of knowledge to engage my relation with Muslim women: (1) critique of representations of Muslim females in the mass media, (2) autoethnographic (Morawski & Palulis, 2009) inquiry into my own processes of othering, and (3) inquiry into the experiences and sense of identity of Muslim, Canadian, female high school students against the backdrop of global tensions (Watt, 2008, 2011a, 2011b, 2012, 2013). Together our voices complicate difference and speak back to schooling and media discourses that construct Muslim women as Other.

My interest in this topic was provoked by the unsettling juxtaposition of lived experience in Pakistan, Syria, and Iran during the 1990s and my experiences back home in Canada shortly before the tragic terrorist attacks of September 11, 2001. As Trinh (1989) suggests, "travelling can . . . turn out to be a process whereby the self loses its fixed boundaries—a disturbing yet potentially empowering practice of difference" (p. 23). In my case, living abroad did provoke new ways to conceptualize the relation of self and other. However, my ability to reread past encounters with difference from postcolonial perspectives in order to comprehend my implication in global power relations was dependent upon access to academic language and concepts. Postcolonial theory is integral to taking on the enormous subjective and societal task of reimagining inter/cultural relations.

LIFE WRITING AS INQUIRY
INTO OUR RELATION TO DIFFERENCE

By writing about our experiences, often in vulnerable, confessional, personal ways, we are creating spaces for others to join us in conversation about their vulnerable and personal stories.
—Chambers, Hasebe-Ludt, Leggo, & Sinner, 2012, p. xxvi

To rewrite my encounters with difference in between *here* and *there*, I draw upon life writing as curriculum inquiry (Chambers et al., 2012; Hasebe-Ludt, Chambers, & Leggo, 2009). Particular stories are chosen to highlight significant shifts in my worldview. Through the writing process, these moments emerge as "unsettling knowledge, [which] are those ideas that disturb the convenient truths through which we organize our thoughts and make meaning of our experience in the world" (Malewski & Sharma, 2010, p. 369). Sumara (2005) contends that taking up decentered, eccentric knowledge in the classroom, the curriculum and educational research may open up possibilities to resist normative discourses and promote social justice, which for the purposes of this chapter I define as the right to be treated with dignity and respect.

Life writing as research is a deeply personal, relational practice that lends itself to inquiries into difference in contexts of teacher education for social justice. Writing self-critically to deconstruct our lived experiences from postcolonial perspectives is "a journey into language and into the world" (Chambers et al., 2012, p. xxvii). The written text becomes a space to engage the tensions and complexities of engaging with decolonizing processes. My narratives disrupt humanist frames widely taken as legitimized knowledge in Western cultures through establishing links between personal experience and broader societal contexts. Interrogating the self may provoke greater awareness of our complicity in the knowledge and structures education for social justice seeks to challenge (He & Phillion, 2008; Sharma, 2009). Personal stories draw attention to what is missing from the official stories circulating in the spaces of schooling, society, and the mass media.

Life writing is "a new kind of scholarly text" (Chambers et al., 2012, p. xxv) that values lived experience as a vital source of inquiry for educators concerned with social justice. It requires us to consider how encounters with difference at the subjective level are linked "to social, political, cultural, and historical dynamics of identity, values, and transformative possibilities" (p. xxvii). The personal text is an invitation to the reader to engage his/her own processes of othering and entanglement in language. Deciding which stories to share and which theoretical frames to apply creates a destabilizing space (Aoki, 2005a, 2005c; Bhabha, 1990; Derrida, 1984; Low & Palulis, 2000) for the author, which may cast doubt on language we take for granted. Decentered knowledge may emerge between reader, writer, lived experience, and text to expand theory and practice in the internationalization of teacher education for social justice.

RE/WRITING THE SELF AS DECOLONIZING PRACTICE

In this text I draw upon memories of encounters with difference abroad, at home in Canada, and in the mass media (Watt, 2011a, 2011b, 2012, 2013). My interest in Canadian, Muslim, female youth arose from a concern with the limited narratives I was hearing and seeing in my everyday life and in

North American media (Watt, 2007), particularly after the terrorist attacks of September 11, 2001. I felt dissonance between my lived experiences in Pakistan, Iran, and Syria and the meanings being circulated in the news and in everyday conversations. Back in Canada, I witnessed the power of media discourses to constitute our subjectivities and readings of difference. I grew concerned about the impact this was having on our social relations and, in particular, on the everyday lives of Canadian, Muslim, female students. I thus re/write my lived experiences of othering to counter narratives connecting terrorism and oppression to essentialized Muslim, female bodies.

Inquiring into our encounters with difference involves giving an account of processes of othering, even if this can only be partial due to the unconscious mind (Butler, 2005). I began autoethnographic (Morawski & Palulis, 2009) inquiries in Dr. Patricia Palulis' graduate course at the University of Ottawa. During the semester we kept journals in which we responded and made personal connections to class discussions and readings. The weekly cycle of reading, writing, and discussion was discomfiting, but ultimately transformative. As I reworked assumptions I had about myself, I began to see how I am implicated in the legacy of colonialism.

Asher (2002) calls into question an exclusive focus on the other without questioning the self. She critiques approaches to multicultural education that focus on difference without engaging critical, reflexive, nonessentialist perspectives necessary to interrogate the relationships of power that shape identities and representations in education. She critiques multiculturalism as a discourse about the other with little examination of the self at the center of the dominant culture. Patriarchal, Eurocentric knowledge is privileged and the notion of self and other as two bordered entities is normalized. Asher calls on educators concerned with social justice to deconstruct processes of othering in relation to curriculum and teaching. Decolonizing pedagogies that deconstruct binaries engage the interstices that emerge at the intersections of different cultures, histories, and locations (Asher, 2005).

Schooling and media discourses tend to represent identities and cultures as static and homogenous in spite of theorizations of these as hybrid, interconnected, and in process (Bhabha, 1987, 1988, 1990, 1994; Hall, 1990, 1996). Assignments given in Canadian school social studies courses, for example, often require students to research and write *about* other peoples and places with little consideration of the cultural lens through which they, themselves, read the Other.

In my own schooling experiences, colonialism was studied as a historical period in the past. We never considered how it continues to frame social relations. Bringing marginalized perspectives into curriculum and society is insufficient if those from the dominant culture remain absent. Aoki (2005c) invites educators to decenter by placing ourselves "in the midst, between and among the cultural entities" (p. 269). The term *inter/cultural* with a slash is used to acknowledge cultures as relational, hybrid, and in process. The slash signifies movement in between cultures and identities, which is a shift to culture-as-verb. Aoki (2005b) suggests that by dwelling here, "newness might emerge" (p. 310). This is a space of engagement where we try to remain open to the Other even when tensions arise, for such tension can be generative and provoke something new (Watt, 2014).

ENGAGING OUR RELATION TO FOREIGN NATIONS

Like a historical process of sedimentation, or a progressive accumulation of toxins,
the concept of difference has been poisoned and has become the equivalent
of inferiority: to be different means to be worth less than. How can difference be
cleansed of this negative charge? Is the positivity of difference... thinkable? What are
the conditions that may facilitate the thinkability of positive difference?
—Braidotti, 2002, p. 4

The binary logic of imperialism is a development in western thought to see the world in terms of oppositions that establish a relation of dominance. In other words, a "simple distinction between centre/margin; colonizer/colonized; metropolis/empire; civilized/primitive represents very efficiently the violent hierarchy on which imperialism is based and which it actively perpetuates" (Ashcroft et al., 1998, p. 24). The Islamic Republic of Iran epitomizes difference for many in the West. It is routinely demonized in media and political discourse. It becomes easy to view Iran in negative terms given that it exists on the inferior side of the binaries, which work to structure thought into simplistic, opposing categories that come to seem natural. Politicans and others readily draw upon the binary language of humanism to justify foreign agendas to the populaces of Western nation-states.

My own relation to Iran and the Iranian people has been a significant site for challenging my own assumptions about difference. When I returned to Canada, I soon realized through everyday conversations that many Canadians are unable to imagine Iran as anything beyond a hostile and dangerous enemy. Before living there for three years I was also caught up in the dominant narratives on Iran. While there may be much to criticize about the Iranian regime, there is also a great deal that remains unsaid in media and political discourse, not to mention the fact there is much to criticize at home as well. This is where I believe teacher education for social justice needs to focus attention.

I traveled all over Iran, usually with one of my female friends. With a basic knoweldge of Persian it was easy to get around. I visited remote cities I had never heard of before arriving in Iran—Bam, Yazd, Mashad, Oroumiyeh—and never once felt afraid or in any danger. On the contrary, Iranians were helpful, kind, and generous. I am not exaggerating when I say I was warmly received everywhere I went. I cannot count the number of times I was invited for tea or a meal in someone's home and offered unsolicited assistance on the street. This was definitely not the Iran I had learned about on television. I would welcome the opportunity to take people to Iran to see this place for themselves. Life for many Iranians was materially less privileged than mine, but that did not lessen the Iranian hospitality and openness toward me, the stranger. Iranian friends have suggested that being a White, Western woman also afforded me a degree of privilege that I did not fully recognize at the time, which may also suggest our entanglement in colonial relations.

The story of any nation and its peoples is complicated and continuously in process. Even though only limited meanings circulate in the school curriculum and the discursive spaces of the North American mass media (Kincheloe & Steinberg, 2004), there is no simple truth about Iran. Most of us know little about how our histories are complexly intertwined. Few can explain the events that led to the American hostage crisis or provide details of the West's involvement in the Iran–Iraq war. Public education has a poor record with regard to providing youth with critical perspectives that counter media and political discourse on nations we consider radically Other, such as Iran (Kincheloe & Steinberg, 2004). Kincheloe (2004) described the classroom as "a central site for the legitimization of myths and silences about non-Western and often non-Christian peoples" (p. 2). He argued that little effort is made to historicize and contextualize the predominantly Islamic world and its relation to the West (p. 3). Like media discourses (Seaton, 2003; Watt, 2008), school representations make little space for complexity (Sensoy, 2007). Before my arrival, I had imposed simple readings on Iran. Three years later, after many face-to-face encounters with Iranians, I believe that when it comes to judging the Other, "one can never be certain, ahead of the event" (Wolfreys, 2005, p. 1). What if teachers could cultivate in their students an openness toward peoples they have never met, themselves?

Teacher candidates need opportunities to consider their entanglement in discourses circulating in cultural sites such as film, video games, and mainstream news and how that constitutes their relation to difference. The Academy Award-winning film *Argo* (Affleck, Clooney, & Heslov, 2012), for example, reproduces familiar stereotypes in the name of Hollywood entertainment. Historical facts surrounding the American hostage crisis are omitted, downplayed, and distorted. There is often a refusal on the part of those with the power to represent to accept reponsibility for their role in the production of meanings about the other. Unfortunately, such meanings constitute a powerful curriculum on Otherness, given they are often reinforced intertextually across multiple cultural sites (Watt, 2011a, 2011b).

These meanings impact our understandings of the self and the other and thus have material effects. When a nation is constructed as Other, for example, those thought to be associated with it risk marginalization.

In her memoir *Lipstick Jihad*, Moaveni (2006) poignantly describes her experiences growing up as an American-Iranian in the United States. In the following excerpt, she gives an account of the first day of school and the discomfort she felt just at having an Iranian name:

> I can still recall with perfect vividness the first day of school each year, when I would squirm miserably in my seat as the teacher called roll. As she approached the K's and L's, I knew the second she slowed down that she had arrived at my name; that she would bludgeon its pronunciation I had already accepted, but I prayed not to be asked in front of everyone else its origins, to have to utter that word, "Iran." (p. 9)

Teachers who identify with the dominant culture might not recognize the pain associated with feeling out of place due to one's family background. Memoirs such as *Lipstick Jihad* offer teacher candidates important insights into how youth from marginalized communities may experience school. In teacher education programs links could be made between (1) teacher candidates' assumptions and where they come from, (2) portrayals of the Iranian people in a popular cultural site such as the film *Argo* (Affleck et al., 2012), and (3) the lived experiences of an American-Iranian such as Moaveni. Such examinations could prompt new teachers to think more deeply about their relation to the Other in complex terms. Iran is only suggested as one example. Learning how to consider another person, nation, or culture from multiple perspectives should be something routine in our educational institutions.

ENGAGING OUR RELATION
TO CULTURAL & RELIGIOUS PRACTICES

Although I do not agree with women being forced to cover, if I wanted to live in Iran I would have to conform. This compromise allowed me to go there and experience the country and people for myself. For three years I was preoccupied with the practice of veiling. It is required by law in Iran, so all women cover, whether they are Muslim or not. While Islamic covering for females has evolved over time in Iran, and under the rule of Reza Shaw was outlawed altogether in the name of modernizing the nation, the common form of covering today is the roopoosh-roosari. The roopoosh (or manteau) is a long, shapeless, dark coat worn over clothes. When we arrived in Iran in 1996, my roopoosh was long, black, and loose. In the past 15 years, coats have become much shorter, colourful, and form-fitting.

The chador is the dress one usually sees in media images of women in Iran, a more traditional covering consisting of one large, dark, piece of fabric worn over the head and body. While in Iran, I wrongly assumed most women would uncover if given the choice. Over time I learned some Iranian women did despise the veil, while others embraced it. Much later when I began autoethnographic inquiries into my practices of othering, I realized that I was reading the veil through a Western cultural lens. Humanism's binaries constituted my seeing. If being uncovered meant freedom, covering signified oppression, plain and simple. My ability to read the veil more complexly evolved gradually.

Meanings associated with cultural and religious practices shift over time and place and are read according to our social, cultural, political, historical, and geographic locations. In the West, veiling is viewed by many negatively. In spite of its semantic versatility (e.g., Alvi, Hoodfar, & McDonough, 2003; Khan, 2002; Shirazi, 2001), it is often read as a sign of radical Islam and women's oppression. Canadian Muslim girls experience the effects of these narrow readings in their daily lives (Watt, 2011a, 2011b). This garment visually marks them as Other, and the meanings associated with the veil become attached to their bodies. They are thus sometimes assumed to be passive and oppressed. Rizvi (2005) observed that when clear differentiations are drawn between them and us, those who are not us do not belong here.

Just as the veil can have multiple meanings for the women who wear it, my headscarf and coat had various meanings for me. When our family agreed to move to Iran for my husband's job, I imagined the veil as an exotic costume I would wear as part of my adventure in a far-off land. People back home in Canada might consider me a courageous explorer. It was a chance to try on a new identity, to play at being the Other. I wondered whether wearing the roopoosh-roosari would offer me insights into Iranian culture and customs. It did allow entry into places I would otherwise have been excluded from, such as mosques and holy shrines. It was convenient to not have to dress up to go to the market or be concerned about the male gaze in crowded bazaars. When I felt at home in Iran, the scarf was a symbol of fitting in, a sign of adaptation. I felt Iranian and embraced the local practice of covering, barely giving it a second thought. However, on difficult days when I was stuck in a Tehran traffic jam on a hot, polluted afternoon, overcharged for vegetables, or simply feeling homesick, it could suddenly feel heavy and oppressive. My readings of covering were not consistent or fixed, but dependent on the context. My relation to the roopoosh-roosari shifted according to how I was feeling about my relation to the places and people I interacted with on a daily basis.

In postcolonial theory, the body is considered a crucial site for inscription. How people are perceived "controls how they are treated, and physical differences are crucial in such constructions" (Ashcroft, Griffiths, & Tiffin,

2000, p. 183). Visible signs of difference are a "prime means of developing and reinforcing prejudices against specific groups" (p. 184). Exclusions are generated for economic reasons or to control the other by emphasizing their difference and constructing them as inferior. If we view the body as text or space on which "conflicting discourses can be written and read" (p. 184), it is possible to see how the discursive forces of imperial power operate on or through people.

The attention that covered Muslim women receive in the West is an example of how power operates on the body through language. This is not to say that bodies are powerless, for they can be part of individual or broader practices of resistance. They may be complexly constructed and play an ambivalent role in the maintenance of and resistance to colonizing power (Ashcroft et al., 2000). Especially since they may be controversial, cultural and religious practices are a compelling site of inquiry for teacher candidates to examine how meanings about the Other are produced and circulated. Teacher candidates' readings of a religious or cultural practice such as veiling can potentially help them learn about themselves (Todd, 1997) through their relation to such difference.

ENGAGING THE SELF AS DIFFERENCE

Faisal Mosque is located in northern Islamabad at the foot of the beautiful Margala Hills, part of the Himalayan Mountain Range. Anyone familiar with the capital city of Pakistan knows this mosque as the iconic symbol of Islamabad. It can be seen from miles around, both day and night. Completed in 1986, the architecture is stunning and unique. Rather than the traditional dome and arches typical of most mosques around the world, this eight-sided mosque is shaped like a desert Bedouin's tent and the cubic Kaaba in Mecca. During the two and a half years we lived in Islamabad, we visited Faisal Mosque a number of times with our two young children.

On one such visit, we were approached by a Pakistani couple who asked to take our photograph. I was surprised by this unusual request, but readily agreed. As we were posing for the photo, a number of other tourists gathered to get their own shots. I could not understand why anyone would want a photo of us. We were so ordinary. I had never considered myself as different, as someone else's Other. This attitude arises from growing up as a member of the dominant culture in Canada. I represented the taken-for-granted norm against which difference was measured. Decolonizing our minds and bodies involves being able to see this fact and the enormous privilege it affords. I have similarly met teacher candidates who view Canada as being without culture. When one experiences life as the unmarked norm, difference becomes something that exists outside the self. This attitude seems common in spite of the fact that many Canadians are not White from European backgrounds. When we see ourselves represented in the school curriculum, our dominance is confirmed and reinforced, while others are constructed on the margins through their absence.

Only a week or two before this incident at Faisal Mosque, I had spent an entire day in the bazaars of Peshawar taking photos of Pakistani and Afghan men and women going about their daily business. It seemed perfectly natural to want photographs of these exotic strangers. Most were dressed in what I assumed to be traditional clothing. Some of the men wore bandoleers strapped across their chests, and many women were fully covered in the shuttlecock burqa typical of that region. I had been hesitant about taking photos of strangers, but at the time thought it must be due to my inexperience as a photographer. I did not yet have the language to frame how I was participating in colonial relations.

In *Orientalism,* Said (1994) establishes that colonial discourse was not just about constructing the colonized other: "The Orient is one of Europe's deepest and most recurring images of the Other. In addition, the Orient has helped to define Europe (or the West) as its contrasting image, idea, personality, experience" (p. 1). Orientalism is "a political vision of reality whose structure promoted the difference between the familiar (Europe, the West, 'us') and the strange (the Orient, the East, 'them')" (p. 43). The existence of an exotic Other reinforces the centrality of the so-called first world. During the 19th century, the exotic and the foreign were associated with stimulating and exciting difference throughout the empire. People or things considered exotic in the metropoles were "a significant part of imperial displays of power and the plenitude of empires" (Ashcroft et al., 2000, p. 95). By constructing Peshawari men and women as exotic, I was constructing myself as ordinary and normal. Back home, my exotic photos would be proof of my adventure. Looking back at these experiences abroad during my graduate studies, I could see how I was caught up in colonial power relations. The more difficult work commenced when I began to consider how this might translate with regards to my relation to difference back in Canada.

ENGAGING MULTICULTURAL DISCOURSE

Teachers may become more global-minded and attuned to difference through opportunities to live and travel abroad (Mahon, 2009; Malewski & Phillion, 2009; Sharma, 2009; Sharma, Aglazor, Malewski, & Phillion, 2011). As my story illustrates, such experiences can provoke decentering processes. Leaving home was an occasion to remove myself from the naturalness of the culture and society I had been immersed in all of my life.

Trinh (1999) explains that the concept of home is sigificant in postcolonial theorizing, for the more we look into our own culture, the more we see there is no such thing as a place that we can return to safely. Leaving home becomes a double journey, for we physically leave the familiar territory of home, as well as the familiar terms of humanism. As Trinh (1999) suggests, "Just as one exiles oneself from one's culture to inhabit it anew, one also returns to it as a guest, rather than as a host or an owner, to hear its voices afresh" (p. 22). That was my experience. When I returned to home after eight years away, I noticed things I had never paid attention to before. Coming home proved as unsettling as moving from Pakistan, to Syria, to Iran.

Canada is sometimes seen by the outside world as an example of how different peoples and cultures might live together since it was the first nation to have an official policy of multiculturalism. In 1971, I was an elementary school student when Prime Minister Trudeau declared Canada's commitment to multiculturalism through state policy, and I grew up taking it for granted as part of what it meant to be Canadian. The Canadian Multiculturalism Act (1988) maintains that all citizens are equal and have the right to preserve their cultural heritage. It promotes the full participation of individuals and communities from all backgrounds in every aspect of Canadian society. Invested in this discourse, I imagined the nation as mostly welcoming and benevolent. However, through the decolonizing process I realized for the first time how my privilege made me resistant to difficult knowledge (Britzman, 1998).

A couple of years after the terrorist attacks of 9/11, one of my adult Muslim, female students told me she and her friends were afraid to go out of the house. Many of them had received hostile looks on the street, or told "*go back where you came from.*" These were frightening experiences for these women given the broader political context, and I found their stories troubling. There had been a backlash across North America, and they worried that their bodies might be associated with the terrorists being portrayed in media. I increasingly felt the need to speak up about my experiences living and traveling in Iran, Syria, and Pakistan.

A recent poll of 2,005 Canadian adults conducted by the Canadian Race Relations Foundation (CRRF, 2014) found that Canadians put respect for human rights at the top of the list of Canadian values. However, 64% believe Canada's multicultural ideals "allow for the pursuit of cultural practices that are incompatible with Canadian laws and norms" (p. 14). When asked to define these incompatible practices, "one in three Canadians said religious head garb and clothing including burqas, hijabs and turbans in public or security settings" (p. 15), and 46% said wearing such items should be discouraged. *Toronto Star* journalist, Nicholas Keung (2015) wrote, "It's a Canadian paradox: We identify human rights and freedoms as among our most important values. Yet many struggle to accept something as simple as a headscarf" (para 1).

Rubin Friedman of the Canadian Race Relations Foundation explained that people are offended by religious clothing such as the veil due to the perceived values associated with this practice (as cited in Keung, 2015). He suggested that public displays of faith are taken as "a symbol of you separating yourself from others, rejecting the rest of us." Canada's Multiculturalism Act (1988) is intended to promote respect and full participation in society. However, it is impossible to mandate attitudes, and cultivating openness to difference requires vigilance. Education will always play a vital role in the promotion of social justice. Negotiating our identities in relation to social conditions, current events, and shifting, contradictory discourses is necessarily an ongoing process.

ENGAGING OUR RELATION TO DIFFERENCE IN MASS MEDIA

My efforts to understand why people seemed to have such a narrow view of Muslim women led me to media discourses as a powerful curriculum on Muslims. My initial inquiries included deconstructing images in print news media (Watt, 2008, 2011b, 2012). Two photographs of covered Muslim women that appeared in a Canadian newspaper caught my attention. They accompanied a headline story on the 2005 Iraqi elections. The front page photo depicted an extreme close-up of a woman wearing a black chador, which is a full body-length garment that covers the head and body. She had a tear in her eye after just having voted. The second photo was of women in a black chador lining up to vote. My first question was why the editors chose to focus the public gaze upon women in chadors rather than on men voting. I also noted that no reference was made to these women in the article. They were not interviewed; only their image appeared. After examining more images and other research (Watt, 2008, 2011a, 2011b), a pattern emerged. Images of covered, Muslim women were repeatedly being used to construct and fix narrow discourses across media sites. Who these women were as individuals was irrelevant; all that mattered was what they stood for (Cooke, 2001) and for whom these particular meanings were contructed.

Given the context of the Iraq war and the election, I read these images of female bodies in chadors as oppressed victims whom the West must free. The narrative of the oppressed Muslim woman is pervasive in media and in education (Sensoy & DiAngelo, 2006), and when reproduced across cultural sites it becomes invested with power and credibility. Dualistic thinking is commonly associated with Muslim women in mainstream media: "[O]n the one hand, there is reason, intelligence, democracy, equality of the sexes, and, on the other hand, religion, stupidity, violence and oppression. It is not surprising that Muslims feel very threatened by this stereotyping" (McDonough, 2003, p. 130).

Teacher education for social justice needs to attend to what narratives are attached to particular bodies, and our entanglement in these discourses. There are oppressed Muslim women out there, just as there are oppressed women in all communities, but reading media representations, one might be led to believe that all Muslim women are oppressed. To essentialize an entire category of women signals that powerful processess of othering are at play. We need to consider whose interests are being served. Boler and Zembylas (2003) have argued that the unfortunate effect of popular history and reductive understandings of difference is that we are "prevented from seeing contradictions, and from inhabiting more ambiguous and less rigid, identities and relations to the world.... The absence of space for contradiction and ambiguity makes resistance to dominant meanings very difficult" (p. 121). Todd (1997) has suggested that representations of otherness be viewed as "not simply concerned with telling falsehoods or truths about groups, but... [as] constructing a sense of who 'we' are, and who 'they' are, and how the society in which we live is understood" (p. 151). Multiple meanings can be generated from any representation. They function differently, depending upon the social context and audience. Teacher education for social justice should therefore be about an "*inquiry into* multiple meanings" rather than "*rectifying*" specific images (Todd, 1997, p. 150, emphasis in original).

Teacher candidates might inquire into how particular messages are produced by investigating the following: (1) the representation; (2) who created it, and why; (3) how those being represented read the message; (4) how other audiences read the message; and (5) where they situate themselves in relation to a particular representation and the multiple readings of others. If student teachers are able to develop critical perspectives on why processes of othering matter, the classroom may become a space where complex inquiries into representation become a taken-for-granted means of knowledge production on difference and our relation to it.

Increasing our knowledge *about* the Other does not go far enough in capturing the complexity of language and social relations in between the personal, the local, and the global. Teachers need critical lenses that question the disinterested discourses of knowledge on difference circulating in schools, society, and mass media, for langauge is never neutral. In addition, if we accept cultures and identities as hybrid and always in process, the notion that a body of fixed, "accurate" knowlege about the other even exists reinforces the notion of cultures as static, monolithic, and homogenous.

Britzman (1998) has pointed out that learning *about* other cultures without engaging the self serves as an invitation to join those of us already at the center, keeping those at the center safe. She critiques the liberal strategy of inclusion by explaining how it perpetuates an unmarked normative order.

Within the frame of inclusion only two subject positions are assumed—"the tolerant normal" and "the tolerated subaltern" (p. 87). Humanist binaries are thus reinforced, along with the colonizing power relations associated with them. The other may be welcomed into the curriculum, but "not because they have anything to say to those already there" (p. 87). This exemplifies how marginalization in education may be produced and maintained in spite of good intentions.

ENGAGING DIFFERENCE
IN TEACHER EDUCATION FOR SOCIAL JUSTICE

As I have attempted to demonstrate in this chapter, academic inquiries into my personal practices of othering led to a profound shift in my sense of identity and how I think about difference and inter/cultural education. Having teacher candidates engage in life writing provides them with a means to critically engage their own encounters with difference in between *here* and *there*. Writing from lived experience creates openings for educators to reimagine inter/cultural education as not exclusively *about the other*, but also about themselves (Sharma, 2009; Watt, 2013). If we do not take up the challenge to deconstruct our relation to difference, our implication in power relations risks being left unsaid; our entanglement in the legacy of colonialism remains unchallenged. What if learning to read the self and other more complexly were to become an urgent priority in the internationalization of teacher education?

NOTE

1. Stack and Kelly (2006) use the term *media* to mean "both the mediums of communication (radio, recorded music, Internet, television, print, film, video) as well as the products or texts of these mediums (journalistic accounts, television shows and film productions, video games, web sites)" (p. 6).

REFERENCES

Alvi, S., Hoodfar, H., & McDonough, S. (Eds.). (2003). *The Muslim veil in North America: Issues and debates.* Toronto, ON: Women's Press.

Affleck, B., Clooney, G., & Heslov, G. (Producers), & Affleck, B. (Director). (2012). *Argo* [Motion picture]. USA:Warner Brothers Pictures.

Aoki, T. (2005a). Imaginaries of "East and West": Slippery curricular signifiers in education. (1996). In W. F. Pinar & R. L. Irwin (Eds.), *Curriculum in a new key: The collected works of Ted T. Aoki* (pp. 313–319). Mahwah, NJ: Lawrence Erlbaum.

Aoki, T. (2005b). In the midst of doubled imaginaries: The Pacific community as diversity and difference (1995). In W. F. Pinar & R. L. Irwin (Eds.), *Curriculum in a new key: The collected works of Ted T. Aoki* (pp. 303–312). Mahwah, NJ: Lawrence Erlbaum.

Aoki, T. (2005c). In the midst of slippery theme-words: Living as designers of Japanese Canadian curriculum (1992). In W. F. Pinar & R. L. Irwin (Eds.), *Curriculum in a new key: The collected works of Ted T. Aoki* (pp. 263–277). Mahwah, NJ: Lawrence Erlbaum.

Aoki, T. (2005d). Language, culture, and curriculum (2000). In W. F. Pinar, & R. L. Irwin (Eds.), *Curriculum in a new key: The collected works of Ted T. Aoki* (pp. 321–329). Mahwah, NJ: Lawrence Erlbaum.

Ashcroft, B., Griffiths, G., & Tiffin, H. (1998). *Key concepts in post-colonial studies.* New York, NY: Routledge.

Ashcroft, B., Griffiths, G., & Tiffin, H. (2000). *Post-colonial studies: The key concepts.* New York, NY: Routledge.

Asher, N. (2002). (En)gendering a hybrid consciousness. *Journal of Curriculum Theorizing, 18*(4), 81–92.

Asher, N. (2005). At the interstices: Engaging postcolonial and feminist perspectives for a multicultural education pedagogy in the South. *Teachers College Record, 107*(5), 1079–1106.

Bhabha, H. (1987). Interrogating identity. In L. Appignanesi (Ed.), *Identity: The real me* (pp. 5– 11). London, UK: Institute of Contemporary Arts.

Bhabha, H. (1988). Cultural diversity and cultural differences. In B. Ashcroft, G. Griffiths, and H. Tiffin (Eds.), *The post-colonial studies reader* (1995) (pp. 207–209). New York, NY: Routledge.

Bhabha, H. (1990). The third space. In J. Rutherford (Ed.), *Identity: Community, culture, difference* (pp. 207–221). London, England: Lawrence & Wishart.

Bhabha, H. (1994). *The location of culture.* New York, NY: Routledge.

Boler, M., & Zembylas M. (2003). Discomforting truths: The emotional terrain of understanding difference. In P. P. Trifonas (Ed.), *Pedagogies of difference: Rethinking education for social change* (pp. 119–136). London, England: RoutledgeFalmer.

Braidotti, R. (2002). *Metamorphoses: Towards a materialist theory of becoming.* Cambridge, UK: Polity Press.

Britzman, D. (1998). *Lost subjects, contested objects: Toward a psychoanalytic inquiry of learning.* Albany, NY: State University of New York Press.

Butler, J. (2005). *Giving an account of oneself.* New York, NY: Fordham University Press.

Canadian Multiculturalism Act. (1988). Ottawa: ON, Government of Canada. Retrieved from http://laws-lois.justice.gc.ca/eng/acts/C-18.7/page-1.html

Canadian Race Relations Foundation. (2014). *Report on Canadian Values.* Toronto, ON: Canadian Race Relations Foundation. Retrieved from http://www.crr.ca/images/Our_Canada/Report_on_Canadian_Values_Billingual-wCOVER.pdf

Chambers, C., Hasebe-Ludt, E., Leggo, C., & Sinner, A. (Eds.). (2012). *A heart of wisdom: Life writing as empathetic inquiry.* New York, NY: Peter Lang.

Cooke, M. (2001). *Women claim Islam: Creating Islamic feminism through literature.* New York, NY: Routledge.

Derrida, J. (1984). *Jacques Derrida: Margins of philosophy* (A. Bass, Trans.). Chicago, IL: University of Chicago Press.

Hall, S. (1990). Cultural identity and diaspora. In J. Rutherford (Ed.), *Identity: Community, culture, difference* (pp. 222–237). London, UK: Lawrence & Wishart.

Hall, S. (1996). Who needs 'identity'? In S. Hall & P. DuGay (Eds.), *Questions of cultural identity* (pp. 1–17). London, UK: Sage.

Hasebe-Ludt, E., Chambers, C., & Leggo, C. (2009). *Life writing and literary métissage as an ethos for our times.* New York, NY: Peter Lang.

He, M. F., & Phillion, J. (2008). *Personal~passionate~participatory inquiry into social justice in education.* Charlotte, NC: Information Age Publishing.

Keung, N. (2015, January 3) Faith is often a visual marker of identity—but also a source of discomfort. *The Toronto Star.* Retrieved from http://www.thestar.com/news/immigration/2015/01/03/faith_is_often_a_visual_marker_o f_identity_but_also_a_source_of_discomfort.html

Khan, S. (2002). *Aversion and desire: Negotiating Muslim female identity in the diaspora.* Toronto, ON: Women's Press.

Kincheloe, J. (2004). Introduction. In J. Kincheloe & S. Steinberg (Eds.), *The miseducation of the west: How schools and the media distort our understanding of the Islamic world* (pp. 1–24). Westport, CT: Praeger.

Kincheloe, J., & Steinberg, S. (Eds.). (2004). *The miseducation of the west: How schools and the media distort our understanding of the Islamic world.* Westport, CN: Praeger.

Low, M., & Palulis, P. (2000). Teaching as a messy text: Metonymic moments in pedagogical practice. *Journal of Curriculum Theorizing, 16*(2), 67–79.

Mahon, J. (2009). Authority and imposition in the study abroad program: A post-structural lens. *Journal of Curriculum Theorizing, 25*(3), 68–83.

Malewski, E., & Phillion, J. (2009). Making room in the curriculum: The raced, classed, and gendered nature of preservice teachers' experiences studying abroad. *Journal of Curriculum Theorizing, 25*(3), 48–68.

Malewski, E., & Sharma, S. (2010). Response to Bernadette M. Baker: The unstudied and understudied in curriculum studies: Toward historical readings of the "conditions of possibility" and the production of concepts in the field. In E. Malewski (Ed.), *Curriculum studies handbook: The next moment* (pp. 365–373). New York, NY: Routledge.

McDonough, S. (2003). Perceptions of the hijab in Canada. In S. S. Alvi, H. Hoodfar, & S. McDonough (Eds.), *The Muslim veil in North America: Issues and debates* (pp. 121–142). Toronto, ON: Women's Press.

Moaveni, A. (2006). *Lipstick jihad: A memoir of growing up Iranian in America and American in Iran.* New York, NY: PublicAffairs.

Morawski, C., & Palulis, P. (2009). Auto/ethno/graphies as teaching lives: An aesthetics of difference. *Journal of Curriculum Theorizing, 25*(2), 6–24.

Pew Research Center. (2011). *The future of the global Muslim population.* Washington, DC. Retrieved from http://www.pewforum.org/2011/01/27/the-future-of-the-global-muslim-population/

Rizvi, F. (2005). Representations of Islam and education for justice. In C. McCarthy, W. Crichlow, G. Dimitriadis, & N. Dolby (Eds.), *Race, identity, and representation in education* (2nd ed., pp. 167–178). New York, NY: Routledge.

Said, E. W. (1994). *Orientalism* (25th anniversary ed.). New York, NY: Vintage Books.

Seaton, J. (2003). Understanding not empathy. In D. K. Thussu & D. Freedman (Eds.), *War and the media: Reporting conflict 24/7* (pp. 45–54). Thousand Oaks, CA: Sage.

Sensoy, Ö. (2007). Social education and critical media literacy: Can Mr. Potato Head help challenge binaries, essentialism, and orientalism? In D. Macedo & S. Steinberg (Eds.), *Media literacy: A reader* (pp. 593–602). New York, NY: Peter Lang.

Sensoy, Ö., & DiAngelo, R. (2006). "I wouldn't want to be a woman in the Middle East": White female student teachers and the narrative of the oppressed woman. *Radical Pedagogy, 8*(1), 1–14.

Sharma, S. (2009). From the red-dot-Indian woman to jet-set-mangoes and all the hyphens in-between: Studying abroad and discovering myself. *Journal of Curriculum Theorizing, 25*(3), 119–136.

Sharma, S., Aglazor, G. N., Malewski, E., & Phillion, J. (2011). Preparing global minded teachers for U.S. American classrooms through international cross-cultural field experiences. *Delhi Business Review: International Journal of Society for Human Transformation and Research, 12*(2), 33–44.

Shirazi, F. (2001). *The veil unveiled: The hijab in modern culture.* Tampa, FL: University Press of Florida.

Stack, M., & Kelly, D. (2006). Popular media, education, and resistance. *Canadian Journal of Education, 29*(1), 5–26.

Sumara, D. (2005). On the importance of the eccentric curriculum. *Journal of the Canadian Association for Curriculum Studies, 3*(1), iii–viii.

Todd, S. (1997). Educating beyond tolerance: Reading media images of the hijab. In J. P. Robertson (Ed.), *Teaching for a tolerant world* (pp. 157–166). Urbana, IL: National Council of Teachers of English.

Todd, S. (2003). *Learning from the other: Levinas, psychoanlaysis, and ethical possibilities in education.* Albany, NY: State University of New York Press.

Trinh, T. M. (1989). *Woman, native, other.* Bloomington, IN: Indiana University Press.

Trinh, T. M. (1999). Painted power, with Homi Bhabha. In T. M. Trinh (Ed.), *Cinema Interval* (pp. 16–31). New York, NY: Routledge.

Watt, D. (2007). Disrupting mass media as curriculum: Opening to stories of veiling. In S. Springgay & D. Freedman (Eds.), *Curriculum and the cultural body* (pp. 147–161). New York, NY: Peter Lang.

Watt, D. (2008). Challenging Islamophobia through visual media studies: Inquiring into a photograph of Muslim women on the cover of Canada's national news magazine. *Studies in Media and Information Literacy Education, 8*(2), 1–14.

Watt, D. (2011a). From the streets of Peshawar to the cover of Maclean's Magazine: Reading images of Muslim women as currere to interrupt gendered Islamophobia. *Journal of Curriculum Theorizing, 27*(1), 64–86.

Watt, D. (2011b). *Juxtaposing sonare and videre midst curricular spaces: Negotiating Muslim, female identities in the discursive spaces of schooling and visual media cultures*

(Doctoral dissertation). University of Ottawa, Canada. Retrieved from http://www.ruor.uottawa.ca/en/handle/10393/19973

Watt, D. (2012). The urgency of visual media literacy in our post-9/11 world: Reading images of Muslim women in the print news media. *Journal of Media Literacy Education, 4*(1), 32–41.

Watt, D. (2013). Auto/ethno/graphic bricolage as embodied inter/culturalism: Dis/locating stories of becoming in encounters with the other. *Journal of Curriculum Theorizing. Special Issue: Cultivating the Multicultural Imagination, 28*(2), 1–19.

Watt, D. (2014). Framing peace as tensioned engagement. In H. Smits & R. Naqvi (Eds.), *Framing peace: Thinking about and enacting curriculum as "radical hope"* (pp. 73–88). New York, NY: Peter Lang.

Willinsky, J. (1998). *Learning to divide the world: Education at empire's end.* Minneapolis, MN: University of Minnesota Press.

Wolfreys, J. (Ed.). (2005). *The J. Hillis Miller reader.* Stanford, CA: Stanford University Press.

CHAPTER 2

PREPARING CULTURALLY RESPONSIVE TEACHERS

An Intercultural Developmental Approach

Helen Marx

ABSTRACT

In the past 20 years, conceptual frameworks have been developed that describe the characteristics of culturally responsive teachers. The concept of culturally responsive teaching developed within teacher education is a discipline-specific articulation of the concept of intercultural competence developed within the field of intercultural communication. The dominant theory that explains the development of intercultural competence, Bennett's (1993) Developmental Model of Intercultural Sensitivity (DMIS), can be used to articulate a more developmentally appropriate approach to teacher education. Such an approach is crucial if teacher educators are to design curricula that address preservice teachers' current levels of intercultural competence and challenge and support them as they transform their worldviews in ways that are necessary for them to become culturally responsive teachers.

Internationalizing Teaching and Teacher Education for Equity, pages 21–38
Copyright © 2016 by Information Age Publishing
21

INTRODUCTION

Preparing culturally responsive teachers is essential if we are to provide equitable educational experiences for all students in culturally pluralistic democracies. A fundamental aspect of culturally responsive teaching is the teacher's ability to attend to the ways that culture—their own and their students'—influences teaching and learning. In the past 20 years, conceptual frameworks have been developed that describe the characteristics of culturally responsive teachers (Gay, 2000, 2002). However, teacher educators do not have a clear theoretical framework that sufficiently explains the developmental processes necessary to help preservice teachers learn to teach in culturally responsive ways (McAllister & Irvine, 2000). In this chapter[1] I suggest that the concept of culturally responsive teaching developed within teacher education is a discipline-specific articulation of the concept of intercultural competence developed within the field of intercultural communication. Further, I propose that the dominant theory explaining the development of intercultural competence, Bennett's (1993) Developmental Model of Intercultural Sensitivity (DMIS), can be used to articulate a more developmentally appropriate approach to teacher education. Such an approach is crucial if teacher educators are to design curricula that address preservice teachers' current levels of intercultural competence and challenge and support them as they transform their worldviews in ways that are necessary for them to become culturally responsive teachers.

NEED FOR CULTURALLY RESPONSIVE TEACHERS

There is a persistent culture gap between teachers and students in U.S. public schools; many classrooms have a student population that is ethnically and racially diverse led by a teacher who is non-Hispanic White (Hodgkinson, 2002; Sleeter, 2001). Currently, over 40% of students in the nation's K–12 schools are students of color, while 83% of teachers are non-Hispanic White (Boser, 2011).

Referred to as the "demographic imperative" (Cochran-Smith, 2005), the culture gap between teachers and students can result in "cultural incongruence" (Irvine, 2003) or "cultural mismatch" (Ladson-Billings, 2005) in students' educational experiences. Jenks, Lee, and Kanpol (2001) contend that dominant culture teachers often fail to see the cultural context of schooling and assume that curricular and instructional decisions are culturally neutral. While these European-American teachers generally hold liberal and humanistic beliefs towards students (Wideen, Mayer-Smith, & Moon, 1998), as members of the dominant culture group with limited intercultural experiences they often have not had to confront issues of racism or prejudice, nor consider their own cultural identity or the cultural hegemony in which they live (Cochran-Smith, 1995). Research indicates that such teachers often marginalize and undervalue the abilities, strengths, and needs of culturally different students; misunderstand and misappropriate culturally appropriate student behavior; and use instructional strategies that are in conflict with the learning and communication styles of some students' home cultures (Gay, 2000; Irvine, 2003; Nieto, 2004; Pohan, 1996; Rogoff, 2003; Sleeter, 2001). The negative impact of the culture gap that exists between many teachers and their students necessitates that teacher educators directly address these ethnocentric beliefs and develop in teachers the abilities to provide all students with equitable and effective education.

INTERCULTURAL COMPETENCE AS THE PREREQUISITE FOR CULTURALLY RESPONSIVE TEACHING

Researchers have focused on identifying teacher beliefs, knowledge, and skills that provide culturally congruent educational experiences for culturally diverse students. Commonly called culturally responsive teaching (also referred to as culturally sensitive, culturally mediated, and culturally relevant teaching), these theories propose that teachers must develop the ability to attend to the ways that culture—their own and their students'—influence teaching and learning. Gay (2000) explains that culturally responsive teachers make use of:

> [T]he cultural knowledge, prior experiences, frames of reference, and performance styles of ethnically diverse students to make learning encounters more relevant to and effective for them. It teaches *to and through* the strengths of these students. It is culturally *validating and affirming*. (p. 29, italics in original)

As such, culturally responsive teachers must understand that both their own and their students' cultural worldviews influence all aspects of teaching and learning and that schools are complex cultural contexts (Gay, 2000).

The theoretical description of culturally responsive teaching is conceptually connected to the definitions of intercultural competence developed within the field of intercultural communication. Kim (1988) defines the field of intercultural communication as theorizing about appropriate and effective communication between individuals who come from different cultural backgrounds. Teacher educators have used similar terms to describe similar concepts within the field of education, such as multicultural competence (Gay, 1994), cross-cultural competence (Jenks et al., 2001; McAllister & Irvine, 2000), intercultural effectiveness (Cushner, 1988), and cultural competence (Trumbull & Pacheco, 2005). A leading theorist in multicultural education, C. Bennett (1995), defines interculturally competent teachers as possessing the skills and knowledge that would allow them to be

> comfortable with their students' cultural styles. They understand their students' verbal communication and body language, preferred modes of discussion and participation, time and space orientations, social values and religious beliefs, and preferred styles of learning. Interculturally competent teachers are aware of the diversity within racial and cultural groups, know that culture is ever changing, and are aware of the dangers of stereotyping. At the same time, they know that if they ignore their students' cultural attributes, they are likely to be guided by their own cultural lenses, unaware of how their culturally conditioned expectations might cause learning difficulties for some children. (p. 263)

This discussion highlights the conceptual relationship between intercultural competence and culturally responsive teaching. The development of intercultural competence should be seen as a necessary prerequisite for culturally responsive teaching, and culturally responsive teaching should be considered a discipline-specific expression of intercultural competence.

A PROCESS APPROACH
TO BECOMING A CULTURALLY RESPONSIVE TEACHER

Teacher educators generally hold that in order to become culturally responsive, preservice teachers must critically reflect upon and become conscious of the cultural dimensions of teaching and learning. Typically, programs seek to provide preservice teachers with opportunities to reflect on culture in multicultural courses and within cross-cultural field placements. However, there is no clear theoretical framework within teacher education that sufficiently explains the development of a culturally responsive teaching mindset.

Articulating a process or developmental approach to becoming a culturally responsive teacher is vital; without this, culturally responsive teaching might be conceived of as a "method" of teaching, with a focus on learning discrete skills and strategies. However, culturally responsive teaching involves more than learning new skills or behaviors; it requires a fundamental shift in a person's worldview or mindset regarding culture. Years ago, Larkin (1995) cautioned that "culturally responsive teaching is not a particular method to be added to a teacher's collection of techniques. Rather, it is a comprehensive approach to the teaching role which informs and guides all aspects of classroom practice" (p. 11). A teacher does not learn to *do* culturally responsive teaching; a teacher must become culturally responsive.

Concurring, McAllister and Irvine (2000) propose that "there is scant research about the process by which teachers develop a cross-cultural competence that enables them effectively to teach diverse students in their classroom" (pp. 3–4) and suggest that teacher education does not adequately address the development of cross-cultural competence. Further, Irvine (2003) cautions that multicultural teacher education must not ignore the "developmental aspects of cross-cultural competence that require time for preservice teachers (many of them young adults) to grapple with, reflect upon, and assimilate complicated issues associated with their own personal, social, cultural, and ethnic identities" (p. 17).

McAllister and Irvine (2000) have suggested that teacher educators should look to theories developed within the field of intercultural communication, where robust models for understanding how intercultural competence is developed have been studied for over 30 years. Further, they believe that the constructivist-developmental approach taken in the field of intercultural communication provides a needed framework to ground the work of teacher educators seeking to increase their students' intercultural competence:

> One conceptual framework that has not been thoroughly examined in multicultural teacher education research is process-oriented models. Some of these models have been used in the fields of counseling and intercultural relations to describe the cognitive, behavioral, and affective changes related to how adults develop cross-cultural competence. The authors recommend the infusion of these models into teacher education. (McAllister & Irvine, 2000, p. 4)

They specifically endorse Bennett's Developmental Model of Intercultural Sensitivity as a framework to be used by teacher educators (McAllister & Irvine, 2000). The focus on the worldview necessary for effective cross-cultural communication and relationships makes the DMIS a useful framework to understand how preservice teachers become culturally responsive teachers.

DEVELOPMENTAL MODEL OF INTERCULTURAL SENSITIVITY

Bennett's (1993) Developmental Model of Intercultural Sensitivity (DMIS) is the most widely used model in the field of intercultural communication. Drawing on previous theoretical work in the field, the DMIS is a developmental stage theory that describes a continuum from ethnocentric to ethnorelative worldviews. The focus of this model is on the ways a person regards cultural difference and how this shapes how a person interacts within cross-cultural contexts and with people who are culturally different. Bennett and Bennett (2004) have explained:

> The underlying assumption of the model is that as one's experience of cultural difference becomes more sophisticated, one's competence in intercultural relations increases. Each state is indicative of a particular worldview configuration, and certain kinds of attitudes and behaviors are typically associated with each such configuration. The DMIS is not a model of changes in attitudes and behavior. Rather, it is a model of the development of cognitive structure. The statements about behavior and attitudes at each stage are indicative of a particular condition of the underlying worldview. (p. 152)

The DMIS is based on the understanding that key to developing intercultural competence is the development of intercultural sensitivity. It is important to understand the relationship between intercultural competence and intercultural sensitivity within this theory. Medina-Lopez-Portillo (2004) explained that in the DMIS, intercultural competence is predicated upon a person's underlying construal of cultural difference—their intercultural sensitivity. Intercultural sensitivity refers to a person's worldview about cultural and cultural difference, whereas intercultural competence refers to their ability to function in effective and appropriate ways (knowledge, skills, and behaviors) within intercultural contexts.

The DMIS delineates six stages of intercultural sensitivity development, from ethnocentric to ethnorelative thinking. Bennett (2004) defines ethnocentrism as "the experience of one's own culture as 'central to reality' . . . the beliefs and behaviors that people receive in their primary socialization are unquestioned: they are experienced as 'just the way things are,'" and ethnorelativism as "the experience of one's own beliefs and behaviors as just one organization of reality among many viable possibilities" (p. 62). In the model, the three ethnocentric stages—denial, defense, and minimization—"can be seen as ways of *avoiding cultural difference*, either by denying its existence, by raising defenses against it, or by minimizing its importance" (Bennett, 2004, p. 63, italics in original). The ethnorelative stages—acceptance, adaptation, and integration—"are ways of *seeking cultural difference*, either by accepting its importance, by adapting perspective to take it into account, or by integrating the whole concept into a definition of identity" (Bennett, 2004, p. 63, italics in original). As a person's worldview regarding cultural difference becomes more sophisticated, nuanced, and ethnorelative, they become increasingly interculturally sensitive and, thus, more interculturally competent.

ETHNOCENTRIC STAGES:
DENIAL, DEFENSE, AND MINIMIZATION

The first ethnocentric stage, *denial*, describes individuals who do not recognize cultural differences and perceive their own culture as the only reality. This would occur if a person experiences cultural isolation, where there is a lack of any experience with differences, or cultural separation, where a culture group is intentionally separated and isolated from others. People in this stage might recognize that other cultures do exist, but they have a very superficial understanding of culture and cultural difference. One common danger is the tendency of people in these stages to see difference as an attribution of deficiency in intelligence or personality, and "outsiders" are typically dehumanized (Bennett, 1993, 2004; Bennett & Bennett, 2004; Hammer, Bennett, & Wiseman, 2003).

The second ethnocentric stage, *defense*, is characterized by the belief that one's own culture is the only viable culture. Bennett (1993) explains that this defensive response to difference is an attempt to preserve a sense of one's own worldview as dominant and true. In this phase, cultural differences are acknowledged but seen in negative contrast to one's own culture. This stage is further divided into three categories. The *denigration* substage evaluates differences negatively and creates negative stereotypes of the "other," typically dehumanizing and finding offensive those who are culturally different. Within the *superiority* substage, people focus attention on an overly positive depiction of their own culture and, by implication, the inferiority of other cultures. In both cases, there is a clear sense of "us" and "them" and a sense that cultural identity is under threat and must be defended. As a third subset of this stage, *reversal* describes those who come to see the "other" culture as superior to their own, often denigrating their own culture. While not seeing the other culture as a threat, a person in the reversal stage still places cultures in an "us" vs. "them" worldview and is still inherently ethnocentric (Bennett, 1993, 2004; Hammer et al., 2003).

The last ethnocentric stage, *minimization*, is characterized by the tendency to minimize differences and overly stress cultural similarities. Within this stage there are two substages: *physical universalism* and *transcendent universalism*. Physical universalism refers to the tendency for some people to minimize cultural difference by looking for biological similarities among people in an effort to focus on what makes us human. From this orientation, a person may overlook or deemphasize the influence of the social and cultural contexts. Importantly, this ethnocentric focus will cause them to generalize about human qualities based on their own cultural experiences of reality; their cultural notions become the norm through which they find human similarities. In transcendent universalism, a person will minimize cultural difference in a belief in universal absolutes, with a firm belief that there are philosophical, religious, or economic concepts that apply cross-culturally and through which they can understand the world (Bennett, 1993, 2004). While much more sensitive to cultural diversity than the previous stages, and less likely to include negative stereotyping and attribution, people at this stage continue to view the world and difference from their own cultural perspective.

While on the surface people at the minimization stage are tolerant of difference, their tendency to view the world and cultural others through their own cultural lens results in cultural hegemony. Bennett (2004) explained:

> Particularly for people of dominant cultures, Minimization tends to mask recognition of their own culture (ethnicity) and the institutional privilege it affords its members. Because people at this stage no longer experience others in a polarized way, they tend to overestimate their racial and ethnic appreciation. While they may be relatively tolerant, people at Minimization are unable to appreciate other cultures because they cannot see their own culture clearly. (p. 67)

In the minimization stage, one's own subjective culture is taken as universal across all cultures. Someone from a minimization mindset can work for years within cross-cultural situations and may appear to function with some level of intercultural competence, particularly when they are members of the dominant culture whose hegemony is rarely questioned by its own members. The problem for cross-cultural relationships for someone within this stage is that, though they might acknowledge and even support the notion of acceptance of cultural differences, their tendency towards universalism protects their notions of the superiority of their own cultural beliefs by elevating these beliefs to the level of an absolute or universal. Within this stage there is little cognizance of the way individual difference is influenced by sociocultural contexts, and issues related to power and privileges are minimized or resisted. People who minimize cultural difference can find intercultural communication difficult, particularly when they must operate outside of their familiar cultural context. Such a worldview results in judging negatively or holding as "deficient" those cultural others who do not abide by what is assumed to be universal beliefs and values.

ETHNORELATIVE STAGES: ACCEPTANCE, ADAPTATION, AND INTEGRATION

At this point in a person's intercultural development, transformative changes in the individual's perception of cultural difference can lead to the three ethnorelative stages: *acceptance, adaptation,* and *integration*. Bennett (2004) describes ethnorelativism as "the experience of one's own beliefs and behaviors as just one organization of reality among many viable possibilities" (p. 62). These ethnorelative stages represent a fundamental shift in an individual's perception of cultural difference, where cultural difference is no longer experienced as an existential threat. Further, cultural difference is understood to be a reality and is often thought to be a desirable element within relationships, groups, and institutions.

The first ethnorelative stage, *acceptance*, is characterized by a recognition and appreciation for cultural differences, both value-based and behavioral differences. There is an understanding that a person's worldview, including one's own, is a relative cultural construct and that there are many viable ways to organize and perceive the world. At this stage, individuals begin to understand more complex cultural constructs that can be used to understand human communication (Bennett, 1993, 2004). The acceptance of the relativity of cultural perspectives is not the same as moral relativism. Hammer et al. (2003) point out that at this stage there is an acceptance of relativity and also an understanding that this does not mean that one must agree with others' perceptions of reality; a person at this stage recognizes that they can "accept the relativity of values to cultural context" (p. 425) and still maintain their commitment to their own ethical and cultural values.

The next stage, *adaptation*, occurs when one is able to experience another culture with the culture's appropriate perception and behavior. This stage involves the development of advanced intercultural communications skills, specifically cultural empathy, which allows one to shift perspectives as cultural contexts shift. This empathetic shift is more than the cognitive shift that might occur in the acceptance stage, but it includes changes in behavior and affect. At this stage, pluralism, described as the ability to have multiple frames of reference and to habitually shift between worldviews, results in a person being bicultural or multicultural (Bennett, 1993, 2004; Hammer et al., 2003).

A person in the last ethnorelative stage, *integration*, would be considered fully intercultural, where "one's experience of self is expanded to include the movement in and out of different cultural worldviews" (Hammer et al., 2003, p. 425). A person at this level struggles with their own "cultural marginality" in that they "construe their identities at the margins of two or more cultures and central to none" (Hammer et al., 2003, p. 425). Bennett does not describe this stage as more desirable than the previous stage, but rather uses it to describe the reality experienced by those who see themselves as possessing "multiple" worldviews, with none dominant. In "encapsulated" form, cultural marginality can be experienced as alienation for the individual, where one does not feel that one "fits" anywhere culturally. In "constructive" form, the individual has the ability to internalize and fully integrate various worldviews.

USING THE DMIS IN TEACHER EDUCATION

The DMIS provides a conceptualization of the process of developing greater intercultural sensitivity that can be used within teacher education to better understand the process of becoming a culturally responsive teacher. An ethnorelative worldview, as defined within the DMIS, is essential in the development of culturally responsive teachers, where teachers are conscious and conscientious of the influence of culture on all aspects of a student's educational experience and teach in ways that provide an optimal learning environment for all students in a classroom. The descriptions of a culturally responsive teacher offered previously clearly imply that such teachers would have an ethnorelative worldview orientation of, at the least, the acceptance stage as described in the DMIS. C. Bennett (2001) described an interculturally competent, culturally responsive teacher as possessing

> dispositions of open-mindedness and the absence of racial or cultural prejudice, and knowledge about the worldviews and funds of knowledge associated with various culture groups, as well as diversity within and across ethnic groups. Also implicit is a sense of cultural consciousness, or the recognition on the part of an individual that he or she has a view of the world that is not universally shared and that differs profoundly from that held by many members of different nations and ethnic groups. It includes an awareness of the diversity of ideas and practices found in human societies around the world and some recognition of how one's own thoughts and behaviors might be perceived by members of differing nations and ethnic groups. (p. 191)

Such a teacher would accept the ways that culture influences teaching and learning and be ready to learn how, as Gay (2000) has suggested, to teach "*to and through* the strengths of these students" (p. 29, italics in original) within cross-cultural classroom and community contexts.

However, there is evidence that many European American preservice teachers are operating from ethnocentric, minimization worldview (Mahon, 2003; Marx & Moss, 2011) and, thus, are not yet able to be culturally responsive. Typical of the minimization stage of the DMIS, many monocultural preservice teachers lack consciousness of culture, have little sense of their own cultural identity or culture as a construct, and tend to minimize cultural differences and accentuate similarities. The culture-blind and colorblind approach to teaching that many preservice students take is indicative of minimization; they often look for ways people are similar at a fundamental level (and by similar, it is meant "just like me"), and believe that to be "fair" everyone must be treated the same (and by the same, it is meant, "as I would like to be treated").

Importantly, a person in the minimization stage has reached a developmental level where they would no longer deny or be defensive about the existence of cultural differences between people; they accept that all people are equally human. The humanistic approach taken by many preservice teachers demonstrates this growth in intercultural sensitivity. However, it is the assumption of similarity that accompanies the understanding of humankind's common humanity that is the developmental challenge of the minimization stage as described in the DMIS. The task, then, for teacher educators working with preservice teachers whose worldview might be within the minimization stage is to help them become conscious of culture and understand that all people construct their perceptions of the world filtered through understandings of reality that are culturally defined.

TRANSITION FROM AN ETHNOCENTRIC
TO ETHNORELATIVE WORLDVIEW

Within the DMIS, the transition from an ethnocentric to an ethnorelative worldview is crucial to being able to develop intercultural competence and is, I argue here, necessary for culturally responsive teaching. Making the transition from ethnocentric to ethnorelative is very difficult. Bennett (1993) explained that between the minimization and acceptance stages there is a "paradigmatic barrier":

> Movement to the next stage represents a major conceptual shift from reliance on absolute, dualistic principles of some sort to an acknowledgement of nonabsolute relativity. . . . For many people in minimization, lack of awareness of their own culture underlies the assumption of cultural similarity. When they can place more of their own behavior in a cultural context, they are less inclined to assume that the behavior is universal. (p. 45)

In the transition out of minimization one must overcome assumptions of similarity and of a single reality that is typical of the minimization stage. In this transition, one must develop an awareness of one's self and others as cultural, confront the assumption of a single reality, and come to accept the relativity of cultural understandings (Bennett, 2004). To make this transition, a person needs to confront the reality that they and culturally dissimilar people operate from fundamentally different cultural perspectives, that these cultural perspectives influence how each person perceives the world and communicates, and that each person's cultural perspective is, for them, viable and "right." This is a difficult and complex transition, with existential repercussions to one's notion of the self, truth, and reality. The transformation of consciousness needed in this transition is referred to as *perspective consciousness* (Hanvey, 1982), though it is often used synonymously with the term *cultural consciousness.*

Consciousness refers to the state of being aware of what is going on around you and your relationship to your environment or context. Flowing from this understanding, cultural consciousness is most often used to refer to an awareness of the cultural context, assumptions, understandings, and knowledge that guides how one perceives the world. The typical understanding of cultural consciousness usually focuses on a type of self-conscious awareness of one's own cultural perceptions and willingness to uncover how one's socialization in identity and cultural groups might influence beliefs, knowledge, values, and one's interactions within various contexts. It is assumed that, through becoming culturally conscious, one will come to understand that one's own cultural perspectives are socially constructed. Thought of in this way, cultural consciousness is self-focused, in that it is focused on becoming aware of the self within a cultural context.

The term perspective consciousness, on the other hand, is *self* and *other* focused. Perspective consciousness refers to our awareness and understanding that cultural others have different and equally valid (if not agreeable) perspectives of reality. Hanvey (1982), one of the first theorists to use the term, described perspective consciousness as:

> The recognition or awareness on the part of the individual that he or she has a view of the world that is not universally shared, that this view of the world has been and continues to be shaped by influences that often escape conscious detection, and that others have views of the world that are profoundly different from one's own. (p. 162)

The term perspective consciousness calls attention to the need to become conscious of one's own and others' cultural perceptions and contexts. This is the challenge in the transition from an ethnocentric to an ethnorelative worldview. In the process of becoming conscious of the Other's cultural perspectives and context, we must also become conscious of our own cultural perspectives. This transition of consciousness is a complex and dynamic process of becoming conscious of culture—our own and cultural others'—and, in so doing, confront the "assumptions of similarity" and the relativity of cultural contexts that are the core challenges in the transition from ethnocentric to enthnorelative worldviews.

SUPPORTING AND CHALLENGING INTERCULTURAL DEVELOPMENT IN TEACHER EDUCATION

Teacher education program seeking to help preservice teacher transition from ethnocentric to ethnorelative worldviews must address their intercultural development. Such programs need to create a supportive environment where students can engage in critical cultural reflection. They also should provide preservice teachers with opportunities to work and live in cross-cultural contexts, both domestically and internationally, and use these experiences as an avenue for critical cultural reflection.

Educational researchers have long drawn attention to the need to have preservice teachers engage in critical cultural reflection (Gay & Kirkland, 2003; Howard, 2003). King (2000) has cautioned that programs that seek to support reflective thinking must be finely tuned to students' readiness needs, including

> underlying respect for students regardless of their level of intellectual development; it acknowledges that the journey is each *student's* journey and that the teacher's role as guide is to choose responses that are adapted to the student's needs. Through respectful but challenging interactions like these, interactions that take account of students' epistemological assumptions, teachers can promote reflective thinking. (p. 25)

Programs that want to support the transformation of students' cultural consciousness must create a safe and supportive space where students can share what are often difficult and confusing thoughts and feeling and take risks as they seek to explore new areas of understanding and consciousness (Parks Daloz, 2000). Berger (2004) described such teachers as the guides who help students as they approach the "growing edge" of their knowledge and consciousness. She suggests that these teachers must help students find and recognize their edge, be good company at the edge, and help to build firm ground in a new place. As teacher educators continue to explore ways to promote critical cultural reflection, we must consider how we guide students, paying careful attention to the ways we create safe spaces from which to grow.

Teacher educators have long proposed the use of cross-cultural field experiences, often in urban schools, as an avenue for the preservice teachers to engage in critical cultural reflection and to learn to work within culturally diverse schools. Though these can be powerful learning experiences, research indicates that even with opportunities for guided reflection during these experiences, many preservice teachers can resist examining the sociocultural dimensions of schooling and discussions related to racism and racial identity (Irvine, 2003).

Study abroad experiences have been promoted as unique opportunities to address preservice teachers' intercultural development (Cushner & Brennan, 2007; Cushner & Mahon, 2002; Malewski, Sharma, & Phillion, 2012; Martin, 2012; Marx & Moss, 2011; Trilokekar & Kukar, 2011). These international experiences can provide significant intercultural challenges that provide the opportunity for monocultural teachers to experience a different cultural context and, with guidance, begin to develop perspective consciousness.

The DMIS provides an understanding of the way international experiences are important elements in the development of intercultural sensitivity and competence. The theory holds that as long as people stay within their own cultural context, they never need to become aware of the way their cultural context affects how they perceive the world or struggle with the reality that others may have very different cultural perceptions (Bennett, 2004). For those with limited intercultural encounters, their "culturalness" can stay out of their awareness; they can be competent communicators within their culture without becoming conscious of culture. However, international intercultural encounters can create the necessity to become culturally conscious in order to function effectively. Bennett (2004) explains that an intercultural experience:

> [G]enerates pressure for change in one's worldview. This happens because the 'default' ethnocentric worldview, while sufficient for managing relations within one's own culture, is inadequate to the task of developing and maintaining social relations across cultural boundaries. (p. 74)

Thus, in the process of becoming ethnorelative, significant encounters with cultural differences are needed in order to develop intercultural sensitivity.

Teacher education study abroad experiences can provide the opportunity for preservice teachers to directly experience a different cultural context and, with guidance, see that members of the other culture have different and equally valid perspectives on what constitutes appropriate educational practices, with the understanding that they do not have to agree with the practices. In the process of becoming conscious of this "other" cultural context, one needs to become conscious of one's own cultural perspectives; for preservice teachers, these experiences bring into relief the fact that they, too, have beliefs about teaching and learning that are culturally constructed and influence the way they teach and learn. This is the developmental challenge in the transition between the minimization and acceptance stages of the DMIS and essential to the development of culturally responsive teaching.

TRANSFORMATIVE INTERCULTURAL TEACHER EDUCATION

The transition from an ethnocentric to an ethnorelative worldview requires an educational program that is ready to support and challenge individuals on a journey of discovery and transformation. The development of perspective consciousness and an ethnorelative worldview is not only about knowing more, it is about knowing differently, and knowing differently is a transformative undertaking. Teacher education programs that take on the task of preparing culturally responsive teachers must be prepared to provide the appropriate levels of support and challenge that this type of transformative learning requires. Kegan (1994) cautions that such developmental and transformative educational programs must be carefully planned, stating:

> People grow best where they continuously experience an ingenious blend of support and challenge.... Environments that are weighted too heavily in the direction of challenge without adequate support are toxic; they promote defensiveness and constriction. Those weighted too heavily toward support without adequate challenge are ultimately boring; they promote devitalization. Both kinds of imbalance lead to withdrawal or dissociation from context. In contract, the balance of support and challenge leads to vital engagement. (p. 42)

Teacher educators who seek to understand preservice teachers' intercultural development must carefully calibrate the support and challenge they design into their programs that might allow for the development of perspective consciousness.

Thus, an intercultural, developmental approach to teacher education means that teacher educators who are working with preservice teachers who might have an ethnocentric worldview not condemn their students for their lack of intercultural experiences or cultural consciousness—a sentiment that runs buried within research related to preservice teachers' beliefs and attitudes. Jenks et al. (2001) have proposed:

> Preservice teacher education programs must be sensitive to such issues as their students' motivations to learn, their prior knowledge about diversity, differences in their learning styles, and differences in the cultural values they being to class. Teacher education fails when it puts on ideological blinders and enacts a hidden curriculum that emphasizes ignorance and guilt, even suggesting moral turpitude. (p. 90)

Developmentally appropriate teacher education practice dictates that we more deeply understand and attend to the intercultural developmental needs of our students, seeking to meet them where they are, and providing well-designed programs that challenge and support them on their way towards interculturally sensitive, culturally responsive teaching. Teacher educators must find ways to create programs that build bridges for students as they transform from ethnocentric towards ethnorelative worldviews, allowing them to begin on the path towards culturally responsive teaching.

NOTE

1. This chapter emanates from sections of my doctoral dissertation, Marx, H. (2008). *Please mind the gap: A pre-service teacher's intercultural development during a study abroad program* (Doctoral dissertation).University of Connecticut, Storrs, Connecticut.

REFERENCES

Bennett, C. I. (1995). Preparing teachers for cultural diversity and national standards of academic excellence. *Journal of Teacher Education, 46*(4), 259–265.

Bennett, C. I. (2001). Genres of research in multicultural education. *Review of Educational Research, 71*(2), 171–217.

Bennett, M. J. (1993). Towards ethnorelativism: A developmental model of intercultural sensitivity. In M. Paige (Ed.), *Education for intercultural experience* (pp. 21–72). Boston, MA: Intercultural Press.

Bennett, M. J. (2004). Becoming interculturally competent. In J. Wurzel (Ed.), *Toward multiculturalism: A reader in multicultural education* (pp. 62–77). Newton, MA: Intercultural Resource Corporation.

Bennett, J. M., & Bennett, M. J. (2004). Developing intercultural sensitivity: An integrative approach to global and domestic diversity. In D. Landis, J. M. Bennett, & M. J. Bennett (Eds.), *Handbook of intercultural training* (3rd ed.) (pp. 147–166). Thousand Oaks, CA: Sage.

Berger, J. G. (2004). Dancing on the threshold of meaning: Recognizing and understanding the growing edge. *Journal of Transformative Education, 2*(4), 336–351.

Boser, U. (2011). *Teacher diversity matters: A state-by-state analysis of teachers of color.* Washington, DC: Center for American Progress.

Cochran-Smith, M. (1995). Color blindness and basket making are not the answers: Confronting the dilemmas of race, culture, and language diversity in teacher education. *American Educational Research Journal, 32*(3), 493–522.

Cochran-Smith, M. (2005). Studying teacher education: What we know and need to know. *Journal of Teacher Education, 56*(4), 301–306.

Cushner, K. (1988). Achieving intercultural effectiveness: Current knowledge, goals, and practices. *Education and Urban Society, 20*(2), 159–176.

Cushner, K., & Brennan, S. (2007). *Intercultural student teaching: A bridge to global competence.* Lanham, MD: Rowman & Littlefield Education.

Cushner, K., & Mahon, J. (2002). Overseas student teaching: Affecting personal, professional, and global competencies in an age of globalization. *Journal of Studies in International Education, 6*(1), 44–58.

Gay, G. (1994). *A synthesis of scholarship in multicultural education: NCREL Urban Education Monograph Series.* Oak Brook, IL: North Central Regional Education Laboratory.

Gay, G. (2000). *Culturally responsive teaching: Theory, research, and practice.* New York, NY: Teachers College Press.

Gay, G. (2002). Preparing for culturally responsive teaching. *Journal of Teacher Education, 53*(2), 106–116.

Gay, G., & Kirkland, K. (2003). Developing cultural critical consciousness and self-reflection in preservice teacher education. *Theory into Practice, 42*(3), 181–187.

Hammer, M. R., Bennett, M. J., & Wiseman, R. (2003). Measuring intercultural sensitivity: The intercultural development inventory. *International Journal of Intercultural Relations, 27*(4), 421–443.

Hanvey, R. G. (1982). An attainable global perspective. *Theory into Practice, 21*(3), 162.

Hodgkinson, H. (2002). Demographics and teacher education: An overview. *Journal of Teacher Education, 53*(2), 102–105.

Howard, T. C. (2003). Culturally relevant pedagogy: Ingredients for critical teacher reflection. *Theory into Practice, 42*(3), 195–202.

Irvine, J. J. (2003). *Educating teachers for diversity: Seeing with a cultural eye.* New York, NY: Teachers College Press.

Jenks, C., Lee, J. O., & Kanpol, B. (2001). Approaches to multicultural education in preservice teacher education: Philosophical frameworks and models for teaching. *Urban Review, 33*(2), 87.

Kegan, R. (1994). *In over our heads: The mental demands of modern life.* Cambridge, MA: Harvard University Press.

Kim, Y. Y. (1988). On theorizing intercultural communication. In Y. Y. Kim & W. B. Gudykunst (Eds.), *Theories in intercultural communication* (pp. 11–21). Newbury Park, CA: Sage.

King, P. M. (2000). Learning to make reflective judgments. In M. Baxter Magolda (Ed.), *Teaching to promote intellectual and personal maturing: Incorporating students' worldviews and identities into the learning process: New directions for teaching and learning* (pp. 15–26). New York, NY: Jossey-Bass.

Ladson-Billings, G. J. (2005). Is the team all right? Diversity and teacher education. *Journal of Teacher Education, 56*(3), 229–234.

Larkin, J. M. (1995). Curriculum themes and issues in multicultural teacher education programs. In J. Larkin & C. Sleeter (Eds.), *Developing multicultural teacher education curricula* (pp. 1–16). New York, NY: State University of NY Press.

Mahon, J. A. (2003). *Intercultural sensitivity development among practicing teachers: Life history perspectives* (Unpublished doctoral dissertation). Kent State University, Kent, OH.

Malewski, E., Sharma, S., & Phillion, J. (2012). How international field experiences promote cross-cultural awareness in preservice teachers through experiential learning: Findings from a six-year collective case study. *Teachers College Record, 114*(8), 1–44.

Martin, L. (2012). *International student teaching in non-Western cultures: Impact on first year teachers* (Doctoral dissertation). Retrieved from Digital Repository at Iowa State University. (12399 http://lib.dr.iastate.edu/etd/12399)

Marx, H., & Moss, D. M. (2011). Please mind the culture gap: Intercultural development during a teacher education study abroad program. *Journal of Teacher Education, 62*(1), 35–47.

Medina-Lopez-Portillo, A. (2004). Intercultural learning assessment: The link between program duration and the development of intercultural sensitivity. *Frontiers: The Interdisciplinary Journal of Study Abroad, 10*, 179–200.

McAllister, G., & Irvine, J. J. (2000). Cross cultural competency and multicultural teacher education. *Review of Educational Research, 70*(1), 3–24.

Nieto, S. (2004). *Affirming diversity: The sociopolitical context of multicultural education* (4th ed.). New York, NY: Allyn & Bacon.

Parks Daloz, L. (2000). Transformative learning for the common good. In J. Mezirow (Ed.), *Learning as transformation: Critical perspectives on theory in progress* (pp. 103–124). San Francisco, CA: Jossey-Bass.

Pohan, C. (1996). Preservice teachers' beliefs about diversity: Uncovering factors leading to multicultural responsiveness. *Equity & Excellence in Education, 29*(3), 62–69.

Rogoff, B. (2003). *The cultural nature of cognitive development.* New York, NY: Oxford University.

Sleeter, C. E. (2001). Preparing teachers for culturally diverse schools: Research and the overwhelming presence of whiteness. *Journal of Teacher Education, 52*(2), 94–106.

Trilokekar, R. D., & Kukar, P. (2011). Disorienting experiences during study abroad: Reflections of pre-service teacher candidates. *Teaching and Teacher Education, 27*(7), 1141–1150.

Trumbull, E., & Pacheco, M. (2005). *Leading with diversity: Cultural competencies for teacher preparation and professional development.* Providence, RI: Brown University and Pacific Resources for Education and Learning.

Wideen, M., Mayer-Smith, J., & Moon, B. (1998). A critical analysis of the research on learning to teach: Making the case for an ecological perspective on inquiry. *Review of Educational Research, 68*(2), 130–178.

CHAPTER 3

IN SEARCH OF FRAMEWORK FOR TEACHING GLOBAL CITIZENSHIP AND SOCIAL JUSTICE

Anatoli Rapoport

ABSTRACT

Global citizenship education is one of the most contested and debated models in the citizenship education paradigm. On the one hand, global citizenship education falls victim to deficient teacher education curricula, lack of knowledge and motivation among educators, or falsely understood patriotism. On the other hand, teachers who are interested in incorporating global perspectives in citizenship education lack pedagogical knowledge and incentives to do so. This chapter demonstrates how global citizenship can be introduced through the framework of social justice. The author argues that by emphasizing the examples and ideas of social justice and equality in courses such as world history, U.S. history, geography and history of the world, world civilizations, economics, or civics, teachers can develop multiple loyalties, perspective consciousness, and multicultural awareness, essential components of global democratic citizenship.

Internationalizing Teaching and Teacher Education for Equity, pages 39–55

INTRODUCTION

Education, particularly its social component, has always been at the forefront of the definition of new boundaries in the development of society. Simply by virtue of being the one, and sometimes the only one, who has to respond to children's questions, the teacher and other education professionals often find themselves in the position where they have to define and make sense of a newly emerging phenomenon and to be able to intelligently, and as uncontroversially as possible, explain its meaning. Two such phenomena in recent classroom discourse are global citizenship and social justice. Numerous studies demonstrate that both of these concepts are far from universally accepted in classrooms, particularly in the United States (Banks, 2004; Gallavan, 2008; Merryfield, 2000; Myers, 2006; Rapoport, 2013; Villegas, 2007). But research has also demonstrated a growing interest among educators in learning more about these two concepts. This volume is a testimony to this interest. Whether this interest is the result of an emerging anticipation of an active social role of educators or a natural reaction to the burgeoning infosphere still remains to be seen. However, it should be admitted that this interest is a positive tendency that requires additional efforts from teacher educators and scholars in facilitating teachers to better understand and eventually internalize the two concepts of global citizenship and social justice.

With the growing interest in supranational categories of citizenship, as well as principles of social justice, the question arises of how we address these and related concepts in schools. Should we incorporate knowledge about different forms of citizenship and theoretical grounds of social justice into school curricula? Is school an appropriate space for instilling the skills necessary for becoming a globally minded, socially just citizen? How well is our education system equipped to teach dispositions attributed to global citizens? These are complex questions that educators are asking themselves more and more often (Merryfield, 2000; Myers, 2006; Rapoport, 2013; Schweisfurth, 2006).

In this chapter, I will demonstrate that global citizenship education and education for social justice are allies in the cause of educating globally minded, responsible, and informed citizens. First, the current debates about both concepts are presented. Next, some challenges of incorporating global citizenship education and education for social justice into curricula are described. Finally, the need of resocialization as a possible framework in current citizenship education will be discussed.

TWO COMPONENTS OF CITIZENSHIP EDUCATION

Historically, citizenship has evolved into a concept that has expanded well beyond its primary legal meaning. As an increasingly contested construct, citizenship has been placed at the center of political, ideological, and cultural debates (Banks, 2008; Barr, 2005; Zajda, 2009). This is because citizenship is seen as a virtue that can be actively practiced by members of society to resist the increasing political apathy and indifference among voters. Citizenship is the measure that helps exercise individual rights against government, and it is citizenship that is perceived as a means for minorities to achieve desirable equality and status. Citizenship is a multifaceted, multifunctional construct that is difficult to define in a traditional manner.

Until recently, at least one aspect of citizenship has been almost universally accepted: Citizenship has been interpreted as an individual relationship with a nation-state when loyalty to the state and building a common identity were at the core of citizenship education (Lawson & Scott, 2002). To be a citizen implied that an individual, at a minimum, had a number of responsibilities to the state and to other members of the community and, at the same time, enjoyed rights that the state awarded him or her as compensation for fulfilling his or her responsibilities. However, as James A. Banks (2008) notes, this basic definition is accurate but it does not reveal the growing complexity and multifaceted nature of citizenship in modern nation-states.

Another area of education that is at the focus of debates is education for social justice. Formal education is a social process. In a democracy, society determines the principal ideas that are institutionalized through education. Thus, schools, particularly public schools, serve as a major institution for educating citizens to internalize not only knowledge and skills but also values and dispositions cultivated and cherished in the society. This functionalistic formula, that in very general simplistic terms describes the symbiotic relations between the society and its system of education, is hardly ubiquitous, although it does normally operate well in democratic societies because these societies, unlike their authoritarian counterparts, have developed dynamic and reliable mechanisms to adequately respond to constant changes. And one of the very important changes in a democracy is that it slowly and gradually becomes more just. Social justice, as a dualistic model of redistribution and recognition (North, 2006), is probably one of the most significant features and, at the same time, achievements of a democratic society.

CHALLENGES TO GLOBAL CITIZENSHIP EDUCATION AND EDUCATION FOR SOCIAL JUSTICE

There are striking similarities in the development of both global citizenship education and education for social justice in U.S. schools. But at a time when social science scholars have been discussing the concepts of global citizenship and social justice at conferences and symposia, practitioners have not been very vocal about these concepts in the classroom. What makes these concepts so controversial? First, it is necessary to note that the ideas of both global citizenship and social justice are still not universally accepted. It is hardly a surprise that much of the criticism is related to their social and political aspects. Wood (2008) denounced global citizenship because citizenship is a technology of governance rather than "an unambiguously emancipatory, empowering institution" (p. 25), and there are no formal political structures at the global level of which citizenship could be a part. Noddings (2005) explained the difficulty of defining global citizenship by pointing out that there is no global government to which we owe allegiance, and there are no international laws that are enacted without nations' endorsement. An absence of relevant global institutions, together with a disbelief in global ethics or in the role of an individual in global affairs, is the primary reason people are skeptical of global citizenship, contends Dower (2003). The emerging global civil society faces several accusations itself: that it is terminologically ambiguous, that its supporters uncritically apply nation-state phenomena to global processes, and that it undermines democracy by weakening the democratic institutions of nation-states (Corry, 2006). Armstrong (2006) argued that the supposedly "global" elements of global citizenship are much less universal and transcendent. Miller (as cited in Carter, 2006, p. 5) calls the idea of global citizenship utopian because "the conditions for global citizenship do not exist and the term is therefore at best metaphorical." Although the role of the nation-state in citizenship education is constantly changing as a consequence of both subnational and supranational forces (Barr, 2005; Ramirez, 1997), the potentially pervasive role of the nation-state in the construction of global citizenship remains problematic due to unresolved tensions in cultural and value-oriented perspectives between Western and non-Western countries (White & Openshaw, 2002).

By the same token, the concept of social justice remains controversial and challenging for many. Justice as a moral category has occupied the minds of philosophers for centuries and even millennia. The term *social justice* was coined by an Italian scholar and Catholic priest, Luigi Taparelli, in 1840. However, the principles of social justice came to attract specific and more critical attention when they became associated with the Marxist idea of a classless society. Austrian philosopher Friedrich Hayek rejected the very idea of social justice as being incoherent. First, he said that justice or injustice can only be attributes of the deliberate actions of individual human beings and not of states of affairs. Second, he argued that the notion of social justice would be unrealizable since there can be no rules of individual action that would guarantee a certain way of wealth distribution. And third, given the wide disagreement in a pluralistic society over the criteria to determine how economic rewards get distributed, there is no principled way in which the ideas of social justice could be implemented consistently. Thus, Hayek concluded, the push for social justice, which he called a mirage, threatens democracy with totalitarianism (Feser, 2005).

According to critics, social justice is an ambiguous and ideologically loaded term with the potential for abuse. Villegas (2007) noted that the opponents of social justice insist that its agenda is nothing more than political indoctrination that distracts educators, particularly preservice teachers, from their real work. Political and ideological criticism of the idea of social justice is also a residual effect of general intolerance to everything that is defined as social. As such, social justice is seen by its critics as only a means of wealth redistribution. Neoconservative and some libertarian commentators directly link social justice to socialism, which for rank-and-file Americans, particularly those who lived through the McCarthyism of the 1950s and the Cold War, is blasphemy rather than a political and governing theory. "What is 'social justice'?" asked Barry Loberfeld (2004) in an article eloquently titled "Social Justice: Code for Communism," answering that it is "the theory that implies and justifies the practice of socialism. And what is 'socialism'? It is domination by the state. What is 'socialized' is state-controlled. So what is 'totalitarian' socialism other than total socialism, i.e., state control of everything?" (para. 14). David Horowitz of the California-based David Horowitz Freedom Center contended that social justice teaching is "shorthand for opposition to American traditions of individual justice and free-market economics" that teaches students that "American society is an inherently 'oppressive' society that is 'systemically' racist, 'sexist,' and 'classist' and thus discriminates institutionally against women, nonwhites, working Americans, and the poor" (Schlafly, 2008, para. 6). It is also noteworthy how critics of ideas of global citizenship and social justice use the narrative of blind patriotism (Staub, 1997) and nationalistic, jingoistic rhetoric to demonstrate the threat of both phenomena to a traditionalistic, conservative audience (Finn, 2007; Fonte, 1997).

The concept of social justice and education for social justice in particular became the target of especially harsh criticism in 2008 during the presidential campaign because one of the candidates, then Senator Obama, was accused of having close ties with William Ayers, a professor of Education at the University of Illinois at Chicago. He had been one of the leaders of the Weather Underground, an organization that was described by the FBI as a domestic terrorist group. Following the ideas of Paulo Freire and being one of the leading scholars in the field of critical pedagogy, Ayers argued that school curricula should be guided by the principles of social justice. Sol Stern (2008), a senior fellow at the Manhattan Institute, called Ayers "not a school reformer [but] . . . a school destroyer" for bringing radical social-justice teaching into our public school classrooms (para. 11).

CONTROVERSIES OF MEANING

Another reason for debates, mostly theoretical, about global citizenship as well as social justice is the absence of a consensus on what these concepts entail. Most authors identify several factors that have caused an increased interest in supranational models of citizenship and consequent changes in citizenship education. The most noticeable among these factors are globalization, increasing cultural and social diversity, erosion of traditional nation-state related models of citizenship, creation of supranational governing bodies, codification of international human rights, proliferation of transnational nongovernmental organizations, and the rise of such phenomena as global ethics, global consciousness, and global law, to name a few (Banks, 2004; Dower, 2003; Gaudelli, 2009; Myers, 2006; Stromquist, 2009). We cannot use a traditional technical definition of citizenship to describe global citizenship, for there is no global government that defines the status of a global citizen. To avoid the "global government" problem, some authors suggest an associational approach (Lagos, 2002; Steenbergen, 1994) in which global citizenship is not defined by legal bureaucratic sanctions but by individuals' associations with the place or polity where they reside, work, or spend time. The European Union is an example of such an association. Dower (2003) argued that the status of a global citizen is made up of three components: (1) normative—as global citizens, we have certain duties that extend to all human beings; (2) existential—we are all members of the global community, whether institutional or quasipolitical in character; and (3) aspirational—as global citizens, we expect basic values to be realized more fully, which requires strengthening communities, institutions, and legal frameworks.

It is also interesting how some authors link the ideas of justice and mutual prosperity with a rationalization for global citizenship. Noddings (2005) suggests that a global citizen is someone who is concerned with the welfare of a nation, region, or globe; is concerned with the well-being of particular physical places; is interested in social as well as economic justice; and supports world peace. McIntosh (2005) proposes a more emotional definition that involves affection, respect, care, curiosity, and concern for the well-being of all living beings. She associates global citizenship with habits and capacities of mind, heart, body, and soul that "have to do with working for and preserving a network of relationship and connection across lines of difference and distinctness, while keeping and deepening a sense of one's own identity and integrity" (p. 23).

Although the term *global citizen* is relatively new, the idea that it represents has occupied minds for centuries. Like any big idea, global citizenship is ostensibly interpreted by people differently due to their own ideologies and contexts. Thus, a discourse, as a primary locus where ideology, language, and context intersect, and where meanings are negotiated and crystallized, becomes a space in which to look for definitions. Discursive typologization is helpful in that it avoids one-dimensional definitions and describes global citizenship as a multifaceted concept. Gaudelli (2009) employs heuristics to define five different discourses of global citizenship: (1) neoliberal, where a global citizen is still affiliated nationally but is governed by a universal market conception; (2) national, where civic identity is a social compact between the nation and the citizen; (3) Marxist, which bases global citizenship on class—primarily proletarian—collectives that transcend national borders; (4) world justice and governance, which rationalizes global citizenship through global human rights, international law, and global civil society; and (5) cosmopolitan, whose framework of global citizenship includes matters of value, morality, and humane treatment. Stromquist (2009) organizes her analysis around major features of the global model of citizenship. She argues that the four discourses that help understand these features are (1) *World Culture*, (2) *New-Era Realism*, (3) *Corporate Citizenship*, and (4) *Planetary Vessel.*

After almost two centuries of its existence, the term *social justice* is still vaguely defined. The same is true about its manifestation in education. The range of definitions of social justice education spans from being about treating all students equally to the dismantling and reconstructing of education from its very core (Hackman, 2005). Education for social justice aims at providing students with a clear understanding of what justice entails in a society. Classical theory of social justice (Gewitz, 1998; Rawls, 1972), which focuses on a distributional orientation of justice, refers to the fact that a just society cannot exist without fair distribution of material and nonmaterial resources. These resources include—among other things—rights, duties, and responsibilities. The relational orientation of justice refers to relationships that shape society. Gewitz (1998) argued that relational justice is critical for understanding "issues of power and how we treat each other, both in the sense of face-to-face interactions and in the sense of macro social and economic relations which are mediated by institutions such as the state and the market" (p. 471).

If we assume that the principal factor in achieving social justice is the consensus that the society and all its components operate fairly and all individuals experience as much freedom as possible given the role they have within society, then "true social justice is attained through the harmonious cooperative efforts of the citizens who, in their own self-interest, accept the current norms of morality as the price of membership in the community" (Zajda, Majhanovich, & Rust, 2006, p. 3). Johannessen and Unterreiner (2010) frame the vision of social justice education as a "set of guiding principles, inspired by democratic values and built on academic experience, critical reflection, and accountability" (p. 81). These principles are personal and professional integrity, caring, respect, commitment to service, and accountability. They tie teaching for social justice with teachers' ethics. Projecting the role of social justice in the development of teachers' disposition, Villegas (2007) concludes that the overriding goal of the social justice agenda in teacher education is to "prepare teachers who can teach all students well, not just those traditionally well served by schools, so that, as adults all are able to participate equitably in the economic and political life of the country" (p. 372). Hackman (2005) argues that social justice education does not merely examine diversity or differences; rather, it creates conditions for careful attention to the systems of power and privilege that allow for social inequality. Education for social justice, according to Hackman, goes beyond the celebration of diversity; it encourages students to critically examine all types of oppression on various levels including institutional, cultural, and individual, as well as to search for opportunities for social action.

GLOBAL CITIZENSHIP
AND SOCIAL JUSTICE IN THE CLASSROOM

Considering the content and programmatic controversies surrounding global citizenship and social justice, it is not surprising that teachers are usually unaware of the curricular materials or instructional strategies related to teaching these concepts (Gallavan, 2008; Gaudelli, 2009; Myers, 2006; Phillion & Malewski, 2011; Quin, 2009; Rapoport, 2009; Robbins, Francis, & Elliot, 2003; Yamashita, 2006). A survey among 187 teacher training and education program graduates in Wales demonstrated that although 76% of the graduates thought that global citizenship should have a high priority in the secondary school curriculum, only 35% felt confident to contribute to a whole-school approach to global citizenship (Robbins et al., 2003). A study in England reported that 700 teachers rated education for global citizenship as important, but had little confidence in their ability to teach it (Davis et al., as cited in Yamashita, 2006). The majority of teacher candidates from a mid-South university in the United States wanted to teach the students to be world citizens, but many also felt unprepared by their teacher education programs or field experiences (Gallavan, 2008). As for the increasing emphasis on social justice in teacher education, this theme causes confusion among teachers. Some teacher education programs focus on teachers' beliefs and identities, while others concentrate on democratic education or multicultural issues (Cochran-Smith, 2010).

There is little doubt that there is an organic connection between education for global citizenship and social justice. Regardless of the origin of both terms, these two concepts possess an internal similarity manifested through a number of values and dispositions attributed to a person who can be considered a socially just, global citizen. It is not all that surprising that scholars who study problems of global citizenship education also write about education for social justice. As White and Talbert have (2005) asserted: "We must prepare children for active participation as global citizens; this means that we have a responsibility to teach for social justice" (as cited in Zajda et al., 2006, p. 2).

Indeed, can a globally minded person who feels responsibility for the global community not be concerned about poverty, hunger, oppression, or discrimination? By the same token, can a person who is genuinely committed to the ideas of justice and fairness not be concerned about whether people are treated justly all over the world? Justice is, by definition, social (Zajda, 2010) in the sense that it ultimately depends on the coordination of individual and institutional efforts. It is impossible to separate the idea of social justice from the idea of global citizenship; therefore, education for social justice is an integral and essential component of global citizenship education. These two areas of education complement each other. Hackman found that a social justice approach in education is characterized by five essential components: (1) content mastery, (2) tools for critical analysis, (3) tools for social change, (4) tools for personal reflection, and (5) awareness of multicultural group dynamics. Not surprisingly, these components are also essential in citizenship education (Banks, 2004; Engle & Ochoa, 1988) and in global citizenship education in particular (Banks, 2004; Merryfield, 1998, 2000; Wilson, 1984, 1986). Classroom teachers involved in implementing international and global education in schools use content and critical analysis in the following ways: (1) to make connections across cultures and civilizations and across global issues, (2) to identify historical antecedents to current world issues and problems, (3) to link global content to the lives of their students, and (4) to teach tolerance and appreciation of cultural differences (Merryfield, 1994). Many experienced teachers use reflection as their teaching strategy. They agree that reflection encourages them to grow and helps them to understand concepts such as culture, perspective consciousness, and global dynamics.

Teacher reflection is an integral step in developing instruction that brings about student reflection so that students begin to see the world around them in new ways (Merryfield, 2000). Reflective strategies or experiential learning assume direct contact with other cultures and peoples essential for understanding multicultural group dynamics. Direct interactions and contact with different cultures, political or educational systems, and representatives of these cultures (1) improve teaching about the places visited; (2) engender educators' responsibilities for passing on the experience, for opening windows on the world for others; and (3) encourage them to try more cross-cultural encounters (Wilson, 1984, 1986). Teaching practices and curricular decisions made by exemplary teachers in global education are usually characterized by cross-cultural experiential learning, students' characteristics, and emphasis on multiple perspectives and perspective consciousness, multiple realities, and multiple loyalties (Merryfield, 2000).

Debates about the essence of global citizenship, or whether or not social justice is too radical, leave little space for a basic question: Where do global citizenship education and education for social justice belong? We routinely say that citizenship education and education for social justice are multi-component systems that involve a number of agencies—government, community, media, parents, peers, and school—which all have their share in socializing a child and in making a child a responsible, informed, and just citizen. However, who particularly should be doing the work? Which agency is best equipped to provide conditions, space, and guidance for developing the knowledge, skills, and dispositions needed to educate globally minded and socially responsible citizens?

It seems that schools can play the leading role in this process, as schools are designed to reflect on and to react to emerging challenges, particularly cultural, social, or ideological. It remains to be seen whether the reaction of many schools is timely and adequate; the public and educators themselves are often skeptical about it. Nevertheless, schools remain the core element of the citizenship education network and education for social justice. But school curriculum, which is a set of ideas, texts, practices, and pedagogies, usually focuses on the disciplines. Global citizenship education and education for social justice, as inherently multi- and interdisciplinary areas, lack what Gaudelli (2009) calls "disciplinary heritage" (p. 78). Although each school discipline has the potential to introduce elements of citizenship or social justice in its content, and many do, the discipline-based approach nevertheless narrows a school's capacity to present any model of citizenship in its entirety. Ostensibly, global citizenship education is usually conceptualized within the frameworks of international education, global education (Davies, Evans, & Reid, 2005), multicultural education (Banks, 2004; Dunn, 2002), peace education (Smith & Fairman, 2005), human rights education (Gaudelli & Fernekes, 2004), or economic education. Education for social justice is usually envisioned as a component of moral education (Johannessen, 2010; Johannessen & Unterreiner, 2010), which is by itself a vaguely defined, nondisciplinary area of education. Practitioners are well aware that none of these approaches, with the possible exception of economic education, has yet secured a position in school curricula. Thus, global citizenship or social justice, if taught as one of the topics within these frameworks, would become even more secondary. Such curricular insecurity discourages even those teachers who are enthusiastic about global citizenship or social justice.

EDUCATING GLOBALLY MINDED AND SOCIALLY JUST
CITIZENS: RESOCIALIZATION FRAMEWORK

The interdependence of the two discourses, those of global citizenship and social justice, in education, their contextual and conventional closeness, as well as the similarity of problems that they face, create conditions in which teaching of one concept inevitably involves teaching the other. Connecting the two paradigms emphasizes important aspects of citizenship when a student learns to comprehend global phenomena not only in geospatial, economic, or cultural terms but also in social terms—that is, in terms of human compassion, empathy, and care. This added emotional dimension of the "simple gesture of humanity" (Johannessen & Unterreiner, 2010, p. 79) in global citizenship education may be a decisive factor in making it ubiquitous and transformative (Banks, 2008). Cochran-Smith (2010) underscores that teaching for social justice is fundamental to the learning and life chances of all teachers and students who are the current and future participants in a diverse, democratic nation and who are able both to imagine and work toward a more just society. By accepting the close proximity or even similarity of objectives in global citizenship education and in education for social justice, we admit that the ultimate goal in applying both orientations in education is raising a socially just global citizen.

Paradoxically, it is easier for an individual to believe that he or she is socially just than to admit to being, or having to behave as, a global citizen. Every human being by the very fact of birth is a member of the global human society. But does this automatically make every human being a responsible global citizen? Probably not. Citizenship status, unlike socially constructed legal citizenship, extends far beyond formal passive membership. It requires very specific knowledge, competences, and qualities that can only be acquired in the process of informal and formal global education and through the development of global consciousness as a result of global socialization. Therefore, the famous phrase of Woodrow Wilson that we are all global citizens and the tragedy is that we do not know about it, can be interpreted differently. We are all members of a global society. The tragedy is that we are still reluctant to become global citizens. It took time for all educational agencies, both formal and informal, to develop a sophisticated system that socializes an individual into a national or communal citizen. This system is not perfect, but it functions. The system of global socialization that can educate a member of a global society into a global citizenship is only starting to emerge. This newly emerging system will face a lot of obstacles, the principal of which is the fact that each individual is no longer an empty vessel or tabula rasa. In other words, global citizenship education works with nationally socialized individuals who will have to acquire knowledge, skills, or dispositions that are sometimes at odds with the knowledge and dispositions associated with national or communal citizenship. Or, as I wrote elsewhere, the task of global citizenship education is to *resocialize* students into becoming global citizens (Rapoport, 2010).

Socialization is a complex process of acquiring norms of behavior accepted in society. It is seen as an ongoing developmental process to acquire and internalize basic knowledge, values, beliefs, and relevant skills. Individuals internalize the society's political value system and ideology and come to understand its symbols and rituals. They become informed about the role of active and passive members of the polity and may participate in political and civic life (Owen, 2008). Although socialization, through its agents such as family, school, or other institutions, constructs and reconstructs identities both locally and globally (Kiwako Okuma-Nyström, 2009; Zajda, 2009), it still remains a predominantly local, area-centered, and nation-centered phenomenon. Traditionally, socialization has been nation-centered ever since the emergence of nations and later, nation-states. Nation-centered socialization has been an important feature of political socialization aimed at instilling in a child traditional cultural and ideological norms characteristic of—and thus limited to—a specific nation. Hence, classical socialization is devoid of engagement in any critical, analytical, or reflective activities; it rather focuses primarily on transmissive and reproductive activities. If we believe that the core of global citizenship education and education for social justice is critical analysis, inclusive practices, and reflective experiential actions (Cochran-Smith, 2010; Hackman, 2005; Merryfield, 1998, 2000; Quin, 2009; Wilson, 1986), then resocialization presents an intriguing and helpful framework for developing new curricula.

Three aspects are critical for understanding the resocialization framework for educating a socially just global citizen: exposure, transferability, and resistance (Black, Niemi, & Powell, 1987; White, Nevitte, Blais, Gidengil, & Fournier, 2008). Each aspect presents both potential and challenge for educators and students. Exposure requires that an individual have as much access to the new environment, phenomena, or knowledge as possible. The more exposure to the new that individuals have, the more they will adapt. Considering the advent of mass communication systems and increasingly expanding global social networks, it is safe to say that the potential exposure of young people to the world is unprecedented.

Through Facebook, Twitter, or around-the-clock real-time news cycles, students have many opportunities to get connected with their peers around the world and to learn about the world without mediation. They also become exposed to numerous cases of inequality, oppression, and injustice, both in the United States and around the world. Not only do contemporary communication systems and networks allow for observation of the cases of injustice or oppression, but they also allow for direct communication with the victims or agencies involved. Another important option for exposure in global citizenship education and in education for social justice is international trips or study abroad programs where sojourners experience the impact of the environment of poverty or oppression (Phillion & Malewski, 2011; Wang, Malewski, Phillion, & Sharma, 2010). Here, the role of educators is not only to provide access to global resources and thus make exposure possible, but also to help children and young adults navigate this sea of possibilities and information.

The transferability component of resocialization refers to the individual's adaptation to the new environment, to his or her ability to draw on past experiences; transfer the knowledge, skills, and dispositions from the old environments; and apply them to the new environments (White et al., 2008). Our students have been objects of citizenship education or, in other words, socialization since the day they were born. This means that they have been within discourses of global citizenship and social justice for a long time. However, these discourses were not in the focus of students' socialization and education. Global ethics, problems of peace, human and civil rights, global environmental problems, and problems of sustainability are, simply put, all problems encompassed by the idea of global citizenship. Also, the problems of equity, equality, resistance to oppression, and other questions that are attributed to social justice are a part of all human ecological systems (Bronfenbrenner, 1979) that surround and impact our students. The task of schools and education is simply to get these questions back into focus and to make them relevant to students.

The third component of resocialization, resistance, is grounded in classical socialization theory. It refers to initial opposition to new phenomena, sometimes unexplained and subconscious, resistance to accept or admit new realities and new environments. Educators and institutions that seriously plan to develop curricula for educating future global citizens concerned about social justice should be prepared to encounter resistance. Classical examples of such resistance are disbelief in the very idea of global citizenship, fear of the principles of social justice, or the tenacity of imaginary elements of reality, such as patriotism or nationalism. However, unlike in classical political socialization theory, where resistance is primarily the function of subjects of resocialization, resistance to global citizenship education or education for social justice is demonstrated by agents (schools, curricula,) rather than subjects (students). Also, we have to keep in mind a correlation between age and resistance: the younger the child is, the less resistant he or she is to the new.

Education is enormously important in combating prejudices and inequalities. Educational institutions can respond to the increasingly complex economic, cultural, moral, and social problems of children and young adults in our globalized world. Schools that are considered crucibles for socialization into democratic citizenship gradually begin to play a critically important role in exposing students to newer ideas of citizenship that span far beyond mere commitment to national symbols. These new ideas are constantly tested and contested because they present new challenges. Educating socially just, responsible, and informed global citizens is one such challenge. It is our duty as educators to find pedagogical tools that would meet and adequately respond to the challenge.

REFERENCES

Armstrong, C. (2006) Global civil society and the question of global citizenship. *Voluntas, 17*(4), 349–357.

Banks, J. (2004). Teaching for social justice, diversity, and citizenship in a global world. *The Educational Forum, 68*(4), 296–305.

Banks, J. (2008). Diversity, group identity, and citizenship education in a global age. *Educational Researcher, 37*(3), 129–139.

Barr, H. (2005). Toward a model of citizenship education: Coping with differences in definition. In C. White & R. Openshaw (Eds.), *Democracy at the crossroads* (pp. 55–75). London, UK: Lexington Books.

Black, J., Niemi, R., & Powell Jr., G. (1987). Age, resistance, and political learning in a new environment: The case of Canadian immigrants. *Comparative Politics, 20,* 70–84.

Bronfenbrenner, U. (1979). *The ecology of human development.* Cambridge, MA: Harvard University Press.

Carter, A. (2006). *The political theory of global citizenship.* London, UK: Routledge.

Cochran-Smith, M. (2010). Toward a theory of teacher education for social justice. In M. Fullan, A. Hargreaves, D. Hopkins, & A. Lieberman (Eds.), *Second international handbook of educational change* (pp. 445–468). New York, NY: Springer.

Corry, O. (2006). Global civil society and its discontents. *Voluntas,17*(4), 303–324.

Davies, I., Evans, M., & Reid, A. (2005) Globalizing citizenship education? A critique of 'global education' and 'citizenship education.' *British Journal of Educational Studies, 53*(1), 66–89.

Dower, N. (2003). *An introduction to global citizenship.* Edinburgh, UK: Edinburgh University Press.

Dunn, R. E. (2002). Growing good citizens with a world-centered curriculum. *Educational Leadership, 60*(2), 10–13.

Engle, S. H., & Ochoa, A. S. (1988). *Education for democratic citizenship.* New York, NY: Teachers College Press.

Feser, E. (2005). Social justice reconsidered: Austrian economics and Catholic social teaching. Retrieved from http://www.edwardfeser.com/unpublishedpapers/socialjustice.html

Finn, C. E. (2007). Teaching patriotism—with conviction. In J. Westheimer (Ed.), *Pledging allegiance: The politics of patriotism in America's schools* (pp. 95–98). New York, NY: Teachers College Press.

Fonte, J. (1997, October 27). Post-West syndrome: When patriotism is threatened, so are the roots of democracy. *National Review,* 38–42.

Gallavan, N. (2008). Examining teacher candidates' views on teaching world citizenship. *The Social Studies, 99*(6), 249–254.

Gaudelli, W. (2009). Heuristics of global citizenship discourses towards curriculum enhancement. *Journal of Curriculum Theorizing, 25*(1), 68–85.

Gaudelli, W., & Fernekes, W. (2004) Teaching about global human rights for global citizenship. *The Social Studies, 95*(1), 16–26.

Gewitz, S. (1998). Conceptualizing social justice in education: Mapping the territory. *Journal of Education Policy, 13*(4), 469–484.

Hackman, H. (2005). Five essential components for social justice education. *Equity and Excellence in Education, 38,* 103–109.

Johannessen, G. (2010). Pedagogical ethics for teaching social justice in teacher education. In J. Zajda (Ed.), *Globalization, education, and social justice* (pp. 3–13). Dordrecht: Springer.

Johannessen, B., & Unterreiner, A. (2010). Social justice pedagogy: Simple gesture of humanity. In J. Zajda (Ed.), *Globalization, education, and social justice* (pp.79–87). Dordrecht, Netherlands: Springer.

Kiwako Okuma-Nyström, M. (2009). Globalization, identities, and diversified school education. In J. Zajda, H. Daun, & L. J. Saha (Eds.), *Nation-building, identity and citizenship education: Cross cultural perspectives* (pp. 25–42). Dordrecht, NL: Springer.

Lagos, T. G. (2002). Global citizenship—toward the definition. Retrieved from http://www.depts.washington.edu/gcp/pdf/globalcitizenship.pdf

Lawson, H., & Scott, D. (2002). Introduction. In D. Scott & H. Lawson (Eds.), *Citizenship education and the curriculum* (pp. 2–6). Westport, CT: Ablex Publishing.

Loberfeld, B. (2004). *Social justice: Code for Communism.* Sherman Oaks, CA: David Horowitz Freedom Center. Retrieved from http://www.discoverthenetworks.org/guides/Z-Social%20Justice-Code%20for%20Communism.htm

McIntosh, P. (2005). Gender perspectives on educating for global citizenship. In N. Noddings (Ed.), *Educating citizens for global awareness* (pp. 22–39). New York, NY: Teachers College Press.

Merryfield, M. M. (1994). *In the global classroom: Teacher decision-making and global perspectives in education.* Paper presented to the American Educational Research Association, April 4, 1994, New Orleans. (ERIC Document Reproduction Service No. ED401249).

Merryfield, M. M. (1998). Pedagogy for global perspectives in education: Studies for teachers' thinking and practice. *Theory and Research in Social Education, 26*(3), 342–379.

Merryfield, M. M. (2000). Why aren't teachers being prepared to teach for diversity, equity, and global interconnectedness? A study of lived experiences in the making of multicultural and global educators. *Teaching and Teacher Education, 16,* 429–443.

Myers, J. P. (2006). Rethinking the social studies curriculum in the context of globalization: Education for global citizenship in the U.S. *Theory and Research in Social Education, 34*(3), 370–394.

Noddings, N. (2005). Global citizenship: Promises and problems. In N. Noddings (Ed.), *Educating citizens for global awareness* (pp. 1–21). New York, NY: Teachers College Press.

North, C. (2006). More than words? Delving into the substantive meaning(s) of "social justice" in education. *Review of Educational Research, 76*(4), 507–535.

Owen, D. (2008, September). *Political socialization in the twenty-first century: Recommendations for researchers.* Paper presented at the Future of Civic Education in the 21st Century conference, Montpelier, VA.

Phillion, J., & Malewski, E. (2011). Study abroad in teacher education: Delving into cultural diversity and developing cultural competence. *Action in Teacher Education: The Journal of the Association of Teacher Educators, 33* (5-6), 643–657.

Quin, J. (2009). Growing social justice educators: A pedagogical framework for social justice education. *Intercultural Education, 20*(2), 109–125.

Ramirez, F. O. (1997). The nation-state, citizenship, and educational change: Institutionalization and globalization. In W. K. Cummings & N. F. McGinn (Eds.), *International handbook of education and development: Preparing schools students and nations for the twenty-first century* (pp. 47–62). New York, NY: Elsevier Science.

Rapoport, A. (2009). A forgotten concept: Global citizenship education and state social studies standards. *Journal of Social Studies Research, 33*(1), 75–93.

Rapoport, A. (2010). We cannot teach what we don't know: Indiana teachers talk about global citizenship education. *Education, Citizenship and Social Justice, 5*(3), 1–11.

Rapoport, A. (2013). Global citizenship themes in the social studies classroom: Teaching devices and teachers' attitudes. *The Educational Forum, 77*(4), 407–420.

Rawls, J. (1972). *A theory of justice.* Oxford, UK: Clarendon Press.

Robbins, M., Francis, L. J., & Elliott, E. (2003). Attitudes toward education for global citizenship among trainee teachers. *Research in Education, 69*(1), 93–98.

Schlafly, P. (2008). *Teaching "social justice" in schools.* Cook, MN: Worldview Weekend. Retrieved from http://www.worldviewweekend.com/news/article/teaching-social-justice-schools

Schweisfurth, M. (2006). Education for global citizenship: Teacher agency and curricular structure in Ontario schools. *Educational Review, 58*(1), 41–50.

Smith, S. N., & Fairman, D. (2005). The integration of conflict resolution into the high school curriculum: The example of workable peace. In N. Noddings (Ed.), *Educating citizens for global awareness* (pp. 40–56). New York, NY: Teachers College Press.

Staub, E. (1997). Blind versus constructive patriotism: Moving from embeddedness in the group to critical loyalty and action. In D. Bar-Tal & E. Staub (Eds.), *Patriotism in the lives of individuals and nations* (pp. 213–228). Chicago, IL: Nelson-Hall Publishers.

Steenbergen, B. (1994). *The condition of citizenship.* London, UK: Sage.

Stern, S. (2008, October 16). Ayers is no education "reformer." *The Wall Street Journal.* Retrieved from http://www.wsj.com/articles/SB122411943821339043

Stromquist, N. P. (2009). Theorizing global citizenship: Discourses, challenges, and implications for education. *Interamerican Journal of Education for Democracy, 2*(1), 6–29.

Villegas, A. (2007). Dispositions in teacher education: A look at social justice. *Journal of Teacher Education, 58*(5), 370–380.

Wang, Y., Malewski, E., Phillion, J., & Sharma, S. (2010). Rethinking poverty, inequality and social injustice: Enhancing preservice teachers' awareness and perceptions through study abroad. *Journal of the International Society for Teacher Education, 14*(2), 17–24.

White, S., Nevitte, N., Blais, A., Gidengil, E., & Fournier, P. (2008). The political resocialization of immigrants: Resistance or lifelong learning? *Political Research Quarterly, 61*(2), 268–281.

White, C., & Openshaw, R. (2002). Translating the national to the global in citizenship education. In D. Scott & H. Lawson (Eds.), *Citizenship education and the curriculum* (pp. 151–166). Westport, CT: Ablex Publishing.

Wilson, A. H. (1984). Teachers as short-term international sojourners: Opening windows on the world. *The Social Studies, 75*(4), 153–157.

Wilson, A. H. (1986). Returned Peace Corps volunteers who teach social studies. *The Social Studies, 77*(3), 100–106.

Wood, P. (2008). The impossibility of global citizenship. *Brock Education, 17*, 22–37.

Yamashita, H. (2006). Global citizenship education and war: The needs of teachers and learners. *Educational Review, 58*(1), 27–39.

Zajda, J. (2009). Nation-building, identity, and citizenship education: Introduction. In J. Zajda, H. Daun, & L. J. Saha (Eds.), *Nation-building, identity and citizenship education: Cross cultural perspectives* (pp. 1–11). Dordrecht, NL: Springer.

Zajda, J. (2010). *Globalization, education, and social justice*. Dordrecht, NL: Springer.

Zajda, J., Majhanovich, S., & Rust, V. (2006). Education and social justice: Issues of liberty and equality in the global culture. In J. Zajda, S. Majhanovich, & V. Rust (Eds.), *Education and social justice* (pp. 1–12). Dordrecht, NL: Springer.

CHAPTER 4

POWER, PRIVILEGE, AND STUDY ABROAD AS "SPECTACLE"

Sandro R. Barros

I deeply respect American sentimentality, the way one respects a wounded hippo.
You must keep an eye on it, for you know it is deadly.
—Teju Cole, 2012

ABSTRACT

This chapter critically examines the short-term cohort model of study abroad within the present context of higher education's commodification of international experiences as a form of curriculum enrichment. Employing Guy Debord's concept of "spectacle" and Augusto Boal's theorization on the social dimension of Western drama, the author analyzes how privilege and power factor in the semiotic structure of study abroad programs and how the organization of study abroad can jeopardize the benefits international experiences can provide to students, particularly in instances when the socioeconomic asymmetry between participants' nations is obvious.

Internationalizing Teaching and Teacher Education for Equity, pages 57–75
Copyright © 2016 by Information Age Publishing

57

INTRODUCTION

Despite a considerable body of research dedicated to study abroad's burgeoning popularity in higher education, little attention has been paid to the short-term cohort model as a curricular experience intrinsically tied to the maintenance of a narrative of power and privilege within the context of higher education. While researchers have examined study programs' contributions to the development of students' linguistic identity (Jackson, 2008), global and U.S. citizenship (Benson, Barkhuizen, Bodycott, & Brown, 2013; Dolby, 2004; Grey, Cox, Serafini, & Sanz, 2015), professional development, employability, and academic performance (Potts, 2015), critical approaches have been scarce. Scholarship in the field has remained distant from directly confronting the social, the historical, and the ideological forces and structures that produce and constrain meaning in study abroad initiatives. This distance is particularly apparent in the lack of studies examining the foreign community's point of view on the study abroad experience. Moreover, the excessive reliance on participants' perspectives has tended to overlook the historical relationships of power between the U.S. and the host countries that direct many study abroad experiences in particular ways. By and large, the flow of discourses about global education continues unevenly, as knowledge traffics from the center to the periphery (Weber, 2007). This observation, therefore, brings to the fore a myriad of ethical concerns related to the nature of U.S. study abroad, citizenship as capital, and mobility as a privilege inherent to study abroad's semiosis.

Indeed, issues of reciprocity in knowledge-based exchanges among participants of study abroad continue to receive scant attention as an organizing ethical principle. Entities such as the Forum on Education Abroad, a nonprofit association serving as a regulating body for standards development in international academic programs, have attempted to implement specific guidelines to be used by participating institutions to affirm "respect for the cultures and values of those communities in which they operate" (Forum on Education Abroad, 2014, p. 15). Despite this acknowledgment, the standards and guidelines for program development make no mention of concrete initiatives and commitments to equalize knowledge-based exchanges between institutions and host nations, particularly where there is an imbalance of economic and social privilege. This imbalance can be exemplified by the lack of second-language preparation in the majority of study abroad ventures. To wit, only 3% of U.S. students currently studying abroad do so for linguistic training purposes (Institute for College Access, 2014). The assumption persists that English as a lingua franca will allow U.S. students to partake in cultural experiences abroad. This assumption, of course, is a dangerous one because it reinforces, at a discursive level, the participant's privileged position as a speaker of English. Concomitantly, the disregard for second language preparation in academic experiences further stresses English as an identifier of power. But as Phillipson (2008) remarks, this curricular position in regards to languages other than English is sustained ideologically. As he notes:

> There is a strong measure of wishful thinking in the projection of those who claim that English is 'the world's lingua franca,' since maximally one-third of humanity have any competence in the language at all. Likewise, the notion that English is the language of science is contradicted by the fact that many other languages are used in higher education and research. But such discourse serves both to constitute and confirm English dominance and American empire, and the interlocking structures and ideologies that underpin 'global' English and corporate interests. Investing in the linguistic capital of English ... is a project that transcends national borders, with the product and processes privileging users of the language in the current world 'order.' (p. 4)

A similar argument about study abroad could be made here in relation to Phillipson's (2008) remarks on English's ideological dominance. The social capital represented by study abroad identifies U.S. students as holding a position of power and privilege in the world. And because of this historically constituted position, it is crucial to examine study abroad's semiosis as a social practice that reaffirms and legitimizes class-based discourses of power and dominance. Such a critical stance allows us to determine the extent to which study abroad programs, particularly short-term ones, mask participants' privilege under a cosmopolitan cloak that is falsely innocuous. In other words, how do power and privilege risk reducing the short-term cohort model of study abroad to an experience in which intercultural competence development, cross-cultural understanding, and empathy are commoditized as learning? How does study abroad's semiosis contribute to the enactment of rationalized and ideologically ambivalent narratives of first-world privilege and interventionism masked as "global learning"?

STUDY ABROAD AS A PROBLEM

For many, study abroad has an unconditional appeal. In times of globalization,[1] this initiative is seen unquestionably as a basic necessity within the professionalizing discourse of higher education. Terms such as "globalized education" and "internationalization of curriculum" have become so ubiquitous in academic debates, along with "multi" adjectives—multicultural, multinational, and so on—that we often take for granted the implications of conflating diversity discourses across contexts and disciplines. Study abroad literature in general underscores globalization as the motivating force for supporting these initiatives in higher education contexts (e.g., Lewin, 2009; Quezada, 2012; Shaklee & Baily, 2012; Weber, 2007).

Yet, despite many allusions to the "global" and the "multi," what is particularly striking within study abroad research is that in many instances scholars overlook the nocive effects of globalization and how this initiative fails to acknowledge mobility and flexibility as elitist traits (Schumann, 2012). A cursory examination of study abroad literature suffices to realize that analyses on the link between globalization, power, and privilege are few (Breen, 2012; Dockrill, Rahatzad, & Phillion, 2016; Matthews & Lawley, 2011; Phillion & Malewski, 2011). For obvious institutional accountability reasons, the research focuses primarily on participants' subjectivities as a means to gauge the success or failure of these academic experiences (e.g., Alfaro & Quezada, 2010; Quezada, 2012). This approach ultimately reveals little to us about the perspective of those with whom students come into contact abroad, what they gain, if anything, valuable from the experience to the same extent that we do. The resulting narratives in study abroad research confirm the stated goals of the programs and their curricula in terms of acknowledging vaguely defined global competencies such as interculturalism, international perspectivism, and cultural knowledge. Indeed, there appears to be a limited number of studies addressing, within the structure of study abroad programs, the "very real set of relationships among those who have economic, political, and cultural power in society... and the ways in which education is thought about, organized, and evaluated" (Apple, 2004, p. 15).

But more importantly, perhaps, stands the fact that we encounter a noticeable dichotomy in the ways study abroad research communicates the enterprise's realized outcomes. In certain fields, such as in teacher preparation, reports on short-term programs display an overwhelming optimism when characterizing students' experiences (e.g., Goldstein, 2007; Kortegast & Boisfontaine, 2015; Olmedo & Harbon, 2010; Page & Benander, 2011; Quezada, 2012; Shaklee & Baily, 2012). Conversely, in other academic areas, we find more nuanced analyses that question study abroad's potential as a transformative pedagogical tool (Breen, 2012; Trilokekar & Kukar, 2011). This registered dichotomy ultimately alerts us to the fact that, as in any educational experience, there are too many variables to reach a replicable conclusion. To propose an optimal study abroad model that guarantees the type of deep, transformative, and socially committed international learning we educators seek for our students represents, at a fundamental level, a task of managing risks (Trilokekar & Kukar, 2011).

Considering that presently there are no studies assessing the long-term impact of study abroad or similar immersive multicultural experiences on students' careers (May & Sleeter, 2010), we should remain skeptical of conclusions on programs' efficacy, as it may be an indication of researchers' undisclosed ideological complicity with what globalization stipulates as a "public curriculum" (Burdick, Sandlin, & O'Malley, 2014). What researchers identify and control for in experiences abroad, the measurable outcomes they determine and classify, ultimately follows those paradigms that suit the belief of the enterprise as an educational commodity in which to be invested. As Twombly, Salisbury, and Tumanut (2012) remark:

> When research can isolate the effects of study abroad independent of input variables and/or can compare equivalent groups of students who study abroad with those who do not, we often cannot control for complexity of program differences much less individual variations in how students experience the sojourn. In fact, compared to the amount of research on study abroad outcomes, there has been very little on the actual experience abroad to help us contextualize outcomes. Finally, and importantly, the beliefs about the positive effects are so deeply ingrained in our higher education narrative that even lukewarm results are interpreted and repeated over and over again taking on fairy tale status. (p. 108)

And while it seems reasonable to suggest that the cross-cultural experiences afforded by study abroad enhance participants' awareness of various global issues, this awareness does not necessarily lead to an examination of the assumptions and experiences that are tied to our social position and the identities we can adopt (Dockrill et al., 2016). Looming around us is always the threat of what Tuana (2006) identifies as a "willful ignorance" towards the other. This type of ignorance is more than acknowledging that suffering and poverty exist; it is "a systematic process of self-deception, a willful embrace of ignorance that infects those who are in positions of privilege, an active ignoring of the oppression of others and one's role in that exploitation" (Tuana, 2006, p. 11). In a context where the educational goals for students are increasingly driven by "understandings of global competitiveness, and the necessity to strategically adapt... to rapidly shifting personal and national contexts" (Mitchell, 2003, p. 388), study abroad constitutes a valuable form of social capital enhancing individualism and privilege against ethical concerns articulated through one's genuine desire to learn—which is no less complicated, of course.

Thus, taking into consideration both the present context of neoliberalization within higher education and research supporting the logic of study abroad, what rationales and semiotic operations underpin the ways in which participants negotiate with the meaning of the "global" and their identity as "global citizens"? What forms of identity politics orient the "multi" prefix and its semantics within academic discourse interfering with study abroad semiosis?

Certainly, it would be absurd to challenge the need for diverse perspectives in higher education curricula, whether these be national or international. At the same time, we are well to wonder if study abroad programs have unduly coopted the "multi" prefix to promote globalization's interests through the reframing of human interactions as commodifiable skills. In other words, in what ways can we see the possibility that the short-term cohort model of study abroad carries out corporate globalization's dirty work? This is an important question to raise because, as Roy (2004) expresses, corporate globalization has instituted a neoliberal cultural logic for our times in which "free elections, a free press, and an independent judiciary mean little when the free market has reduced them to commodities available on sale to the highest bidder" (p. 3). In this sense, we may further probe: In what ways does study abroad operationalize the "multi" by transforming it into a fetishized product, a spectacle for the viewing pleasure of first- world audiences? How does study abroad and its ensuing body of research inadvertently contribute to this extracurricular experience as "spectacle" by disregarding problematic assumptions inherent to its structure? These assumptions relate specifically the normalization of

> the selling off of public goods to private interests; the attack on social provisions; the rise of the corporate state organized around privatization, free trade, and deregulation; the celebration of self-interests over social needs; the celebration of profit-making as the essence of democracy coupled with the utterly reductionist notion that consumption is the only applicable form of citizenship. But even more than that, it upholds the notion that the market serves as a model for structuring all social relations: not just the economy, but the governing of all of social life. (Giroux, 2014, para. 3)

STUDY ABROAD'S SPECTACLE AND PRIVILEGED CONSUMPTION

As an immigrant teacher involved in study abroad programs in various capacities for the past 15 years, I have confronted difficult questions related to its inherent theatricality. I have asked myself on numerous occasions whether or not the short-term cohort model of study abroad, which is the principle target of my critique here, is ultimately worth the price. This critical inquiry is merited, especially when currently 71% of our students graduate from four-year colleges in debt (Institute for College Access and Success, 2014). As a former third-world[2] citizen, however, my doubts with respect to study abroad's hype—its assertions of providing essential opportunities for students' intercultural development—also derive from my personal history. At both ends of the experience, as a participant and director, I became aware that host communities did not always profit as much as participants do, whether financially, intellectually, or emotionally. Our global mobility, after all, signals our identity as cosmopolitan, privileged subjects to others. And this identity marker implies that our relationships are always embedded in the kinds of power we represent and are able to exercise at the personal and collective level through inherent or conquered privileges (Bourdieu, 1984).

As Mengestu (2012) asserts, privilege is both the source of power and the origin of our burden as first-world citizens. This is to say, the intersection of multiple identities bestowed upon us from birth—such as citizenship, Whiteness, sexual identity, and so on—can represent a celebration of our power in the world, the radicalization of our position in society. Our investments as lifelong learners are intrinsically tied to the maintenance of what we inherit and our ability to assume a myriad of social positions (Bourdieu, 1984). It is therefore plausible to state that we are born into societal relationships inasmuch as we work for or against their constitution, arguably spending our lives acquiring various forms of capital to benefit our ability to conveniently position ourselves in the social networks through which we traffic. Put another way, we buy—whether through symbolic or monetary forms of capital—our way into legitimacy, assuming in the process a myriad of identities that reflect the positions we relationally come to occupy in society. Drawing on the work of Lucal (1996), McIntosh (1988), and Robinson (1999), Black and Stone (2005) identify five core components that provide defining boundaries for privilege as a concept. As they argue:

> Privilege is a special advantage; it is neither common nor universal. Second, it is granted, not earned or brought into being by one's individual effort or talent. Third, privilege is a right or entitlement that is related to a preferred status or rank. Fourth, privilege is exercised for the benefit of the recipient and to the exclusion or detriment of others. Finally, a privileged status is often outside of the awareness of the person possessing it. (p. 243)

As for study abroad, our privileged identification as participants represents the very purchasing of a cosmopolitan identity. This identity affords us more privilege inasmuch as it legitimizes our social position as witnesses *of* and *for* the "global," which reinstates the synecdochical encounter with the foreign as a commoditized experience. Peirce (1995) suggests that learners invest in international/intercultural experiences with a clear understanding that these experiences afford them a range of symbolic resources—such as language education, friends, and so on. Upon acquiring social capital in the form of symbolic resources, learners reassess their position in society, not necessarily based on humanitarian values, but rather because these acquired, culturally and contextually based resources are generally perceived as adding value to those identities one is able to assume (Norton & Toohey, 2011). As an acquisitional item, an extracurricular "purchase," study abroad celebrates a form of exceptionalism through what global mobility affords participants—provided that one pays for it and is socially positioned to enjoy the benefits it provides. To those who can partake in study abroad experiences, the world can be a playground for self-experimentation, an opportunity for unquestioned personal growth that is "open to the education consumer whose ability to pay is predetermined by economic privilege, which is further empowered by the differentiating subtleties of private [or public] universities" (Breen, 2012, p. 84).

In a sense, then, study abroad is inherently artificial; it represents a restructured reality commoditized as a foreign experience. As such, study abroad transforms the foreign space into a "staging" for the global. Consider, for instance, the relative safety of the environment in which most programs take place, the provisions for students' supervision and wellbeing, and the access to local translators and a range of services that otherwise, in independent experiences, might have brought students to closer sense of "normality" better representative of life abroad. Seen through this prism— admittedly not an optimistic one—study abroad assumes a characteristically spectacular quality. Consumers' expectations, and even emotional responses, are built upon at the sphere of study abroad's production, the design of its curriculum, the instituting of its rules. As Debord (1994) explains, the spectacle in modern society

> is both the result and the project of the existing mode of production. It is not a supplement to the real world, an additional decoration. It is the heart of the unrealism of the real society. In all its specific forms, as information or propaganda, as advertisement or direct entertainment consumption, the spectacle is the present model of socially dominant life. It is the omnipresent affirmation of the choice already made in production and its corollary consumption. The spectacle's form and content are identically the total justification of the existing system's conditions and goals. The spectacle is also the permanent presence of this justification, since it occupies the main part of the time lived outside of modern production. (p. 13)

If we follow Debord (1994) here, we see just how much study abroad's curricular and pedagogical decisions excise ambiguity to deliver upon predetermined learning objectives as products. The experience must do so in order to fulfill its promises, to provide student-customers with a rewarding experience above all, a commodity for which they paid. This commodity comprises a series of organizational steps that are taken on behalf of participants to ensure the maximization of their investment in the form of an expected outcome. In this sense, the goal within study abroad is not to open its curriculum to new and unpredictable possibilities as it is claimed; rather, the spectacle requires closure so that the experience itself can be properly evaluated and controlled for re/production. Some may optimistically say that they gained much from the experience. However, a closer discursive analysis of student data in many study abroad programs reveals that, for participants, "me" and "them" continues to imply a worldly division (Dockrill et al., 2016; Goldstein, 2007; Olmedo & Harbon, 2010).

Given the complex institutional organization of study abroad, it is difficult to refrain from understanding its pedagogical impetus outside an accommodating response to global capitalism's ironic instatement of hyperreal choice. Higher education follows suit by delivering learning "choices," regulated experiences that, ironically enough, do not constitute choices at all. As previously argued, because the outcome of study abroad is decided upon production—as is the case with conventional education—the resulting experience leaves little to imagination.

To understand study abroad as a hyperreal spectacle, a map discursively constructed before the territory—as Baudrillard (1995) would have it—it would be useful to understand what Bryman (2004) identifies as a "Disneyzation" production logic in today's "society of the spectacle" (Debord, 1994). As Bryman (2004) explains in relation to Disney products, global organizations have begun to project production in a way that their products interlock in a consumption chain. In other words, one act of consumption invariably leads to another. For instance, when one frequents a Disney theme park, one realizes that products are arranged in such a way as to encourage hybrid forms of consumption. Merchandising is developed to stress memory and locality, while employee behavior is meticulously scripted and managed to project an ideal of happiness and satisfaction that elicits a specific emotional response from the consumer. What is sought under this model, Bryman (2004) argues, is product variation and the illusion of choice through an apparent individualization. Nevertheless, what becomes concealed in this process is that being at a Disney park, eating Disney food, and buying Disney souvenirs are preplanned, meticulously designed occurrences. More than simple consumption, corporations like Disney design for interrelated and associative experiences vis-à-vis that which their products can provide at an emotional level. Bryman (2004) draws this helpful analogy to explain this production-consumption circuit as the operative logic of our times, which extends to how universities operationalize curricula within a mass-market logic:

> Eating in a standard McDonald's or Burger King may have the advantage of filling a basic need (hunger) cheaply and in a predictable environment, but Disneyized restaurants are likely to provide an experience that gives the *impression of being different* and even a sense of the dramatic while being in a location that perhaps increases the likelihood that the consumer will *engage in other types of consumption,* such as purchasing merchandise or participating in other activities in a hybrid consumption setting. Hybrid consumption environments themselves frequently take on the *characteristics of the spectacular because of the sheer variety of consumption opportunities* they offer and especially when accompanied by theming. To a significant extent, then, Disneyization

connects with a post-Fordist world of variety and choice in which *consumers reign supreme.* (p. 5, italics added)

Thus, just as the Disney company interlocks a series of events and products to better customize experiences and elicit a particular emotional response from the public—from the amusement park attractions and its connections to movies, restaurants, and merchandising—so do study abroad programs. By and large, these are structured to create dispositions towards globalization's variety—the multi-fill-in-the-blanks—in ways that confirm its logic at an atomistic, social behavior level. To ensure this activity's predictable sequence, a myriad of semiotic procedures ascribe affective dispositions towards travel abroad, invoking the "signs" of the global as example of foreign authenticity. We can see study abroad's semiosis, particularly in short-term cohort models, operationalized as follows through Bryman's Disneyzation framework:

- Theming: the curricular dispositions suiting academic interests of participants in connection with their specific disciplines.
- Hybrid consumption: the structuring of the educational experience in a way that students' multiple experiences are interlocked with the curricular focus—for example, visits to tourist sites related or marginal to one's profession and the very time built in for "pleasure."
- Merchandising: the articulation of a valuable workforce skills tied to globalization discourse vis-à-vis what the trip enables.
- Performative labor: the emotional work done by organizers at pre-departure, onsite, and postdeparture events, the discursive activity that directs and attempts to control for the "mood" of the international experience.

The simultaneous coordination of the above elements works to sustain for study abroad participants a rather predictable hyperreal experience of foreign alterity. To be clear, I am not suggesting that participants come to read the foreign experience in the same exact way. What I am suggesting, however, is that there are aspects of study abroad—herein described through Bryman's Disneyzation scheme—that orchestrate as and frame this event planning around a theatrical catharsis. As such, this experience builds upon participants' emotional predispositions to control for desired goals scripted previously to the departure. This script certainly counts on existing discourses and the knowledge they are able to produce constructed from the viewpoint of the first-world participant. On rare occasions is this theatricalized production short from "magic."

The following section delves into this theme in more detail.

STUDY ABROAD AS THEATER

As Boal (1985) argues, one of the primary goals of theater within Western traditions has been to induce an experience of catharsis. This desired emotional response, however, extends beyond the early Aristotelian assumptions on the purification of negative emotions through art: that is, our identification with the characters in a given dramatic plot enabling us to vicariously expunge negative feelings. As a desired dramatic response, catharsis inaugurates the symbolical reinstatement of social order. Through it we reaffirm our commitment to those hierarchies that we use to justify or prevent moments in which our desire gets the best of us. The spectacle's discursive function thus serves as a conduit for our conscious and unconscious tendencies; it enables us to reaffirm a myriad of symbolic structures that we believe to safeguard what we imagine social organization to be like, which for me is akin to Foucault's concept of governmentality (c.f. Foucault, 1980; Lemke, 2011).

Within the theatrical as medium, the transgressions of our human desires take place in a safe alternate reality. The punishment for our transgressions comes through the vicarious experience of the other, within the safety of the spectacular environment's artificiality. Our empathy for the other, the dramatic characters on stage with whom we identify, at lesser or greater degree, constitute reminders, remote possibilities of ourselves.

It is empathy, Boal (1985) explains, that unites spectator and protagonists—the latter prosthetically implants him/herself in the spectator through what s/he desires. When, for instance, the audience hears the tragic hero's confession, they make a confession of their own. It is the protagonist's job to sort out the audience's behavior, to straighten out what is crooked (Boal, 1985). The staged event reaffirms, in a way, the audience's moral superiority, the knowledge of the rules. But underneath it, the spectacle shows us our immorality, the guilty pleasures we vicariously experience through our enjoyment of the sinful transgressions of the characters.

Certainly, Boal's *ars dramatis* sought to intervene in the classic deployment of catharsis both as a distancing and identifying mechanism. The mediating character of the jester that Boal breathes life into in his *Theater of the Oppressed* (1985) is envisioned as a way to disrupt the audience's reception of the spectacle as a cathartic inevitability. The audience's intervention becomes part of the theatrical reality's static reaffirmation of societal order.

In Boal's *ars dramatis*, the joker subverts the spectacle; s/he obscures easy answers, expectations; its presence as an artifice questions "what passes as reality to discourage a kind of heroism that mythifies essential facts, and, finally, to deem submissiveness and tranquility untenable" (Babbage, 2004, p. 147). More than that, Boal's joker reminds us that the spectacle isn't always as it appears. It is our intervention in the pre-established order that makes reality "real." In this sense, the spectacle in Boal's theater is redimensionalized outside Debord's (1994) *panis et circensis* analysis, as the audience's complacency is thwarted towards the apparent chaos of a theater now unscriptable. This "chaos" does not constitute disorder but is rather an ever-emerging new "order," one that albeit designed has no predetermined outcomes. It is the audience who is constantly reordering, reconstructing dramatic sequences, events, and character actions by recasting assumptions, becoming what Boal terms "spect/actors." Catharsis' alienating potential becomes if not deterred, at least minimized, as the breaking of the fourth wall requires emerging commitments between actors and audience through dialogic interaction. The spectacle itself is risky. Life is no longer represented but lived in a worldly stage.

I am bringing Boal's observations on Western drama here—more specifically Aristotelian tragedy—as a means to reflect upon how study abroad's theatricality risks the same cathartic complacency observed in traditional theater. Although participants in study abroad, especially in short-term cohort model programs, could in principle rewrite the rules of the spectacle, act to transform the experience of the foreign into something other than what educators and program administrators expect, what is overwhelmingly reported by research as an adherence to expected outcomes, moments misread as *conscientização* (Freire, 2000), as an embodied awareness of the living *with/as* alterity. These "awakening" moments, certainly, can indicate myriad things, particularly if lack of reciprocity guides the international experience as an event at a distance. This complacency is noticeable in the silence that the majority of study abroad programs maintain concerning their own instrumentality in sustaining privileged knowledge afforded and legitimized through one's academic global mobility. Study abroad traces, then, a fine line between representing an opportunity for participants to see the world differently and a framing mechanism to see the "world" reaffirmed through a class-based vantage point. Put another way, study abroad is a mirror in which we see reflected the very hierarchical representation of society to itself (Debord, 1994). The denial of this inherent representability issue constitutes, perhaps, the greatest risk to study abroad as a project that, instead of challenging students to see the world differently, ultimately confirms our disinterest towards intervening in it. We may claim empathy, but ours is the same empathetic response experienced in Western theater. There is an end to the spectacle.

EMPATHY IN STUDY ABROAD' SPECTACLE

As Foucault (1982) reminds us, "if everything is dangerous, then we always have something to do. So [our] position [should not lead] to apathy but to a hyper and pessimistic activism" (pp. 231–232). I share this sentiment when examining study abroad's claims in teacher education programs, particularly through the articulation of its promises of developing dispositions in teachers to become more interculturally aware and empathetic towards the diverse populations they teach at home. For instance, do we need or benefit equally from teaching and learning about children in Mexico to understand domestic diversity? How does a short-term, localized experience abroad, averaging five or six weeks, enhance a White, middle class teacher's understanding of the other and shape his or her development of empathy towards this other? My answer is, certainly, we cannot know. But I would like to rehearse a few observations that may bring to light the "business" of empathy in education literature and its complications to study abroad research.

Empathy, particularly cultural empathy, is argued in study abroad literature as one of the most salient goals of these types of initiatives (Bennett, 2009; Goldstein, 2007; Root & Ngampornchai, 2013; Shaklee & Baily, 2012; Vande Berg, Paige, & Lou, 2012). However, as scholars across disciplines have noted, it has been difficult to determine empathy's multidimensionality, that is, whether it is a process or a content, whether it is something that can be "exercised" or activated as an emotional response (Bubandt & Willerslev, 2015; Oxley, 2011).

While I am not interested in examining if empathy is good or bad for society (c.f. Bloom, 2014), I do feel it is important to examine its promotion as a skill afforded by international excursions. I believe empathy, as a desired educational outcome in teacher preparation programs, constitutes a problem. It represents a problem not only because this term is biased and has acquired multiple definitions and categorizations across disciplines (Oxley, 2011), but also because it guides teacher education within a humanist rationale. In this rationale, curriculum and pedagogy operate towards ideologizing "feeling as/with the other," as if this means something is universally experienced in the same way by all members of society, independently from culture and the relationships of power that culture establishes. For example, in the field of teacher education, empathy is often discussed as an important skill. Many argue that this "skill" is essential for educators to work with the diverse and multinational population of U.S. schools (Boyer, 2010; Cruz & Patterson, 2005).

Yet, if we see empathy as an acquisitional item, or as something sold and enabled by the experience abroad, we are framing it as a rationalized expectation—indeed, a strategic response. This strategic response suggests that teachers manipulate students into learning as they see fit. In this case, empathy appears recast as a weapon akin to a martial arts move. Practiced enough, this "move" will be naturalized and the professional will be better for it. However, as Delgado (1996) argues, empathy can only exist in a just world, where our experiences and social histories "are roughly the same, unmarked by radical inequality. In such a world, we would have things to trade. There would be reasons for needing to get to know others, for understanding what they feel and need. But... we don't live in such a world" (p. 94). Delgado's (1996) observation coincides with what some researchers have examined as "tactical empathy." Bubandt and Willerslev (2015), for instance, note that while empathy has served as an umbrella term to designate positive, altruistically emotional responses, there are instances in which "the empathetic incorporation of an alien perspective contains, and in fact is motivated by, seduction, deception, manipulation, and violent intent" (p. 6).

We are left to wonder, then, if the reactions commonly reported as intercultural learning in study abroad research might, in fact, correspond to an exemplar of self-deception or a strategic empathy towards alterity. Warren and Hotchkins (2014) ask this same question while noting that false empathic responses are most evident in instances when more powerful subjects "place their needs, desires, and points of view... above those needs, desires, and points of view" of less privileged beings (p. 279). In this sense, and in light of the preceding sections' discussions, how can we not be skeptical of the claim of empathetic responses in study abroad as overwhelming evidence of its value in relation to its cost? How can we disregard empathy, within the spectacular, as a covert validation of first-world privilege?

If anything, empathy is a double-edged sword; it "relies on, but also destabilizes, the association among persons and their experiences" (Shuman, 2005, p. 4). In the context of study abroad, this assertion brings to the fore a myriad of ethical concerns related to who holds the right to self-representation in international narratives, whose histories, and under whose terms these histories are represented. As argued elsewhere in this chapter, study abroad research has fallen short from investigating how U.S. participants' experiences operate in relation to power and the social positions they occupy. Unless we account for empathy in this mix as being also implicated in situations and positionalities of power, any internationalization initiative in higher education, particularly study abroad, will continue to represent a "a site of failed promises" (Shuman, 2005, p. 4).

FINAL THOUGHTS

As educators invested in multilingual/multicultural curriculum development, we are morally obligated to acknowledge study abroad as, among many things, the reflection of a dire reality. This reality informs us that half of the world's wealth is held by 1% of the population (Treanor, 2015). As long as study abroad organizers insist upon dismissing reciprocity in knowledge-based exchanges as an organizing principle, programs will fall prey to the spectacular and reproductive organization described throughout this chapter.

In times when scholars have called for interventionist models to guarantee the "success" of study abroad as a disciplinary enterprise (Kortegast & Boisfontaine, 2015; Vande Berg et al., 2012), I would argue for the opposite: freedom from structures that risk framing the experience to students as a Debordian spectacle. The challenge, of course, is to create the necessary curricular conditions making the experience abroad more "freeing," negotiable, and accessible, not only to those who can afford it, but also to all students who wish to participate in its academic configuration. I do not believe, for the reasons specified herein, that study abroad programs fashioned as cohorts, regulated with little attention to linguistic training, and devoid of self-criticality towards globalization are as useful as argued. When criticizing the power that the U.S. represents on the global stage, Cole (2012) makes a statement that I find particularly relevant to the context of this conclusion: "If we are going to interfere in the lives of others, a little due diligence is a minimum requirement" (para. 1).

I do not doubt that many educators working within study abroad today are conscious of the ideological risks involved in this extracurricular activity and, therefore, work diligently to ensure their programs' ethical realization. Yet, what concerns me in today's environment is that, in our due diligence, we may forget to make apparent to ourselves and to our students our social position as first-world citizens, and what this position entails in terms of unwittingly supporting discourses perpetuating structural inequalities. As Foucault (1975/1996) remarks, "to reveal relations of power is . . . to put them back in the hands of those who exercise them" (quoted in Fendler, 2003, p. 23). If we follow Foucault here, we may conclude that study abroad participants and stakeholders are the ones who ultimately hold the power to transmute this event's semiosis into a process that can potentially become more creative than cathartic. not a play exclusively staged for participants' pleasure, but an event that actually establishes commitments by disrupting the harmful effects of globalization and what it produces as reality.

For those of us who are committed to the "multi" as a futuristic project of democratic possibilities, the issue at hand is the necessary confrontation of the ideological risks that are inherent to the discourses we practice as the "global." Rather than advancing study abroad as the promised land of intercultural competence development, we would be advised, *a priori*, to unmake globalization's ideological web by deconstructing our first-world participation in international academic programs as a privilege. Moreover, we would do well to examine the extent to which this privilege blinds our experiences abroad in ways that covertly satisfy our sentimental needs over the urgency of taking responsibility for what our first-world privilege sanctions and legitimizes as (academic) knowledge. As it currently stands, the popular short-term cohort model for study abroad can teach students little beyond their known universe. Yet it risks much when providing an experience that cathartically alienates people from a genuine opportunity to commit to "the global" and the challenging intertwined realities we find therein.

NOTES

1. Although the concept of globalization is not short on definitions, and its genealogy is indeed complex across various fields of study (James & Steger, 2014), I employ the term here to mean the increasingly interdependence and continued exploitation and concentration of the means of production at a global scale, aided by what emerging technologies enact and make viable in social life. The process is marked by economic agents' defense of free trade, free flow of capital, and the tapping of cheaper foreign labor markets, which provoke profound alterations in cultural processes and patterns of human migration.

2. Throughout this chapter I employ the terms "first" and "third" world as a means to reclaim the postcolonial subject's identity within academic debates. I do so in the same way many appropriate the adjective "queer" to highlight the axiological construction of colonial subjectivities' within the continuum of what is defined as North and South, East and West epistemologies.

REFERENCES

Alfaro, C., & Quezada, R. L. (2010). International teacher professional development: Teacher reflections of authentic teaching and learning experiences. *Teaching Education, 21*(1), 47–59.

Apple, M. W. (2004). *Ideology and curriculum* (3rd ed.). New York, NY: Routledge.

Babbage, F. (2004). *Augusto Boal.* New York, NY: Taylor & Francis.

Baudrillard, J. (1995). *Simulacra and simulation* (S. F. Glaser, Trans.). Ann Arbor, MI: University of Michigan Press.

Bennett, M. J. (2009). Defining, measuring, and facilitating intercultural learning: A conceptual introduction to the Intercultural Education double supplement. *Intercultural Education, 20*(sup1), S1–S13.

Benson, P., Barkhuizen, G., Bodycott, P., & Brown, J. (2013). *Second language identity in narratives of study abroad.* Hampshire, UK: Palgrave Macmillan.

Black, L. L., & Stone, D. (2005). Expanding the definition of privilege: The concept of social privilege. *Journal of Multicultural Counseling and Development, 33*(4), 243–255.

Bloom, P. (2014, September 10). Against empathy. *Boston Review.* Retrieved from https://bostonreview.net/forum/paul-bloom-against-empathy

Boal, A. (1985). *Theatre of the oppressed.* New York, NY: Theatre Communications Group.

Bourdieu, P. (1984). *Distinction: A social critique of the judgement of taste.* Cambridge, MA: Harvard University Press.

Boyer, W. (2010). Empathy development in teacher candidates. *Early Childhood Education Journal, 38*(4), 313–321.

Breen, M. (2012). Privileged migration: American undergraduates, study abroad, academic tourism. *Critical Arts: South-North Cultural and Media Studies, 26*(1), 82–102.

Bryman, A. (2004). *The Disneyization of society.* Thousand Oaks, CA: Sage.

Bubandt, N., & Willerslev, R. (2015). The dark side of empathy: Mimesis, deception, and the magic of alterity. *Comparative Studies in Society and History, 57*(1), 5–34.

Burdick, J., Sandlin, J. A., & O'Malley, M. P. (Eds.). (2014). *Problematizing public pedagogy.* New York, NY: Routledge.

Cole, T. (2012, March 21). The white-savior industrial complex. *The Atlantic.* Retrieved from http://www.theatlantic.com/international/archive/2012/03/the-white-savior-industrial-complex/254843/

Cruz, B. C., & Patterson, J. (2005). Cross-cultural simulations in teacher education: Developing empathy and understanding. *Multicultural Perspectives, 7*(2), 40–47.

Debord, G. (1994). *The society of the spectacle.* New York, NY: Zone Books.

Delgado, R. (1996). Rodrigo's Eleventh Chronicle: Empathy and false empathy. *California Law Review, 84*(1), 61–100.

Dockrill, H., Rahatzad, J., & Phillion, J. (2016). The benefits and challenges of study abroad in teacher education in a neoliberal context. In J. A. Rhodes & T. M. Milby (Eds.), *Advancing teacher education and curriculum development through study abroad programs* (pp. 290–305). Hershey, PA: IGI Global.

Dolby, N. (2004). Encountering an American self: Study abroad and national identity. *Comparative Education Review, 48*(2), 150–173.

Fendler, L. (2003). Teacher reflection in a hall of mirrors: Historical influences and political reverberations. *Educational Researcher, 32*(3), 16–25.

Forum on Education Abroad. (2014, August 22). Standards of Good Practice. Retrieved from https://forumea.org/resources/standards-of-good-practice/

Foucault, M. (1980). *Power/knowledge: Selected interviews and other writings, 1972–1977.* New York, NY: Pantheon Books.

Foucault, M. (1982). *Michel Foucault: Beyond structuralism and hermeneutics* (H. L. Dreyfus & P. Rabinow, Eds.). Brighton, UK: Harvester Press.

Freire, P. (2000). *Pedagogy of the oppressed.* New York, NY: Continuum.

Giroux, H. A. (2014). Henry Giroux on the rise of neoliberalism. Retrieved from http://www.truth-out.org/opinion/item/26885-henry-giroux-on-the-rise-of-neoliberalism

Goldstein, T. (2007). Educating world teachers for cosmopolitan classrooms and schools. *Asia Pacific Journal of Education, 27*(2), 131–155.

Grey, S., Cox, J. G., Serafini, E. J., & Sanz, C. (2015). The role of individual differences in the study abroad context: Cognitive capacity and language development during short-term intensive language exposure. *The Modern Language Journal, 99*(1), 137–157.

Institute for College Access and Success. (2014). Retrieved from http://ticas.org/

James, P., & Steger, M. B. (2014). A genealogy of "globalization": The career of a concept. *Globalizations, 11*(4), 417–434.

Jackson, J. (2008). *Language, identity, and study abroad: Sociocultural perspectives.* Oakville, CT: Equinox Publishing.

Kortegast, C. A., & Boisfontaine, M. T. (2015). Beyond "It was good": Students' post-study abroad practices for negotiating meaning. *Journal of College Student Development, 56*(8), 812–828.

Lemke, T. (2011). *Foucault, governmentality, and critique.* Boulder, CO: Paradigm.

Lewin, R. (Ed.). (2009). *The handbook of practice and research in study abroad: Higher education and the quest for global citizenship.* New York, NY: Routledge.

Lucal, B. (1996). Oppression and privilege: Toward a relational conceptualization of race. *Teaching Sociology, 24*(3), 245–255.

Matthews, J., & Lawley, M. (2011). Student satisfaction, teacher internships, and the case for a critical approach to international education. *Discourse: Studies in the Cultural Politics of Education, 32*(5), 687–698.

May, S., & Sleeter, C. E. (Eds.). (2010). *Critical multiculturalism: Theory and praxis.* New York, NY: Routledge.

McIntosh, P. (1988). *White privilege and male privilege: A personal account of coming to see correspondences through work in women's studies. Working paper No. 189.* Wellesley, MA: Center for Research on Women, Wellesley College.

Mengestu, D. (2012, March 12). Not a click away: Joseph Kony in the real world. Retrieved from http://www.warscapes.com/reportage/not-click-away-joseph-kony-real-world

Mitchell, K. (2003). Educating the national citizen in neoliberal times: From the multicultural self to the strategic cosmopolitan. *Transactions of the Institute of British Geographers, 28*(4), 387–403.

Norton, B., & Toohey, K. (2011). Identity, language learning, and social change. *Language Teaching, 44*(4), 412–446.

Olmedo, I., & Harbon, L. (2010). Broadening our sights: Internationalizing teacher education for a global arena. *Teaching Education, 21*(1), 75–88.

Oxley, J. C. (2011). *The moral dimensions of empathy: Limits and applications in ethical theory and practice.* New York, NY: Palgrave Macmillan.

Page, D., & Benander, R. (2011). Promoting cultural proficiency through reflective assignments in study abroad. *International Journal of Arts & Sciences, 4*(25), 205–216.

Peirce, B. N. (1995). Social identity, investment, and language learning. *TESOL Quarterly, 29*(1), 9–31.

Phillion, J., & Malewski, E. (2011). Study abroad in teacher education: Delving into cultural diversity and developing cultural competence. *Action in Teacher Education, 33*(5–6), 643–657.

Phillipson, R. (2008). The linguistic imperialism of neoliberal empire. *Critical Inquiry in Language Studies, 5*(1), 1–43.

Potts, D. (2015). Understanding the early career benefits of learning abroad programs. *Journal of Studies in International Education, 19*(5), 441–459.

Quezada, R. L. (Ed.). (2012). *Internationalization of teacher education: Creating globally competent teachers and teacher educators for the 21st century.* New York, NY: Routledge.

Robinson, T. L. (1999). The intersections of dominant discourses across race, gender, and other identities. *Journal of Counseling & Development, 77*(1), 73–79.

Root, E., & Ngampornchai, A. (2013). "I came back as a new human being": Student descriptions of intercultural competence acquired through education abroad experiences. *Journal of Studies in International Education, 17*(5), 513–532.

Roy, A. (2004). *An ordinary person's guide to empire.* Cambridge, MA: South End Press.

Schumann, C. (2012). Boundedness beyond reification: Cosmopolitan teacher education as critique. *Ethics & Global Politics, 5*(4), 217–237.

Shaklee, B. D., & Baily, S. (Eds.). (2012). *Internationalizing teacher education in the United States.* Lanham, MD: Rowman & Littlefield.

Shuman, A. (2005). *Other people's stories: Entitlement claims and the critique of empathy.* Urbana, IL: University of Illinois Press.

Treanor, J. (2015, October 13). Half of world's wealth now in hands of 1% of population. *The Guardian.* Retrieved from http://www.theguardian.com/money/2015/oct/13/half-world-wealth-in-hands-population-inequality-report

Trilokekar, R. D., & Kukar, P. (2011). Disorienting experiences during study abroad: Reflections of pre-service teacher candidates. *Teaching and Teacher Education, 27*(7), 1141–1150.

Tuana, N. (2006). The speculum of ignorance: The women's health movement and epistemologies of ignorance. *Hypatia, 21*(3), 1–19.

Twombly, S. B., Salisbury, M. H., & Tumanut, S. D. (2012). *Study abroad in a new global century: Renewing the promise, refining the purpose.* San Francisco, CA: Jossey-Bass.

Vande Berg, M., Paige, R. M., & Lou, K. H. (Eds.). (2012). *Student learning abroad: What our students are learning, what they're not, and what we can do about it.* Sterling, VA: Stylus Publishing.

Warren, C. A., & Hotchkins, B. K. (2014). Teacher education and the enduring significance of "false empathy." *The Urban Review, 47*(2), 266–292.

Weber, E. (2007). Globalization, "glocal" development, and teachers' work: A research agenda. *Review of Educational Research, 77*(3), 279–309.

CHAPTER 5

TEACHING SOCIAL JUSTICE WITHIN OTHER COMMUNITIES

Study Abroad Coordinators' Perspectives on the Impacts of Community Practice in Honduras, India, and Tanzania

Kadriye El-Atwani

ABSTRACT

This chapter examines the perspectives of three study abroad coordinators from the same university who coordinate three different short-term study abroad programs in Honduras, India, and Tanzania. In this reflective chapter, the author discusses the evaluation of each study abroad program from the coordinators' perspectives and explores the reflections of coordinators about how community of practices in Honduras, India, and Tanzania importantly affect the understanding the relationship between society and education. This study exemplifies qualitative research and includes interviews of three study abroad program coordinators in a college of education where most of the students are White, conservative, and lacking in international experiences. The findings of this study suggest that international teaching experiences that require community of practice in different educational settings accommodate meaningful experiences to help understand critical issues in education such as race, class, language, and social justice.

Internationalizing Teaching and Teacher Education for Equity, pages 77–90
Copyright © 2016 by Information Age Publishing

INTRODUCTION

Since the beginning of 20th century, the ethnic structure in the United States has been changed by immigration waves from the various nations in Asia and Latin America (Banks, 2006). The effects of immigration are perhaps most evident in U.S. schools (Marx & Moss, 2011). The classrooms of public schools are becoming tremendously diverse in terms of race, ethnicity, and language (Banks, 2006; Darling-Hammond, French, & Garcia-Lopez, 2002). While minority students represent the numerical majority of students in urban public schools (Darling-Hammond et al., 2002), the cultural gap between White, middle-class teachers and the children of "others" who are immigrants, low-income, and racial, ethnic, and religious minorities in the U.S. still remains (Ladson-Billings, 2001; Lee, 2002; Phillion & Malewski, 2011). According to Sleeter (2001), this situation is a result of the fact that preservice teachers in the U.S. have limited cross-cultural experience and thus lack understanding of multicultural teaching.

There is significant research that suggests that study abroad experiences in teacher education are a potential way to develop culturally competent teachers. Recent research in study abroad in teacher education suggests extensive knowledge about the impacts of short-term study abroad programs generally on participants, specifically how study abroad programs can make a difference in understanding cross-cultural learning and culturally responsive teaching, and in reconceptualization of self-identity, social justice, and global understanding. However, there is limited research about the perspectives of teacher educators who lead study abroad programs. The overarching purpose of this study was to explore the perspectives of study abroad coordinators about the role of designing a study abroad program that includes community-based teaching experiences in conceptualization of teaching preservice teachers about critical issues in education such as race, class, and gender.

STUDY ABROAD LITERATURE IN TEACHER EDUCATION

Karsan, Hakim, and Decker (2011) have discussed how the study abroad experiences of U.S. college students enriched students' lives and helped them recreate a way to see the world through others' eyes. A general benefit of study abroad programs is that international experience allows participants to improve their self-confidence, adaptability, flexibility, and other skills like navigating unfamiliar settings (Cushner, 2007). Specifically in teacher education programs, field experiences in international settings provide an environment where preservice teachers can understand the social context of education. According to Faulconer (2003), observing educational contexts in host countries during international field experiences plays a critical role for preservice teachers in breaking down their taboos and prejudices toward different cultures. Furthermore, a study abroad program that requires immersion in a host community helps preservice teachers to conceptualize their social, racial, and gendered identities (Phillion, Malewski, Sharma, & Wang, 2009). Related to this, the disorienting experiences of preservice teachers who live in host communities during study abroad trips allow preservice teachers to think about "racial dynamics," "outsider status," "power relations," and "risk-taking behavior," which requires critical self-reflection (Trilokekar & Kukar, 2011). A case study by Marx and Moss (2011) exemplifies how a U.S. preservice teacher reported a transformed worldview, from ethnocentric to ethnorelative, during a study abroad program. Similarly, Herbers and Mullins Nelson (2009) found that the opportunity for critical personal reflections during a study abroad program caused significant changes in participants' perspectives about cross-cultural practice and experiences.

Coryell (2011) found that instructors have more opportunity to know their students and their students' learning needs when they are on a study abroad trip compared to when they teach same classes on a university campus. While the existing research has explored the role of study abroad faculty members in the intercultural development of their study abroad students (Goode, 2008; MacNally, 2002; Sunnygard, 2002), the role of study abroad program design in social identity development has been underestimated.

In this study, answers were sought to the following research questions:

1. In what ways do study abroad program coordinators consider the role of host communities in teaching critical issues in education?
2. How do study abroad coordinators evaluate the role of community practice in preservice teachers' understanding the social aspects of teaching?
3. What suggestions do study abroad program coordinators have about increasing the learning of preservice teachers within host communities during study abroad programs?

BACKGROUND INFORMATION
OF STUDY ABROAD PROGRAMS

This research is a part of larger study abroad research that focuses on risk factors of study abroad programs. In this study, the researcher considered three different study abroad programs in a college of education where most of the students are predominantly middle-class, White, and lacking in cross-cultural experiences. Although the college of education at this particular university provides seven study abroad programs, this research focused on three short-term study abroad programs that each offer teaching experiences in local schools in the host countries. These study abroad programs take place in India, Honduras, and Tanzania. All three programs are open to all preservice teachers, allowing them to earn credits in foundational and core education classes and a global studies minor. The reason for researching these study programs rather than other programs in the same college is that all three programs provide community-based teaching experiences and school experiences in several educational settings in their host countries. All three study abroad programs, which have run between 4 and 10 years, spend approximately three weeks in their host countries, and all incorporate cultural or sightseeing activities. Since the study abroad programs are housed within different departments in the college of education, the contents of each program vary. For example, while the Honduras study abroad program offers introductory courses for the teaching profession, the Tanzania study abroad program offers a method course for teaching mathematics. All three programs are based largely on school field experiences. Although the course contents differ in each program, the assignments and classroom activities in three study abroad programs show similarities such as discussion-based teaching and reflective observation journals. Finally, the courses taken in each study abroad program are also offered on campus during the academic year; therefore, the program coordinators are able to compare the development of preservice teachers who study abroad with those preservice teachers who take classes on campus.

RESEARCH METHOD AND THEORETICAL FRAMEWORK

The research method of this study is phenomenology, informed by Van Manen (1997). The core of hermeneutic phenomenology is lived experience, which in this study is ideal for examining the study abroad program coordinators' perspectives about the impacts of their study abroad programs on preservice teachers' understanding of social contexts in education. This method was chosen because it is a "research methodology aimed at producing rich textual descriptions of the experiencing of selected phenomena in the life world of individuals that are able to connect with the experience of all of us collectively" (Smith, 1997, p. 80).

In addition to phenomenology, this study was also guided by community of practice theory (Lave & Wenger, 1991). In community of practice theory, participation in community leads to both organizational and individual learning. However, community of practice theory requires strong participation through which learners acquire rich and deep involvement in community. Wenger (1998) explained the characteristics of participation as referring "not just to local events of engagement in certain activities with certain people, but to a more encompassing process of being active participants in the *practices* of social communities and constructing *identities* in relation to these communities" (p. 4, emphasis in original). Short-term study abroad programs like the ones examined in this study allow preservice teachers to practice international field experiences, which are intended to help them develop essential and organic interactions within a host community.

Wenger (1998) defines community of practice in three dimensions: *mutual engagement*, which includes common practices that hold learners together; *joint enterprise*, in which learners negotiate their practices and engage in discussion based on gained experiences; and *shared repertoire of practice*, where the community is no longer central but learners share historical and social resources, tools, and stories that are gained during practice of community with others and make it memorable for their identity. The study abroad programs examined here offer preservice teachers an appropriate practical environment to be involved in community-based learning.

DATA COLLECTION ANALYSIS

Semi-structured interviews were chosen as a data collection method. Each program coordinator was interviewed once. Interviews lasted approximately one hour and were audio-recorded. Data analysis for this study was an example of the data analysis spiral that Creswell (2007) describes in three parts. The first part, organization of data, requires the transcription of interviews by the researcher and coding of transcripts. During the second part, description and classification of data, the researcher reads the transcripts several times to immerse him- or herself in the details of data. This process helps the researcher to create codes according to the research questions. The final step, interpretation of data, helps the researcher understand the data coding for each program and also conceptualize how three different study abroad programs share common purposes and outcomes to stress the role of community practice in the conceptualization of critical issues in education such as race, class, gender, and culture.

RESEARCH FINDINGS

Research Question 1:
In what ways do study abroad program coordinators consider the role of host communities in teaching critical issues in education?

In this study, the interviews of three different study abroad program coordinators highlighted that, for these faculty study abroad coordinators, there are two main factors related to host communities that reinforce a more sophisticated or nuanced understanding of critical issues in education. Based on the perspectives of the study abroad coordinators, choosing a non-English-speaking country and providing various educational settings in the host community are the main factors that enrich the experiences of preservice teachers to capture the relationship between society and education. For example, the inability to speak Hindi during the India study abroad trip resulted in disorienting experiences (Trilokekar & Kukar, 2011) for the preservice teacher participants and allowed them to think about the role of language in teaching. The study abroad coordinator who created and runs the program, an Indian male living in the U.S., described one such example of a disorienting experience:

> When we go for a city walk and to restaurants, they always walk together, which is very discomforting for them as lots of shopkeepers and waitresses do not necessarily speak English so that they cannot communicate.

Similarly, the coordinator of the Honduras study abroad program, a Canadian female, pays attention to how preservice teachers experience "otherness" when they cannot communicate with elementary school students, though many of the mentor teachers in the Honduran school they visit are from the United States.

> The students experience frustration from the simplest communication for your basic needs to more complex things around education that they can't say. They are confronted with that during this experience.

Although the Tanzania study abroad coordinator, a U.S.-American female, explained that language is not a significant problem for the preservice teachers in her program as majority of people in Tanzania are able to converse conversationally in English, her interview revealed that preservice teachers in this program often expressed difficulty understanding the situation of English being spoken in schools in Tanzania.

> Tanzanian teachers are not fluent in English, but they are expected to teach the content in English. Also, the students are not fluent in English. They share a language in school in which they are all fluent [Swahili], but they are not allowed to use it. So it is a real challenge for my students, which I think helps them to understand things better.

One conversation on this topic can provoke involves the colonial legacy of English being used as the language of instruction in a nation where Swahili is the native language. Preservice teachers can be encouraged to think about—and question—the hegemony of English as a global language, and how this circumstance came to be constructed.

Another factor that was mentioned by all of the study abroad coordinators in this study related to providing different educational settings in Honduras, India, and Tanzania. All three coordinators mentioned that the primary goal of their programs is to give preservice teachers an opportunity to engage in schools that have very different settings than the ones with which preservice teachers are typically familiar. Two of the study abroad coordinators specifically pointed out that their programs were unlike tourist visits and during all of the interviews, the study abroad coordinators elaborated on how preservice teachers reflect on their school experiences in host countries in relation to the educational issues in the United States. For example, in India:

> We go to a school in India which is for homeless kids in New Delhi. There are different sides of school. One side is where you make initial contact with the students. What they do is, basically, they have carpet and milk and students come and eat. So at least you can eat, at least one meal a day, or do whatever. Then we go to younger kids. The school is as big as my office or maybe one and half size of that. There is nothing. There is no air conditioning and kids sometimes sleep there. When we walk in Delhi we walk to a third type of school which is bigger and with an air cooler but still without desks. Kids, they sit on the floor. We also go to private school in Delhi where kids come with uniforms and they have air conditioned music rooms and so on. Preservice teachers see the contrast and it pushes them to think about the issues of accessibility and poverty and how those same issues also exist in this country [the U.S.], like rural schools and inner cities.

Many times throughout the interviews, the study abroad coordinators expressed their amazement at the strength of observation experienced by preservice teachers in impoverished school areas; however, they did not only emphasize poverty. For example, the Honduras study abroad coordinator described how the educational policy of the cooperating school in Honduras plays a critical role in the conceptualization of social justice by the preservice teachers.

> I think the school context is terribly important. Because of that I try to place students as much as possible in a school where the overarching mission is social justice. So our students are getting exposure to that. In the classes that they are in, the school does lots of community-based projects with a social justice focus that our students partially can join.

Research Question 2:

How do study abroad coordinators evaluate the role of community practice in preservice teachers' understanding the social aspects of teaching?

The overall responses of participants of this study indicate that the short-term study abroad programs in Honduras, India, and Tanzania had impacted the preservice teachers' understanding of the relationship between society and education. As documented in the literature (e.g., Karsan et al., 2011), all three study abroad program coordinators emphasized that from their perspective, school experiences in the host countries had given preservice teacher participants an opportunity to experience community of practice and prepared them to be better able to teach in culturally diverse classrooms. At the same time, these experiences reinforced the concept of social justice in education. The testimony of the Tanzanian study abroad coordinator is revealing in this regard:

> I have no evidence, but I know that it makes a difference. These students are qualitatively different when they come back from Tanzania. The time that they spend there is something that opens more in them. I do not know what is quantitatively different, and I do not know how to measure it, but I stay still in contact with anyone who went to Tanzania with me and I see it. For example, Heather[1] who went to Tanzania in the first year, she just applied for the Project for Invisible Children in Uganda.... Another student, Mark, who has grown up in the suburbs, applied for Teach for America to teach in urban schools. Maybe study abroad program allowed them to ask themselves why the world is so unjust, and what can I do? How can I make a difference?

This statement echoes the perspectives of the other study abroad coordinators. It also articulates the argument that study abroad experiences allow participants to think critically about taboo dynamics (Trilokekar & Kukar, 2011). Cooper (2007) has noted that the cultural immersion experiences that preservice teachers have in host communities can challenge their prior beliefs. Relevant to this, the Honduras study abroad coordinator suggested that preservice teachers' community of practice experiences in Honduras increased their political awareness. She stated:

> Honduras is a developing country and our students can learn to think about issues in the U.S. that they have never been exposed to or forced to think about before because most of them are primarily local, primarily White, primarily Christian, and primarily conservative, and maybe primarily Republican. So they haven't thought to critique U.S. involvement in any country in the world.

The India study abroad coordinator provided a similar perspective:

> Typically, students that come from our university have never experienced those schools. They come from middle-class schools and all their friends are White. Suddenly they go to a country for the first time in their life where they are the minority. Those students do not know what being a minority is. And they have never felt what being a minority is. Suddenly, they find that they are the minority in these schools and in the city. And they find that little kids who have never

seen White people are pointing at them to the parents, as they do not look like the rest of India. I think that is another powerful experience for them, and hopefully that will have an impact on their teacher identity in future.

As to the question of whether community of practice experiences in their programs changed or reinforced preservice teacher participants' understanding of social contexts, the study abroad coordinators grounded their responses by reflecting on the opportunities that preservice teachers have to be engaged in the host communities while on the trip. Two of the study abroad coordinators articulated the power of community involvement. In Tanzania:

> I do not want to teach the same course that I would teach here. When we go to Tanzania, we stay in an outpost, teach at the same schools, go on safari to see animals, and then come home. Even though people go there for safari, when my students write their reflections, safari gets a very small piece. What get lots of space are the relationships they formed with the teachers and the kids in the schools, with the people in the orphanage, and with the people at the outpost where they stayed. Those are at the center for them.

From Honduras:

> I want them to learn from community rather than textbooks and classes. It is two weeks of community immersion in Honduran culture and seeds are planted during that time. At least some of them will flourish.

Research Question 3:
What suggestions do study abroad program coordinators have about increasing the learning of preservice teachers within host communities during study abroad programs?

The study abroad coordinators interviewed in this study offered their reflections on the limitations of study abroad programs and provided their perspectives on an ideal study abroad program that might reinforce better understandings of the social aspects of teaching for preservice teachers. Similar to the literature that states that the impacts of short-term study abroad on preservice teachers are not sustainable if preservice teachers are not involved in further opportunities to strengthen what the learned in study abroad programs (e.g., Mahon, 2007), all of the study abroad coordinators stressed that preservice teachers might learn more in terms of the social aspects of teaching if their study abroad programs were longer. For example, the Indian study abroad program coordinator emphasized designing a study abroad program that allows preservice teachers to see different educational settings in different countries.

> I would do study abroad experiences for six months but in different sites with the same group of students but in different places every month. For me personally, it would be looking at the educational settings of different places.

The responses of the study abroad coordinators also provided some interesting insights into areas less explored by the literature, particularly regarding how preservice teachers should be immersed in host community culture to provide more sophisticated understandings of the host country. As the perspectives of study abroad coordinators in this study suggest, study abroad programs can include experiences that provide full engagement of preservice teachers in the host community that may create more complex and cultivated relationships between the host community and preservice teachers. The study abroad coordinators reflected that although such a study abroad program may not be suitable for most students, the benefits provided by such a program could promise lifelong changes in preservice teachers' understanding of the complexity of education, teaching, and social justice. The Honduras study abroad program stated her ideas in this way:

> I would like to go for a semester, for example to a country vastly different. Also, I would make my students way independent more than I do now. We could organize a lot if we were there for a semester. For example, there are rooms and little apartments, why don't we put our students over there? We would let students shop by themselves, make them kind of community members. I could try that. The time length is really important.

EDUCATIONAL SIGNIFICANCE

The findings of this study suggest that the chance of practicing community-based learning during study abroad programs plays a critical role for preservice teachers to conceptualize social aspects of teaching and education. Although all the programs were not ideal at maintaining "life-changing" experiences and sophisticated social understanding, it was evident that community of practice (showing different educational settings in the host community, creating informal classroom settings to discuss preservice teachers' school experiences, allowing preservice teachers to engage in some activities with teachers, students, or people in the host community) ensured in the Honduras, India, and Tanzania study abroad programs have helped preservice teachers to understand the relationship between society and teaching in a broader sense, especially when compared to the campus-based courses. Additionally, the perspectives of the three study abroad coordinators in this study may help to answer the question raised by Quezada and Cordeiro (2007): "How can teacher education programs provide the opportunities for teacher candidates to student teach abroad in order to attain competence as a global teacher?" (p. 4). Although "global teacher" was not a term specified by the participants in this study, all of the participants mentioned terms like "culturally responsive teaching" and "cultural awareness" several times. At the same time, data analysis suggests that the Honduras and Tanzania study abroad coordinators defined the preservice teachers' engagement in the same way Wenger (1998) describes "participation" in community of practice, and both coordinators encouraged preservice teachers to be active in the host community. The India study abroad coordinator also advocated active engagement in the host community but not to the same degree as the other programs. In Delhi, the preservice teacher participants had various opportunities to explore different educational settings; however, they were not as involved in community events as the students in the Tanzania and Honduras study abroad programs because of safety concerns.

All of the study abroad coordinators in this study require preservice teachers to sign consent forms and assure the safety of preservice teachers to their parents. In all three programs, safety is typically a considerable concern for preservice teacher participants and their parents, speaking to the sheltered backgrounds from which many of them come. Although community of practice theory does not inform the role of safety, the results of this study shows that the safety of the host community is a priority of the study abroad coordinators when promoting community of practice in host communities. Furthermore, research findings illustrate that the informal classroom settings, which are maintained in all the study abroad programs in this study, effectively helped to sustain better *shared repertoire of practice*, as described by Wegner (1998).

All of the study abroad coordinators talked about the benefits of scheduled predeparture meetings that inform preservice teachers about the cultures, schools, and program schedules. These meetings seem to prepare preservice teachers to be more active in the host communities they visit as they are less concerned with logistical or schedule issues that have already been taken care of. Data analysis of responses to the third research question also indicated that the study abroad coordinators believe that providing a year-long preparation prior to the trip (e.g., learning the native language of the host country) might assure more powerful community involvement for preservice teachers to strengthen the understanding the relationship between society and education.

CONCLUSION

In conclusion, the results of this study suggest the following educational implications of community of practice theory in study abroad programs: First, the role of community of practice in host communities should be considered by study abroad coordinators as a critical way to improve preservice teachers' understanding of critical issues in education; second, study abroad programs should be well-structured and designed to increase educational opportunities that provide preservice teachers with involvement in different educational settings and engagement in host communities; third, semester-long study abroad programs should be encouraged for preservice teachers in colleges of education to sustain more sophisticated understanding of the social aspects of teaching. Finally, more opportunities should be provided for study abroad coordinators to share and discuss the outcomes of different study abroad programs in colleges of education to improve the application of community of practice theory in teacher education. Informing study abroad program coordinators about community of practice theory is helpful in building more sophisticated and comprehensive understanding of multicultural education and social justice for preservice teachers in teacher education programs. This study provides preliminary discussion about re-addressing the roles of study abroad program coordinators to promote more inclusive learning for preservice teachers during study abroad experiences to comprehend the roles of society, community, and schools in teaching.

ACKNOWLEDGEMENTS

I wish to thank all of the study abroad coordinators who participated in this study and generously shared their experiences. I also wish to thank Jubin Rahatzad, who provided assistance during interviews.

NOTE

1. All names are pseudonyms.

REFERENCES

Banks, J. (2006). *Cultural diversity and education: Foundations, curriculum, and teaching.* New York, NY: Pearson Education.
Cooper, J. E. (2007). Strengthening the case for community based learning in teacher education. *Journal of Teacher Education, 58*(3), 245–255.

Coryell, J. E. (2011). The foreign city as classroom: Adult learning in study abroad. *Adult Learning, 22*(3), 4–11.

Creswell, J. (2007). *Qualitative inquiry and research design: Choosing among five traditions* (2nd ed.). Thousand Oaks, CA: Sage.

Cushner, K. (2007). The role of experience in the making of internationally minded teachers. *Teacher Education Quarterly, 34*(1), 27–39.

Darling- Hammond, L., French, J., & Garcia-Lopez, S. P. (Eds.). (2002). *Learning to teach for social justice.* New York, NY: Teachers College Press.

Faulconer, T. (2003, April). *These kids are so bright! Pre-service teacher's insights and discoveries during a three-week student teaching practicum in Mexico.* Paper presented at the annual meeting of the American Educational Research Association, Chicago, IL.

Goode, M. L. (2008). The role of faculty study abroad directors: A case study. *Frontiers: The Interdisciplinary Journal of Study Abroad, 15,* 149–172.

Herbers, M. S., & Mullins Nelson, B. (2009). Using the disorienting dilemma to promote transformative learning. *Journal on Excellence in College Teaching, 20*(1), 5–34.

Karsan, L., Hakim, A., & Decker, J. (2011). Honors in Ghana: How study abroad enriches students' lives. Journal of the National Collegiate Honors Council, *12*(1), 33–36.

Ladson-Billings, G. (2001). *Crossing over to Canaan: The journey of new teachers in diverse classrooms.* San Francisco, CA: Jossey-Bass.

Lave. J., & Wenger, E. (1991). *Situated learning: Legitimate peripheral participation.* New York, NY: Cambridge University Press.

Lee, J. P. (2002). Racial and ethnic achievement gap trends: Reversing the progress towards equity? *Educational Researcher, 31*(1), 3–12.

MacNally, S. (2002). The role of the faculty director. In S. E. Spencer & K. Tuma (Eds.), *The guide to successful short-term programs abroad* (pp. 173–190). Washington, DC: NAFSA: Association of International Educators.

Mahon, J. (2007). Overseas student teaching as a catalyst towards internationalizing teacher education. *Teacher Education Quarterly, 34*(1), 133–149.

Marx, H., & Moss, D. M. (2011). Please mind the culture gap: Intercultural development during a teacher education study abroad program. *Journal of Teacher Education, 62*(1), 35–47.

Phillion, J., Malewski, E. L., Sharma, S., & Wang, Y. (2009). Reimagining the curriculum: Future teachers and study abroad. *Frontiers: The Interdisciplinary Journal of Study Abroad, 18,* 323–339.

Phillion, J., & Malewski, E. (2011). Study abroad in teacher education: Delving into cultural diversity and developing cultural competence. *Action in Teacher Education, 33*(5–6), 643–657.

Quezada, R. L., & Cordeiro, P. A. (2007). Guest editors' introduction: Internationalizing schools. *Teacher Education Quarterly, 34*(1), 3–7.

Sleeter, C. E. (2001). Preparing teachers for culturally diverse schools research and the overwhelming presence of whiteness. *Journal of Teacher Education, 52*(2), 94–106.

Smith, S. J. (1997). The phenomenology of educating physically. In D. Vandenburg (Ed.), *Phenomenology and educational discourse* (pp. 119–144). Johannesburg, South Africa: Heinemann.

Sunnygard, J. (2002). If you cross over the sea...: Program leadership for intercultural development. In S. E. Spencer & K. Tuma (Eds.), *The guide to successful short-term programs abroad* (pp. 191–201). Washington, DC: NAFSA: Association of International Educators.

Trilokekar, R. D., & Kukar, P. (2011). Disorienting experiences during study abroad: Reflections of pre-service teacher candidates. *Teaching and Teacher Education, 27*(7), 1141–1150.

Wenger, E. (1998). *Communities of practice: Learning, meaning, and identity.* New York, NY: Cambridge University Press.

Van Manen, M. (1997). From meaning to method. *Qualitative Health Research, 7*(3), 345–369.

CHAPTER 6

COMMUNITY SCHOOLING IN HONDURAS

A Simulated Dialogue With Freire, Dewey, and Pinar

Eloisa Rodriguez, Suniti Sharma, and JoAnn Phillion

ABSTRACT

This chapter reports on a three-year study that examined a Honduran school as an international field placement site for promoting U.S. American preservice teachers' cross-cultural understanding of place-based grassroots community schooling. Dewey's vision for democratic education and learning-by-doing, Freire's theory of critical consciousness and community action, and Pinar's notion of place-based learning and understanding curriculum presented a critical cross-cultural lens for exploring the opportunities and challenges of a place-based grassroots community school in Honduras. Participants comprised the founding director of the school, two teachers, and four members of the community. Data consisted of recorded observations and interactions, interviews, informal conversations, and off-site activities. Findings evidence that cross-cultural place-based learning and grassroots community schooling offer U.S. American preservice teachers opportunities for acquir-

Internationalizing Teaching and Teacher Education for Equity, pages 91–106
Copyright © 2016 by Information Age Publishing
All rights of reproduction in any form reserved.

91

ing diverse knowledges and critical skills, understanding their own location within the community and the world, and heightened awareness of the social and economic realities that impact education with potential for informed actions aimed at supporting social justice in schools and community.

INTRODUCTION

For the last 12 years, the authors of this chapter have contributed to a study abroad program in Honduras in different capacities. JoAnn Phillion, a teacher educator in the United States (U.S.), started the program in 2003 and organizes it each year; Eloisa Rodriguez, a teacher educator in Honduras, has coordinated the program from its inception; and Suniti Sharma, a teacher educator in the U.S., serves as a researcher for the program. The study abroad program in Honduras offers opportunities to preservice teachers from a Midwestern public university to gain cross-cultural experience through an international field placement early in their teacher preparation. International field placements offer preservice teachers opportunities for developing multicultural competencies in the following areas: cross-cultural knowledge of alternative school systems in communities different from their own; critical skills for examining and addressing educational inequities; diverse pedagogies informed by cross-cultural experiences and exposure to multiple world views; and dispositions informed by local and global perspectives.

Over time, we have developed relationships with several rural schools in Honduras including Esperanza School (pseudonym meaning hope), where preservice teachers spend two weeks in an immersion experience. Located in Zamorano, a small Honduran town, Esperanza School offers place-based grassroots community schooling with a strong social justice mission. In this chapter, we focus on place-based learning through grassroots community schooling as a possible response to educational inequity embedded in the public and private school systems of Honduras. In expanding preservice teachers' cross-cultural learning in real-world contexts, Esperanza, a place-based grassroots community school, serves as an important site that opens spaces for crossing ideological borders that underscore school missions and goals, critiquing assumptions about traditional education, and developing alternative knowledges excluded from school curriculum.

LITERATURE REVIEW

A grassroots community school is grounded in place-based learning and is built on a set of partnerships between the school and the community that emphasize real-world experiences and group problem-solving for the common good (Melaville, Berg, & Blank, 2006). According to Melaville, Berg, and Blank, place-based learning is based on a philosophy of integrated school curricula, health and service learning, community development, and community engagement aimed at improving student learning, strengthening school and family ties, and promoting effective citizenship for a democratic society. Rather than a scripted curriculum, place-based learning uses the unique history, environment, culture, and the economy of a particular site to provide a context for learning and its application toward addressing the needs of the community.

Several communities around the globe—in Africa, Europe, and South America, for example—have been educated in grassroots community schools with success in preparing students to meet community needs through place-based learning. Place-based grassroots community schools provide education that is designed to meet the needs of communities in over-exploited countries, growing out of far-reaching educational and societal concerns such as poverty and illiteracy, which are global issues with causes that are in part unique to nation and place (Pagani, Boulerice, Vitaro, & Tremblay, 1999; Welshman, 2002). Also, there is the self-fulfilling cycle of a lack of education that perpetuates poverty, which, in turn, leads to a lack of educational opportunities (Howard, Garnham, Fimister, & Viet-Wilson, 2001). This cycle of inequality is particularly apparent in the two-tier public/private school system that is characteristic of Honduras, including the community where Esperanza School is located.

Grassroots community schools have been found to be a particularly effective vehicle for addressing educational inequality, providing increased opportunities for those in poverty to attend school (Farrell, 2008). Grassroots community schools are often small (100–200 students) and classes have low pupil–teacher ratios (Lee & Smith, 1995) compared to public schools. Students in small, community-based schools make more progress toward completing their education without dropping out or leaving school (McMullan, Sipe, & Wolfe, 1994). The structure of grassroots community schools encourages community participation and support and offers curricula directly connected to community values and ways of knowing and being (Pittman & Haughwout, 1987). Committed to cultural and economic development at the grassroots level, community school curricula imparts place-based education for improving the quality of life for the local community and providing real-world experiences responsive to local needs.

As part of our study abroad program, in the past we have offered opportunities to preservice teachers to gain cross-cultural experience through diverse field placements in Honduras that have included different types of schools as well as organized activities and events for interacting and getting familiar with local communities. We have also conducted research for program development in teacher preparation through international field experiences and to facilitate cross-cultural awareness of preservice teachers in a range of diverse social, cultural, and educational environments. Expanding our previous scholarship focused on developing multicultural awareness in preservice teachers committed to educational equity and social justice (Malewski & Phillion, 2009), in this chapter we explore a critical aspect of preservice teachers' experiences—the location of their field placement, Esperanza School—as a site for place-based grassroots community schooling with a social justice mission. This focus on place-based learning, a new facet of ongoing study abroad program research, addresses a gap in the literature on study abroad in teacher education, that is, the importance of place to the teaching and learning process (Kincheloe, 2004; Kincheloe & Pinar, 1991).

We base this chapter on a three-year study examining Esperanza as site for place-based grassroots community schooling with a social justice mission. We examined two questions: How does Esperanza provide place-based grassroots community schooling as a response to the inequitable education embedded in the current public/private two-tiered school system in Honduras? How does Esperanza School contribute to preservice teachers' cross-cultural understanding of place-based grassroots community schooling in Honduras? Specifically, we examined four key principles that underscore the goals, core beliefs, curriculum, and pedagogy of Esperanza School for imparting place-based grassroots community schooling: (1) community values, (2) community needs, (3) community program planning, and (4) community development.

In order to highlight the critical importance of place, we contextualize the study by providing background information on Honduras, information on the educational system of Honduras, and details on Esperanza as a community school guided by the principles of place-based learning. We also provide the framework and the methodology for our study followed by our findings and a brief discussion.

BACKGROUND AND CONTEXT

Honduras: The Country

Honduras, the third poorest country in the Americas behind Haiti and Nicaragua, has an unequal distribution of income and high unemployment (United Nations Development Programme, 2009). With a population of about 8 million, Honduras has struggled to meet the needs of its citizens. Half of the people in Honduras live in cities and the other half mainly in rural areas. The labor force is divided as follows: 39% government services,

39% in agriculture, and 20% in industry (Central Intelligence Agency, 2009). The economy relies primarily on exports of bananas and coffee; its natural resources are timber, gold, silver, copper, lead, zinc, iron ore, antimony, coal, and fish (USAID, 2010). The yearly average salary in Honduras is $1900; around 50% of households are living in poverty, and 30% in extreme poverty (World Bank, 2014).

Honduras depends economically on the United States (Merrill, 1995). According to Merrill, in spite of U.S. investment in improving the economic infrastructure through land reforms, health programs, and educational reforms, a key issue facing the country is how to improve the education system and raise literacy rates. The lack of appropriate schooling in Honduras has been a challenge for the Honduran government and its people. Raising the literacy rate and decreasing the school drop-out rate would help alleviate poverty, and this can best be achieved by providing better quality education.

Honduras Education: Two-Tiered System

The educational system in Honduras is composed of public and private schools regulated by the Ministry of Education under the Honduran government. Public schooling is informally referred to as the "free education system," and the private system the "expensive education system." Public and private school systems in Honduras report to the Ministry of Education, follow a standard curriculum established in the 1990s (Currículo Nacional Básico), have year-long student learning objectives, are mandated to fulfill the same plan of study across schools, and require 200 days of class per school year.

In the public education system, the government states that Hondurans are to receive educational support such as free tuition, books, and a meal during the school day (Secretaria de Educacion de Honduras, 2014). The public school system, however, is not able to meet these requirements. In addition, there are issues such as a lack of schools, understaffed schools, underpaid teachers, outdated teaching methods, poor administration, and a lack of physical facilities. Accordingly, over the last several years, teachers have gone on strike for weeks at a time, which leads to school closings, thus depriving children of an education. While in session, teachers are responsible for classes of 60–100 students, often working without supplies or furniture in their classrooms. Many communities express that the government is failing the public school system, which in turn is failing the community it serves.

With an inadequate public school system, since 1970 there has been a proliferation of private schools in Honduras (Merrill, 1995). The private school system is for-profit and provides secure instruction (all mandated school days are followed) and English immersion education at the cost of about $200 a month. Although exact figures are unavailable, only a small fraction of the total population has access to education through private schooling due its high cost (World Bank, 2014).

Esperanza School: Place-Based Community Schooling

Esperanza School, the focal school of this chapter, is a unique grassroots community school as it was founded by the local community and supported by donations through a foundation making it different from both public and private schools in Honduras. Many aspects of the school make it a grassroots community school. The school has a strong social justice mission to educate all local students guided by passionate and participatory partnerships across the local community. It provides K–6 instruction and has a 98% graduation rate (Esperanza School, 2010). Forty percent of students attend on a full scholarship (such as children from a nearby orphanage); the rest pay tuition on a sliding scale (such as people who work in the local area) with some paying full fees of $2,500 per year (such as children of faculty at the agricultural college, the campus location of Esperanza School).

The school provides a bilingual education program, which enables students to become fluent in English and Spanish. All courses are taught in English with the exception of Spanish and Spanish social studies; however, both languages are applied to a wide range of educational, cultural, and recreational activities. The school follows a student-centered approach to teaching and learning. With a maximum of 15–18 students per class, teachers establish a learning environment conducive to meeting the needs of each student. The school has recently become internationally accredited, enabling students to take standardized U.S.-based tests. The curriculum is adopted from various U.S. states, and while textbooks are not used as main class texts, they are resources for teachers. Many of the teachers are born and educated in the United States.

The mission of the school is to provide children of diverse socioeconomic and cultural backgrounds a stimulating and challenging educational environment that fosters intellectual, social, and emotional growth. The social justice mission of the school is to provide free education to students from economically disadvantaged rural communities; train teachers for rural schools; and provide scholarships, books, food, and equipment to a local orphanage. Core beliefs of the school include high standards of excellence, student-centered inquiry-based learning, learning-by-doing, and commitment to the community.

THEORETICAL FRAMEWORK: DEWEY, FREIRE, AND PINAR

Building on the philosophies of John Dewey, Paulo Freire, and William Pinar, we used a critical framework to examine Esperanza School—its goals and core beliefs—as an exemplary educational site for place-based learning, which includes developing and sustaining a robust grassroots community school. Dewey's vision for democratic education and learning-by-doing, Freire's theory of critical consciousness and community action, and Pinar's notion of place-based learning and understanding curriculum present cross-cultural lenses for exploring the opportunities and challenges of a place-based grassroots community school in Honduras.

RESEARCH METHODOLOGY: NARRATIVE INQUIRY

We used narrative inquiry to position ourselves as inquirers with participants as equal inquirers (Phillion & He, 2008). This created an equitable environment for the researchers and participants to negotiate meanings of the participants' lived experiences. Participants comprised the founding director of the school, two teachers, and four members of the community. Over a period of three years (part of a longer-term 12-year study), the researchers were immersed in Esperanza School to observe participants' experiences, actions, and feelings. These observations and interactions were recorded along with interviews, informal conversations, and off-site activities, allowing the researchers to triangulate participant narratives with the simulated dialogues connecting theories, philosophies, and perspectives to the goals and core beliefs of Esperanza as a place-based grassroots community school. For the analysis of data, we turned to a cross-cultural lens to examine the critical interplay of culture, ideology, and educational equity within the school and community.

We present our analysis and findings through a simulated dialogue among Dewey, Freire, Pinar, and Eloisa—critical scholars committed to social and educational change. The simulated dialogue offers preservice teachers exposure to cross-cultural theorizing of complex overlapping and sometimes divergent ideologies and philosophies in relation to the pedagogies and practices of place-based grassroots community schooling with a social justice mission. We simulated a form of dialogue as an interchange of perspectives on the ideological and educational experiences in the context of community schooling to further our understanding of inequality within over-exploited nations and how critical educators might respond to educational inequality in their classrooms, schools, and communities.

RESEARCH FINDINGS:
A SIMULATED CROSS-CULTURAL DIALOGUE

We selected Esperanza School as the site for preservice teachers' international field placement as the school is grounded in community principles with a strong social justice mission[1] aimed at addressing inequalities in the local community. The philosophy and mission of the school are based on core beliefs reflecting a diverse range of scholars from Dewey and Freire to Pinar. Therefore, we were interested in researching how the school brings together diverse thinkers to address the needs of the local community. Our findings opened up critical questions that we examine in this section: How does Esperanza school, a school that values place-based learning, promote community knowledge and values though U.S. language, curriculum, and pedagogy? How do the school's core beliefs translate into planning and development that address the needs of the community, especially inequities in social, economic, and educational processes? How does the school balance place-based schooling for community development with global influences that privilege and/or oppress? How does Esperanza School offer preservice teachers opportunities for developing a more complicated understanding of cross-cultural teaching and learning that promotes social justice?

In the next section, we draw from our findings to answer the above questions through a simulated cross-cultural dialogue among Freire, Dewey, Pinar, and Eloisa. We position Eloisa in the dialogue as she has been a K–12 teacher in Honduras, is currently a teacher educator in Honduras, serves as a coordinator for the study abroad program, has worked with U.S. preservice teachers, and has been educated in Honduras and the U.S.; therefore, she has a range of educational experiences within the K–12 and higher education systems in both countries.

> **Eloisa:** Paulo, John, and Bill, throughout this research, we learned about Esperanza School and how place-based learning in grassroots community schools offers a response to addressing inequality in the Honduran education system. Part of what a democratic education entails is for people to be critical about the larger issues that impact educational processes and outcomes. In Esperanza School, the employees, parents, students, and the local community accept what the school offers without questioning any of the school's goals, core beliefs, and practices. What do you think about education in Esperanza School, knowing that the school is committed to place-based learning promoting community knowledge and values, yet simultaneously privileges U.S. language, curriculum, and pedagogy?
>
> **John [Dewey]:** This school reaches out to the community and believes that the knowledge and values of the family, and the family history of the children in the school, will enhance teachers' understanding of

where the children are coming from so that curricula and pedagogy can be designed around their academic needs and how they learn.

Eloisa: In other words, a school whose educational goal is providing quality education based on individual needs need not attend to the economic and social needs of the community. For example, the curriculum at Esperanza is planned and implemented under bilingual education with emphasis on English rather than students' home and community language, Spanish, which presents two challenges: First, the curriculum, specifically language, reflects and embodies culture, so privileging the English language implies promoting knowledge and values different from that of the local community, which seems contradictory to place-based grassroots community schooling committed to promoting community knowledge and values. Second, when children become proficient in English, they cannot continue with their education within the local community where the medium of instruction is Spanish. Therefore, they must move to the city or outside the country to study and work in an English-speaking environment. To me, this move to the city or another country conflicts with place-based community schooling that is focused on addressing the community's needs.

John: As I have always maintained, "democracy is not an alternative to other principles of associated life. It is the idea of community life itself" (1927, p. 148; see also 1938). I must say that communities are part of the larger world communities, so in terms of addressing the community's needs, Esperanza School has good intentions by linking the local to the outside world. The school follows democratic principles of equality and education for all in the community who worked for a placement in the school, which is commendable. Also, I was impressed by the commitment of the teachers and the principal of the school on the value they placed on the practice of democratic education, learning-by-doing, and inquiry-based experiential learning. The school has high expectations from its teachers, students, and parents as they seem to work in partnership as a community of practice.

Eloisa: On one level, I can see how the school has created a sense of community, involved parents to be active members of the community, and welcomed parents on the school premises every day. On another level, I am interested in knowing why rural communities in Honduras want to be educated in a bilingual system that privileges English above local languages. Would you consider bilingual education in a local community in Honduras an imposition or a form of oppression?

John: In terms of the English language, you informed us about the evolution of curriculum in Esperanza School, their struggle for accreditation, and how that is seen as the route to success. This school transformed from a fully Spanish-speaking school to earning accreditation from SACS (Southern Association of Colleges and

Schools). Why is it so important for a school like Esperanza School to be accredited?

Eloisa: There is a delicate balance between wanting accreditation (reasons stated in participants' interviews) and having standardized questions in yearly tests that the students in Esperanza School have to abide by because of the SACS accreditation. It is troubling that the school is using U.S. American textbooks that mention dollars and not lempiras (Honduran currency), with examples of snowmen and snowflakes in a warm country that sees only a rainy and a dry season. It is also troubling to see that most of the school's personnel are from the U.S., opening possibilities for students to go and visit or study in the U.S. rather than contribute by staying within the community. It seems that students at Esperanza are living someone else's reality, harboring false hopes of striving to get to the U.S., which is their idea of success.

Paulo [Freire]: I can see the issue around bilingual education is an ongoing concern you have, Eloisa. In order for the community of Esperanza School to be oppressed by the English language, this community would had to have been forced to enter that schooling system, to adopt the other culture's practices, or been prevented from choosing between the private system and the public system to which they belonged before (Freire, 2003). In this case, oppression would manifest itself in authoritarianism where no dialogue or partnership existed between the school and the community. I do not see Esperanza School as one where the community has been silenced by the board, principal, or school teachers. In my opinion, Esperanza School is community-based and is a work in progress as it strives to attain its social justice mission as a grassroots community school. A community school foresees the needs of all the community members and strives to attain them. On the other hand, Esperanza School originally concentrated on addressing the needs of the four families who started the school and allowed the Agricultural College to exercise dominance over their decisions because of land and funding needs. A place-based community school will be able to figure how to be sustainable so that the community's knowledge, values, and interests are not compromised.

Bill [Pinar]: I must admit, in my handbook (Pinar, 2003), I failed to include a curriculum for small, local communities in relation to place-based education. Eloisa, you describe some of the communities around Esperanza School as rural, where most of the jobs relate to farming and the land. With little exposure to city life, belonging to rural areas and working on the land with crops, the sociocultural realities and experiences must be different from families and communities living in the cities. I wonder about the kind of curriculum that would attend most closely to the specific experiences and needs of the local community of Esperanza School without

emulating the standardized educational system in the U.S. that
dehumanizes certain groups of students and communities.

Eloisa: The curriculum in most bilingual schools in Honduras follows U.S.
American content and assessment standards and uses U.S. American textbooks. Esperanza School's curriculum does not include
detailed history, geography, literature, and the arts of Honduras,
nor does it reflect the social, cultural, and economic realities of its
communities. I see a gap between place-based community schooling focused on producing the next generation of community
leaders with the capacity to address the needs of the community
and plan for its growth and development on the one hand and a
curricula that is taken out of a U.S. American education context,
on the other. Paulo, how would you address this issue?

Paulo: I think we have to remember that education is not limited to curriculum plans to be implemented in the classroom. A curriculum
based on the "banking model of education" (Freire 2000, p. 73–81)
is limited to knowledge transferred through the tyranny of rote
learning from textbooks. However, education as the practice of
freedom opens opportunities to learn from and about the real world
of students and their communities. Students need critical tools to
be able to use experience and learning for addressing the needs
of their communities, and use their knowledge and skills to act as
cultural workers who fight for educational and social change (Freire
& Macedo, 1998; Freire, 1998a, 1998b). I firmly believe that *conscientization*, or raising consciousness toward inequities in the social,
economic, and educational systems, and empowerment through
critical dialogues and cooperative action among communities are
the cornerstones of a liberating education (Freire, 1973b, 2004). A
community cannot exist on its own and is impacted by the outside
world. In the case of Honduras, local inequities are part of the capitalist processes that generate inequities around the world and create
categories of rich and poor. So a school with a social justice mission
addresses inequitable distribution of wealth on many fronts. Let's
look at the different dimensions of education at Esperanza School to
see how their ideology and philosophy of education fits with place-
based community schooling committed to social justice.

Bill: I agree with Paulo that education, whether in Honduras or in the
U.S., should not be about rote learning and transmission of dominant cultural knowledge and values. Rather, education is about
validating the knowledges and experiences of those who have
been traditionally outside mainstream culture of schooling (Pinar,
2012). A mechanistic system in which knowledge is produced and
transferred by the teacher to the students is not democratic education. In other words, democratic education is about recognizing
the alternative knowledges and values of communities marginalized from dominant school knowledge and social processes. So if
we as educators aim to address inequities in educational practices,

we need to have complicated conversations on how different ideologies and perspectives can come together toward building an inclusive educational system that benefits all students and communities. Eloisa, I see your concerns, but what if Esperanza School could function as a separate community school and more branches like it could exist in Honduras? Could it serve as an alternative model for education that does not have the price tag that comes attached to a private school and gives quality education as a place-based community school committed to social justice? What if philanthropic businesses sponsor one public school and commit to offer quality education for the community in the area? Of course, this takes us back to the question of what is quality education in the context of the local communities around Esperanza?

John: Bill, I think you have a great idea that brings schools and society in close partnership. I have always believed in education as the vehicle for social reform through democratic participation of all members of the community. Democratic participation is more than just a political role, though; it is democracy as a mode of working with others in a society towards a common interest. It is in the interest of the community to promote social justice and true democratic participation by counteracting the free-market capitalist forces that produce oppression and inequities. From my philosophical perspective, Esperanza School teachers do this and much more with their students. In my laboratory school, we developed the power of inquiry in my students, and the role of reflection was to construct meaning (Dewey, 1902, 1916). So I have to say that Esperanza School is a unique model. Can you imagine the impact on Honduran society if the disadvantaged were empowered with quality education and knew that the community was looking after them?

Paulo: I see Esperanza School students being curious about the world and empowered by what they are learning. They reflect upon their acquired knowledge and how it impacts their community. Maybe Esperanza School is not asking students to critically reflect on their position on the economic ladder or the Honduran political system and what powerful countries are taking from Honduran sweatshops, but I do not think any school in Honduras does that. I even wonder if the community schools do that.

Bill: I have to agree with both Paulo and John on this statement—Esperanza School is not a community school that makes the community reflect upon their reality but one that is concerned with exposing the community to a world of possibilities through diverse curricula that includes bilingual education. I wonder about the curriculum discourses around Esperanza School. Is it offering a hidden curriculum that makes the community believe that a U.S. curriculum is superior?

Paulo: That is precisely what I expect from grassroots community schooling—an awakening of critical consciousness through dialogue

(Freire, 1973a). But if instead schools continue to create masses who believe the world is a perfect place, then how can we implement social, economic, and educational reform and reconstruct a socially just society?

John: Why do we have to opt for dualistic thinking and choose whether a school can teach individuals how to be part of a society *or* how to be critical of the world that surrounds them? In the complex world of schools and society, we need critical tools that enable us to value the communities we belong to, be pragmatic enough to critique what needs to change, and act toward social, economic, and educational reform.

Bill: That is the critical piece that is missing in many school contexts around the world. I have talked in my writings about curriculum being a political, social, and a racial text (Pinar, Reynolds, Slattery, & Taubman, 1995). I think we agree that all teacher educators, teachers, teacher education students, and K–12 students should have the knowledge and skills to critique philosophies by analyzing the ways in which curriculum discourses have been used in specific places as an instrument of cultural assimilation and domination that in turn promote inequities. Critically conscious teachers are mindful of domination and oppression and are aware of current events around the world that affect the lives of their students and impact the place and community in which they live and teach.

Eloisa: Paulo, John, and Bill, I want to thank all of you for your time, and I appreciate your thoughtful input on Esperanza School as a place-based grassroots community school and helping us to understand the opportunities and challenges posed by the school's goals, core beliefs, curriculum, and pedagogy. This dialogue also made me realize that educational change is a continuous process of distilling the best in educational research, theoretical orientations, and pedagogical practices from around the world in relation to addressing local community needs that in turn make a difference in attending to national challenges.

DISCUSSION: OPPORTUNITIES OR/AND CHALLENGES OF PLACE-BASED COMMUNITY SCHOOLS

We brought a dialogic format presenting theories and philosophies of Freire, Dewey, and Pinar, without privileging any one ideology over any other, to allow for the full participation of cross-cultural perspectives and worldviews to bring together a meaningful set of ideas guiding place-based grassroots community schooling with a social justice mission. Dewey, Freire, and Pinar envision education as the means to social change and eradication of injustices. All three scholars argue for a place-based education system where students are not passive recipients of knowledge but active participants in the classroom, school, and community. A central theme of Freirian pedagogy is what he calls conscientization, or developing a critical consciousness toward one's position in an oppressed society and the tools for taking action. In Deweyan terms, democratic education translates into experiential learning and reflective thinking combined with pragmatic action (Dewey, 1961, pp. 184–186). Key to Pinarean philosophy for understanding curriculum is lifelong and place-based learning inclusive of the knowledges and histories of all students. When teachers and students are involved in the process of doing, they bring their experiences to the classroom, research together, ask questions, examine and analyze issues, work in partnership with community—these actions involve critical thinking skills that help them make "informed" decisions that are for the common good.

Cross-cultural, overlapping, and divergent philosophies and theories help us understand that education is a process in which individuals as active members of society have a say in its planning and development and are mindful of the critical importance of place to educational processes and outcomes. Place-based learning and grassroots community schooling offer opportunities to teachers and students to acquire diverse knowledges and critical skills for taking action for the common good. Place-based community schooling promotes active learning, fosters critical thinking as a means to understanding oneself and others, and involves dialogue to enable teachers and students to become fully aware of their own location within the community and the world. Critical thinking and dialogue are forms of conscientization and praxis premised on becoming aware of the social, economic, and educational realities in one's community and taking informed actions to transform community. Active learning takes place when students, through dialogue and critical thinking, understand the inequalities and injustices in their lives and communities and in so doing take practical action for ending all forms of oppressions.

CONCLUSION

There is a gap between Esperanza School's vision for social and educational change in Honduras and the social, economic, and educational inequity that exists in local communities. At the same time, schools like Esperanza offer a vision of education to students, teachers, parents and community toward addressing the gap. Esperanza, a place-based grassroots community school, extends unique opportunities to future teachers invested in cross-cultural knowledges and pedagogies as students, teachers, and the community take a more critical and activist stand toward social justice.

NOTE

1. During interviews, the school founder and U.S. American teachers reinforced their belief of Esperanza School's social justice mission and worked to get involved with and for the community.

REFERENCES

Central Intelligence Agency. (2009). Retrieved from https://www.cia.gov/library/publications/the-world-factbook/geos/ho.html

Dewey, J. (1902). *The child and the curriculum.* Chicago, IL: University of Chicago Press.

Dewey, J. (1916). *Democracy and education.* New York, NY: Macmillan.

Dewey, J. (1927). *The public and its problems.* New York, NY: Holt.

Dewey, J. (1938). *Experience and education.* New York, NY: Touchstone.

Dewey, J. (1961). *Democracy and education: An introduction to the philosophy of education.* London, UK: Macmillan.

Esperanza School. (2010). Retrieved from http://alisonbixby.org/about/history

Farrell, J. P. (2008). Community education in developing countries: The quiet revolution in schooling. In F. M. Connelly, M. F. He, & J. Phillion (Eds.), *Handbook of curriculum and instruction* (pp. 369–389). Thousand Oaks, CA: Sage.

Freire, P. (1973a). *Education for critical consciousness.* New York, NY: Continuum Publishing.

Freire, P. (1973b). *Education: The practice of freedom.* London, England: Writers and Readers Publishing Cooperative.

Freire, P. (1998a). *Teachers as cultural workers: Letters to those who dare teach.* Boulder, CO: Westview Press.

Freire, P. (1998b). Pedagogy in process. In A. Freire & D. Macedo (Eds.), *The Paulo Freire reader* (pp. 111–162). New York, NY: Continuum Publishing.

Freire, P. (2000). *Pedagogy of the oppressed.* New York, NY: Continuum Publishing.

Freire, P. (2003). *Pedagogy of the oppressed.* New York, NY: Continuum Publishing.

Freire, P. (2004). *Pedagogy of hope: Reliving pedagogy of the oppressed.* Trans. Robert Barr. New York, NY: Continuum Publishing.

Freire, P., & Macedo, D. (1998). *Literacy: Reading the word and the world.* South Hadley, MA: Bergin & Garvey.

Howard, M., Garnham, A., Fimister, G., & Viet-Wilson, J. (2001). *Poverty: The facts.* London, UK: Child Poverty Action Group.

Kincheloe, J. L. (2004). The knowledges of teacher education: Developing a critical complex epistemology. *Teacher Education Quarterly, 31*(1), 49–66.

Kincheloe, J., & Pinar, W. (Eds.). (1991). *Curriculum as social psychoanalysis: The significance of place.* Albany, NY: State University of New York Press.

Lee, V. E., & Smith, J. B. (1995). Effects of high school restructuring and size on early gains in achievement and engagement. *Sociology of Education, 86*(4), 241–270.

Malewski, E., & Phillion, J. (2009). International field experiences: The impact of class, gender and race on the perceptions and experiences of preservice teachers. *Teaching and Teacher Education, 25*(1), 52–60.

McMullan, B. J., Sipe, C. L., & Wolfe, W. C. (1994). *Charters and student achievement: Early evidence from school restructuring in Philadelphia.* Philadelphia, PA: Center for Assessment and Policy Development.

Melaville, A., Berg, A. C., & Blank, M. J. (2006). *Community-based learning: Engaging students for success and citizenship.* Washington, DC: Coalition for Community Schools.

Merrill, T. (Ed.). (1995). *Honduras: A country study.* Washington, DC: GPO for the Library of Congress.

Pagani, L., Boulerice, B., Vitaro, F., & Tremblay, R. E. (1999). Effects of poverty on academic failure and delinquency in boys: A change and process model approach. *Journal of Child Psychology and Psychiatry, 40*(8), 1209–1219.

Phillion, J., & He, M. F. (2008). Multicultural and cross-cultural narrative inquiry in educational research. *Thresholds in Education, 34*(1), 2–12.

Pinar, W. (Ed.). (2003). *International handbook of curriculum research.* Mahwah, NJ: Lawrence Erlbaum.

Pinar, W. (2012). *Curriculum studies in the United States: Present circumstances, intellectual histories.* New York, NY: Palgrave Macmillan.

Pinar, W. F., Reynolds, W. M., Slattery, P. G., & Taubman, P. M. (1995).*Understanding curriculum: An introduction to the study of historical and contemporary curriculum discourses.* New York, NY: Peter Lang.

Pittman, R. B., & Haughwout, P. (1987). Influence of high school size on dropout rate. *Educational Evaluation and Policy Analysis, 9*(4), 337–343.

Secretaria de Educacion de Honduras. (2014). Retrieved from http://estadisticas. se.gob.hn/portal/portal.php, and http://www.se.gob.hn

United Nations Development Programme. (2009). Retrieved from http://www. undp.org USAID. (2010). *Report No. 1-522-10-007-P.* Retrieved from http:// oig.usaid.gov/node/442

Welshman, J. (2002). The cycle of deprivation and the concept of the underclass. *Benefits, 10*(3), 199–205.

World Bank. (2014). Honduras overview. Retrieved from http://www.worldbank. org/en/country/honduras/overview

CHAPTER 7

RETHINKING TECHNOLOGY—
"TECHNOLOGY
AS A PUBLIC GOOD"

Examining the Korean Government's
Policy for Bridging Digital Inequality

Sunnie Lee Watson

ABSTRACT

The South Korean government's policy of bridging the digital inequality in society is a notion of "technology as a public good." South Korea's Master Plan for Closing the Digital Divide first launched in 2001 and has been continually renewed and updated for implementation for over a decade. In 2012, the Korea Communications Commission reported that 82.3% of all households in South Korea had broadband access (Park & Kim, 2014). Overall, this policy has been considered very successful in its implementation, becoming a uniquely successful example of information and communication technology (ICT) development through government policy implementation. In this chapter, I examine the notion of "technology as a public good" through the Master Plan for Closing the Digital Divide policy and explore how the policies

Internationalizing Teaching and Teacher Education for Equity, pages 107–123
Copyright © 2016 by Information Age Publishing
107

were implemented and appropriated in the Korean cultural context. I also argue for the need for an enhanced understanding of the complex connections between digital divide policies, adoption of ICT use, and socioeconomically disadvantaged populations.

INTRODUCTION

In a society where knowledge-intensive activities are more and more important, the distribution of information across the population is increasingly related to divisions and stratification. Many optimists and information technology advocates have argued for the promise of information communications technology (ICT) in reducing social inequality, describing the current inequities in ICT access as temporary. These optimists and advocates, such as Rogers (1983), have argued that the benefits of technology will reduce inequality by decreasing the hurdles to information access, allowing people of all backgrounds to advance their human capital, strengthen their social networks, search for and find better jobs, and overall improve their quality of life by having the ability to access opportunities and information. However, others have warned that the rapid and uneven spread of Internet access across the population leads to increasing inequalities, advancing the situations of those who are already in privileged positions while disallowing the underprivileged opportunities for equal access (Hargittai, 2003).

Researchers, policymakers, and information technologists have paid attention to which parts of the population have access to the Internet and what sort of effects these trends have on society. Findings and arguments are mixed based on contextual factors, and the research clearly reflects that while the Internet has positive effects, it can also lead to further or new divides and inequalities (DiMaggio, Hargittai, Celeste, & Shafer, 2004; Van Dijk, 2012; Warschauer, 2004).

In this chapter, I review the implementation studies of the South Korean government's policies on closing the digital divide. I specifically focus on their first digital divide policy, the 2001 Master Plan for Digital Divide Solution, which has been the most impactful and which takes the stance of "technology as a public good" in bridging the digital inequality in society.

THE DIGITAL DIVIDE

The term "digital divide," often also referred to as "information gap" or "information inequality," is used to refer to the inequality between those people with effective access to powerful information technologies and those without access to it, particularly as embodied in the Internet (Norris,

2001). While the precise definition of digital divide can vary by the context in which it is being used or the group of people discussing it, the meaning of digital divide includes the discrepancies in physical access to ICT as well as the inequalities in resources and skills needed to effectively use digital information or participate in the digital society (Cho, 2001; Korean Ministry of Information and Communication, 2001; Seo, 2001). In other words, it is the unequal access by some members of society to information and communications technology and the unequal acquisition of related skills. Groups often discussed in the context of a digital divide include those grouped by socioeconomic status, gender, race, age, or region/geography. In this discussion, I will use the term "digital divide" to mean discrepancies in access to or use of ICT services because of economic, regional, physical, or social situations.

The most common understanding of the notion of digital divide has been to divide Internet access according to geographical or regional lines, such as the North–South divide or the "Western countries and the others" (Guðmundsdóttir, 2005). Digital divide exists within every nation or region between the affluent minority and the rest of the population, and its negative impact on society in general and education in particular has already been recognized in many ICT-advanced countries (Schradie, 2011; Van Dijk, 2012).

WHY THE KOREAN CASE?

South Korea has made major strides in information and communication technology (ICT). In 1960, after the Korean War, Korea had a telephone penetration of 0.36 per 100 inhabitants, barely one tenth of the then-world average. Even after the rapid economic development between the 1960s and 1990s, South Korea had less than one Internet user per 100 inhabitants in 1995 (International Telecommunication Union [ITU], 2003). And yet in 1999, Korea's Internet user rate surpassed the developed nation average, and by the end of 2002, it was the world's fifth largest Internet market, with 26 million users. Furthermore, in 2007 the number of Internet users in South Korea increased to over 34 million (World Internet Statistics, 2007), and by 2012, 82.3% of all households in South Korea had broadband access (Park & Kim, 2014).

Demographically, Korea is not the ideal candidate to have one of the highest Internet penetration rates in the world, or even the highest in Asia. Among the so-called Four Tigers (South Korea, Hong Kong, Singapore, and Taiwan), Korea has the largest land area and the largest population. Korea's population stands twice as large as Taiwan, seven times bigger than

Hong Kong, and more than 11 times larger than Singapore, which makes ICT access to the general public a more significant challenge.

Korea cannot be viewed as the best candidate economically either, as the World Bank classifies Korea as an upper-middle income country, one category down from the high-income classification. Therefore, Korea's high level of Internet penetration is not strongly correlated to its income level. Another discouraging factor against Korea's ICT development is Hangul, the Korean alphabet, which uses a pictographic font that is not suited to computerization (ITU, 2003).

What, then, are the reasons behind South Korea becoming a leading ICT strong nation with an ICT access of over 70% of the general public? There are various factors that will be discussed in the following section that have helped contribute to the growing impact of ICT in the Korean economy and society. Among these various factors, however, international ICT researchers refer to the government's policies on ICT as the most important factor in Korea's success (Han, 2003; Picot & Wernick, 2007). Over 20 of the reviewed case studies and implementation studies of both domestic and international policies for digital divide show that the Korean government ensured a high level of confidence and assurance for the general public and private companies by establishing and communicating a clear vision and strategy for ICT as a public good.

THE POLICY: "MASTER PLAN FOR DIGITAL DIVIDE SOLUTION"

While Korea has worked on incremental information society plans since the 1980s, the real push was in 1994 when the Korean government made major structural transformations in the government and changed the Ministry of Postal Service into the Ministry of Information and Communication (MIC), modeled after the national information infrastructure of the United States.

The first full-scale information society initiative was Cyber Korea 21 (1999–2002). In March 1999, it was announced that Cyber Korea 21 was to be implemented. Cyber Korea 21 presented the following three policy objectives: building information infrastructure for a knowledge-based economy, improving nationwide productivity using knowledge and information foundation, and increasing employment using information infrastructure. Among detailed strategies for Cyber Korea 21 were upgrading information and communications networks, establishing and revising the legal support systems for an information-age society, bridging the digital divide by building a computer-literate nation, building a small but effective e-government, facilitating e-commerce, and establishing a sound and secure information culture (Choi, 2003; Korean Ministry of Information and Communication, 2001).

However, as soon as the full-blown Cyber Korea 21 policy was rolled out, the government came to recognize the increasingly unequal distribution of access to ICT and felt the need to set forward a set of policies on closing the digital divide if the Cyber Korea 21 policy was to become a success. Therefore, in March of 2001, the 2001 Master Plan for Digital Divide Solution was announced by the government and led by the Ministry of Information and Communication. The policy set goals to achieve the following six main objectives: (1) ensure high-speed broadband Internet through providing Asymmetric Digital Subscriber Lines (ADSL) in every single village, town, and city in the entire nation; (2) provide free computers and five years of high-speed Internet in 50,000 homes of children-led families (families of children on welfare with no parent or foster parent direction), people on welfare or with disabilities, and social service centers; (3) ensure access to people with disabilities; (4) provide 550 public libraries that still did not have computers and Internet access with digital resource centers for facilitating all citizens' Internet use; facilitate the opening of at least 14,000 Personal Computer Cafes (PC Bang) nationwide, at a price lower than one U.S. dollar an hour; (5) provide low-income families and people with disabilities the ADSL service at a 50% discount through government support; and (6) based on the successful program implementations through 1988–1999 on digital literacy for children, housewives, people with disabilities, and low-income families, expand the program for 10 million citizens, including the elderly, small business owners, and farmers/fishermen in less developed regions.

In addition, the plan was to establish at least one or more free Internet center in every village and to provide basic digital literacy education opportunities to all citizens. Content for e-learning was to be developed and distributed to those of certain demographic groups that were traditionally excluded from information technology such as people with disabilities, the elderly, and farmers and fishermen. Detailed policies for access to ICT for people with disabilities were to be laid out later that year, and a development and research center of ICT for persons with disabilities was also to be established.

SOURCES AND FUNDING FOR THE POLICY

The 5-year plan was to be supported with 2.3 trillion *won* (approximately 2.3 billion U.S. dollars) by the government. Although the use of funding was not described or planned in detail at the time of the policy's announcement, each government department was to be provided with money that could be allocated to support this initiative. Most departments were required to directly participate in the policy rollout by planning specific programs that would be a good fit with their area of interest and also transform the department to be an organization more appropriate for an information society. In addition, tax cut incentives, subsidies, direct underwriting, loans, and other types of financial support for construction of new high-capacity computer hardware and private high-speed broadband Internet companies were supported in order to facilitate the equitable distributions of computer hardware and high-speed Internet services (Choi, 2003).

THE IMPLEMENTATION OF POLICY

Overall Policy Mechanisms

The 2001 Master Plan for Digital Divide Solution policy is a redistributive policy that tries to address the unequal distribution issues raised by the developmental Cyber Korea 21 government policy. This redistributive policy used a variety of methods for the policy implementation. As the detailed plans for the policy rolled out and the implementation process unfolded, the results showed that the policy was mainly using mandates for public organizations and institutions and incentive-based inducements for private business owners. Mandates were used as enforcement of law for compliance in government-based or public institutions; regulations were mandated to provide free Internet services and basic digital literacy education. Inducement mechanisms such as tax cuts and loan support were also used for private companies such as Hanaro Telecom and Korea Telecommunications (KT) to provide computer hardware resources and services to the disadvantaged, to low-income families, and to those living in rural areas. As for individual level participation in digital literacy education and requests for physical resources and services, incentives such as the provision of software were popular and effective in the majority of the departmental programs (Korean Ministry of Information and Communication, 2001).

Key Complementary Factors and Actors

Government Commitment
Clearly, the Korean government played the most significant role in providing investment and commitment for closing the digital divide. Han (2003) and Picot and Wernick (2007) found in their studies that the public good character of broadband and Internet access was emphasized by the Korean government granting subsidies to providers that offered broadband in rural or less developed regions on a national level. The Korean government not only assisted in building a network infrastructure by acting as a

catalyst that encouraged private companies to invest in large projects but also provided side stimulants by marketing the educational benefits of digital literacy and ICT to the less developed business sectors and regions (Han, 2003). The government ensured a high level of confidence and assurance for private companies and the general public by establishing a clear vision and strategy.

Departmental Implemented Programs and Funding

The 5-year plan was to be supported with 2.3 trillion won (2.3 billion U.S. dollars) by the government. The policy had a very clear mission statement in six categories but did not have detailed plans for specific allocation of funding. The specific programs and plans for funding were designed in collaboration with all representatives of all departments. Table 7.1 details a brief overview of how much funding was provided to these departments to carry out their programs regarding the digital divide policy.

Public Private Partnership

While the Korean government's leadership and strong commitment towards the issue of digital divide brought this plan to life, it is not a far stretch to claim that the private sector has done most of the heavy lifting in achieving Korea's current status as a world leader in ICT access, providing affordable prices to the general public, and also providing free or discounted services to the disadvantaged. The collaboration of the government and private companies has been a notable one, and different companies have turned the guidance provided by the Ministry of Information and Communication into action. Choudrie and Lee (2004) and Han (2003) analyzed this to mean that a little government spending can go a lot further in achieving objectives than in other countries where there is a more adversarial relationship between the government and the private sector.

Competition of Broadband Internet Companies

The Korean government has also consistently facilitated competition among Internet provider businesses, based on deregulation and market principles (Choudrie & Lee, 2004). Individual home users of the Internet had a maximum connection speed of dial-up service until the late 1990s. However, this changed when the government's push and incentives toward the use of ADSL technology encouraged companies such as Hanaro Telecom and KT to join the broadband provider competition. In just three years after the policy announcement in 2004, the number of home users with broadband Internet access exceeded 11 million, which covers more than 70% of the households in Korea. The Korean government recognized that to be successful, broadband access would need to be priced at affordable

TABLE 7.1   Funding for Implementation of Policy of Departmental Programs

Category	Program	Funding (10,000,0000 Won)
Ministry of Education, Science and Technology	Provision of low income family PC and Internet services (50,000 homes)	133
	Teacher training for information technology	30
Ministry of Foreign Affairs and Trade	Aid for closing digital divide in developing countries (sending experts, volunteers abroad)	172
Ministry of Justice	Juvenile correction facilities' information technology centers	49
Ministry of National Defense	150,000 soldiers' basic digital literacy education	N/A
Ministry of Public Administration and Security	Information village (more than 100)	430
	Digital Literacy education (250,000–50,000 people)	260
Ministry of Culture, Sports and Tourism	Development of a national digital library for people with disabilities	16
Ministry for Food, Agriculture, Forestry and Fisheries	AFFIS.NET—development of agricultural information technology	23
	Digital literacy education (60,000 people).	27
	PCs for farming areas	4
	E-commerce development	6
	Product support system expansion	10
	Distance conferencing system	1
Ministry of Knowledge Economy—Small and Business Administration	Small business owners' digital literacy education	11
	Small business areas' broadband systems	30
	Unions' information access system	28
Ministry for Health Welfare and Family Affairs	Elderly digital literacy education (35,400 people)	7
	People with disabilities' digital literacy education	13
Ministry of Labor	Digital literacy education for laborers	658
	People with disabilities' employment information system	9
	People with disabilities' digital literacy education	280
Ministry of Gender Equality	Cyber women IT professional training	10
	Women human capital and citizen digital literacy education	2

(continued)

TABLE 7.1 Funding for Implementation of Policy of Departmental Programs (continued)

Category	Program	Funding (10,000,0000 Won)
Ministry of Maritime Affairs and Fisheries	Fishermen digital literacy education (10,000 people)	26
	Fishing area Internet rooms (250 rooms)	
Ministry of Information and Communication	Provision of broadband Internet service in excluded areas (KT)	680
	Free Internet centers support	N/A
	Used PC distribution	17
	People with disabilities' access to Internet technology research	16
	Digital literacy education for the elderly	10
	Digital literacy education for people with disabilities	40
	Education centers at post offices	28
	E-Korean education	60
	Small business owners' education	315
	Low-income families' children's digital literacy education	60
	Housewives' e-Biz education	62
	Distance education system support	6
	Digital literacy training specialist training and support	12
	People with disabilities and elderly content development for ICT	6
	East Asian Digital Divide Special Collaboration program	7
	World Bank Digital Divide Act support	18
	IT leader invitation training	8
	Teens abroad for volunteer work	16
	Next generation IT leader invitation education	5
	Long term IT expert support	26
	Developing countries' IT center development	14
	Foreign media specialist IT tour program	3
	Digital divide current status research	2
	Campaign for closing the digital divide	0.5

Source: Adpated from "Korea's characteristics of digital divide and its solution" (Choi, 2003).

levels for middle-income households. This was estimated to be less than 30 U.S. dollars per month.

Geography

The geographic features of Korea are certainly a factor that contributed to the commitment to free and discounted broadband services and digital literacy education programs. The dense housing patterns delivered significant economies of scale for broadband network deployment (Choudrie & Lee, 2004). A favorable characteristic for the cost-effective deployment of the broadband infrastructure is the fact that much of the South Korean population lives in large apartment complexes. As a product of building regulations in the 1970s, the majority of apartments have a single communications room in the basement, making it very cost effective for operators to provide broadband access for the whole area. The very high degree of urbanization and dense housing patterns reduced the cost of network building and allowed the rapid deployment of discounts and free services for the public.

Education Fever

The rapid diffusion of the demand for Internet access and the successful turnouts for the digital literacy programs nationwide in Korea can be attributed in part to some characteristics of the Korean "education fever." The literacy rate and tertiary enrollment rate in Korea are among the highest in the world (Hawkins & Su, 2003) and, for various reasons, Korean parents are very committed to providing the best education possible for their children, spending a significant proportion of their income for educational activities. The Korean government capitalized on the "education fever" as part of their strategy to stimulate demand for broadband services. As well as ensuring the rapid connection of all schools to broadband, the government encouraged the integration of the Internet into daily school life.

According to the Korea Education and Research Information Service (KERIS), relatively simple initiatives such as encouraging school teachers to post their homework assignments on their own personal websites and requiring students to submit their assignments by e-mail created a feeling among parents that the Internet was a necessity for their children's education. Service providers such as Hanaro and KT also focused on educational benefits in their advertising campaigns to encourage parents to invest in broadband connections for their children (Choudrie & Lee, 2004). In addition, Korea's major corporations, leading universities, lifelong learning institutions that operate through the Ministry of Education, and even K–12 schools showed immense momentum for building cyberspace for online education and education resources.

PC Bangs (Internet Cafes) and Online Simulation Games

Another important factor was the fact that PC Bangs (Internet cafes) that provide the general public with Internet access began to appear. PC Bangs can be described as a business model in which constant access to the Internet is open to the public through leased lines (Park & Lee, 2002). PC Bangs are equipped with high-speed leased lines and multimedia computers. They offer high-speed access to the Internet at around one dollar per hour. The first domestic Internet cafe opened for business in Seoul in 1995, and the online war simulation game *Starcraft* became immensely popular with the younger male population by 1998. The gaming in PC Bangs concept proved to be massively popular, and the number of PC Bangs increased to more than 21,000 by 2001, making PC Bangs not simply a place to access the Web and play online simulation games, but also a place for socializing.

Many Korean users were first exposed to high-speed access to the Internet using PC Bangs. The users became so accustomed to using high-speed services that they were not satisfied with returning to dial-up methods. This was one important factor that drove the general public to become broadband subscribers. As the numbers of affordable PC Bangs increased with the facilitation of the government's digital divide policy, it could be said that PC Bangs and the younger male population contributed greatly to the distribution of affordable Internet access.

"Keeping Up With Your Family and Community" Culture

The Korean culture of "keeping up with the family and community" significantly influenced the rapid increase of digitally literate housewives and the elderly population, as they saw the Internet as a very effective means for keeping up with their friends, family, and community. The rapid development of strong online communities based around the personal interests of users in areas as diverse as online games, geographical areas, hobbies, music, sports, and even politics were also influenced by this characteristic of the Korean culture. The Korean government built on this culture of "keeping up with family and community" and strongly pushed the marketing of the digital literacy programs to be relevant and advantageous to housewives and the elderly population.

DISCUSSION

Decrease in Divides

The evaluation studies conducted on Korea's master plan for closing the digital divide show that the implementation of the policy process has been positive. Han (2003) found that Internet access had become a virtually universal service in Korea, and that the overall number of people who were able to access ICT had risen significantly. In 1995, Korea had less than one

Internet user per 100 inhabitants. By 2007, Korea had an Internet penetra-tion rate of over 70% with 34 million users. In 2012, 82.3% of Korean house-holds had broadband access (Park & Kim, 2014).

Numbers in self-reported ICT access data showed that the significant di-vides had somewhat decreased during the policy rollout period. According to the National Information Society Agency, the divide in gender decreased to 11.6%, with males at 65.2% and females at 53.6% ICT access. The divide in the less educated population had also decreased, as the ICT access rate among the population who had less than an elementary education had in-creased around 450% by 2001–2002. In one year, occupation divides had also decreased, as homemakers' ICT access had increased to 37.3%, and production workers also had increased to 30%, compared to 31% and 25% respectively in 2001 (National Internet Development Agency, 2007). The divide between regions had decreased significantly as well, as Ulsan city and Gyungi suburb regions' ICT access had increased to 67.7% and 66.9%, even higher than Seoul's 66% access (Kim, 2004).

Digital Literacy Programs for Disadvantaged Populations

Another positive result that all agreed on with the success of the policy was the implementation of digital literacy programs. Programs targeted homemakers, the elderly, military personnel, farmers, and excluded social sectors such as low-income families, the disabled, and prisoners. The gov-ernment established the Ten Million People Internet Education project in June 2000–2001, which aimed to provide Internet education to 10 million people via a range of different programs. This promotional activity contrib-uted towards the nationwide Internet boom as 4 million people, including one million homemakers, were trained in basic Internet skills (Picot & Wer-nick, 2007; Yun, Lee, & Lim, 2002).

Among the programs for computer and Internet literacy, the programs designed for homemakers were the most successful. The MIC set "home-makers," who are predominantly married women who are not employed, as one of its main targets for digital literacy education. The rationale for targeting homemakers was that they controlled the household budget and had a strong influence upon purchasing decisions within their family. Implementers believed that without the homemakers' faith and approval of the Internet, its diffusion among households would not happen. Most importantly, the program identified the shared feeling among homemak-ers of "being left behind" or "being ignored by their own children," and so it stimulated a hidden demand for the Internet, particularly for its use in their children's learning. Government subsidies were granted to private

IT/Internet training institutes for training homemakers, which allowed the homemakers to participate in Internet courses without any cost, or at an affordable price. The program was a success and created an Internet boom among homemakers.

ICT Access in Schools

Many of the implementation studies also show how the government's active promotion of the use of the Internet in schools was successful as well. Discounts for physical resources such as computer hardware and computer software applications were provided to all schools through the Ministry of Education and the provision of the high-speed Internet in schools under a special agreement with KT. This led to 100% of schools obtaining broadband connections by 2003 (Choudrie & Lee, 2004; International Telecommunication Union, 2003).

Perceptions of IT Use by the General Public

Studies show that the once upper-class privilege of Internet access has now become a general public good, and average Koreans do not hesitate to express the benefits and value they gain from the Internet. To them, the benefits are obvious. Internet users almost always refer primarily to educational opportunities and then access to information and entertainment as the benefits. They have adopted broadband Internet because it is useful and easy to use while the resources it requires are at a tolerable level. Koreans realize that the Internet is not a temporary trend and that it has a profound impact on their daily activities. Online access to educational resources and opportunities are clearly proving to be a necessity in all areas and age groups (Choudrie, Papazafeiropoulou, & Lee, 2003).

Technology As a Public Good: Meeting the Policy Goals

In terms of implementing the programs for closing the digital divide, the Korean government and other researchers seem to be fairly satisfied with the fact that the 2001 Master Plan for Digital Divide Solution policy has contributed strongly to the growth of Korea's ICT access. The fact that Korea's Internet penetration rate has grown to over 70% in less than 10 years says a lot about the Master Plan for Digital Divide's policy. Clearly, as examined earlier, the digital divide between groups defined by age, gender, occupation, disability, and SES groups have decreased. However, inequalities still remain within those categories, and new kinds of divides, such as purpose of usage, knowledge and skills, and content quality inequalities are emerging.

In addition, it is very hard to conclude whether the 2001 Master Plan for Digital Divide Solution policy implementation was a success. This is because the Korean government, when announcing the policy in March of 2001, never really set a goal for achievement that enabled the policy implementers, evaluators, or researchers to measure the success. Many critics have argued that the policy was always a rather symbolic policy and that there is a strong need to make specific plans for addressing more specific goals on closing the digital divide in the future. These arguments have made their way into the updates on the policy, providing more specific and detailed goals and suggested solutions for addressing the issues of the digital divide (Ministry of Information and Communications, 2006; Park & Kim, 2014).

Further Support and Research

Internationally, research and evaluations on digital divide policies are mostly looked at from a macro-level perspective at the national level, and this was the same for the Korean policy on developing a policy of technology as a public good. It is true that the Korean government's plan for reducing the digital divide was successful in bringing positive results. However, by taking on this macro-level perspective and dealing with Korean users as an aggregate population, evaluations and research for digital divide policies were largely dictated to only aim for collecting and evaluating large-scale, macro-level data.

There is a critical need to explore this issue of digital divide with a more micro-level perspective for a richer understanding of these various factors and how they interact (Picot & Wernick, 2007). Both macro- and micro-level studies should be pursued together in order to help policymakers understand a theoretical framework that encompasses many of these various factors within the policy. Research is needed that studies the impact of user behavior, demographic and educational factors, pricing of services, private sectors' competition, and public good-oriented governmental strategies, in a more holistic, comprehensive way.

It is also surprising to see how little effort there is in trying to understand the impacts of digital divide policies on the beneficiaries' lives. What kinds of programs were more successful, and why were they successful in that context? What factors were most important for certain groups? What kind of impact did ICT access have on their small business revenue or household? Are they more likely to use online banking and make transactions online for their business? Did the revenue of the business or household income rise by any measures?

More research on free-of-charge computers and high-speed Internet support for disadvantaged youth, schools, and their experience in those programs is also needed. How often do students use these programs and what do they use them for? What has this done for their schoolwork and homework and their searching for information and strategies for accessing college applications? Are they more likely to set higher aspirations and goals that require higher technology skills in their jobs because of their exposure to ICT? Did they become more interested or feel inclined to participate in online discussions on social issues or political matters? These are important questions that need to be considered in future research on digital divide policies, not only in Korea but also in the international community as a whole.

CONCLUSION

Clearly, the South Korean government's approach of "technology as a public good" raises many issues that need to be investigated about digital divide policies. In particular, attempting to understand a theoretical framework that encompasses many of these various factors within the policy implementation process would be worthwhile. Such research efforts should be aimed at collecting and evaluating both macro-level data and micro-level studies that give us a richer understanding of these various factors and how they interact.

ICT researchers should also engage in research that can facilitate social change and contribute to more equitable and empowering use of ICT at the local grassroots level. An important goal here is to learn how policymakers, practitioners, and researchers can together, in collaboration, contribute to working towards decreasing digital inequity.

The notion of "technology as a common good" presents a case to consider the notion of ICT as a public good, and its consequences for enhanced quality and equality in life and educational opportunities through technology use. Further exploration on this topic is needed to identify what has worked well for disadvantaged population in adopting ICT into their lives, and connecting that to help shape other policies in other countries with similar digital divides.

REFERENCES

Cho, J. (2001). 정보격차 현황 및 정책의 발전 방향 [Trends in digital divide and policy development direction]. *Digital Policy, 8*(2), 74–91.

Choi, D. (2003). 우리나라 정보격차의 특성 및 정보격차 해소를 위한 정책 과제 [Korea's characteristics of digital divide and its solution]. *Korean Information Culture Center Publication*, 1–19.

Choudrie, J., & Lee, H. (2004). Broadband development in South Korea: Institutional and cultural factors. *European Journal of Information Systems, 13*, 103–114.

Choudrie, J., Papazafeiropoulou, A., & Lee, H. (2003). A web of stakeholders and strategies: A broadband diffusion in South Korea. *Journal of Information Technology, 18*, 281–290.

DiMaggio, P., Hargittai, E., Celeste, C., & Shafer, S. (2004). Digital inequality: From unequal access to differentiated use. In K. Neckerman (Ed.), *Social inequality* (pp. 355–400). New York, NY: Russell Sage.

Guðmundsdóttir, G. B. (2005, December). *Approaching the digital divide in South Africa.* Paper presented at the NETwork for Research and Evaluation on Education and Development (NETREED) Conference, Beitostølen, Norway.

Han, G. (2003). Broadband adoption in the United States and Korea: Business driven rational model versus culture sensitive policy model. *Trends in Communication, 11*(1), 3–25.

Hargittai, E. (2003). The digital divide and what to do about it. In D. C. Jones (Ed.), *New economy handbook* (pp. 821–839). San Diego, CA: Academic Press.

Hawkins, J. N., & Su, Z. (2003). Asian education. In R. F. Arnove & C. A. Torres (Eds.), *Comparative education* (pp. 338–356). Lanham, MD: Rowman & Littlefield.

International Telecommunication Union. (2003). Broadband Korea: Internet case study. Retrieved from http://www.itu.int/itudoc/gs/promo/bdt/cast_int/85867.html

Kim, Y. (2004). 정보격차의 추이분석과 향후 과제 [An analysis of digital divide and future assignments]. Busan, South Korea: Kyungsang University Press.

Korean Ministry of Information and Communication. (2001). *2001 master plan for closing the digital divide solution.* Retrieved March 23, 2008 from www.mic.go.kr/eng/index

Korean Ministry of Information and Communication. (2006). *2006 master plan for closing the digital divide solution.* Retrieved March 23, 2008 from www.mic.go.kr/eng/index

National Internet Development Agency. (2007). *NIDA 2007 Internet user report.* Retrieved from https://www.kisa.or.kr/eng/main.jsp

Norris, P. (2001). *Digital divide: Civic engagement, information poverty, and the internet worldwide.* New York, NY: Cambridge University Press.

Park, J., & Lee, J. (2002). The prospect and policy directions of the broadband Internet market. *Telecommunication Market, 40*, 73–88.

Park, S., & Kim, G. (2014). Lessons from South Korea's Digital Divide Index (DDI). *Info: The Journal of Policy, Regulation and Strategy for Telecommunications, Information and Media, 16*(3), 72–84.

Picot, A., & Wernick, C. (2007). The role of government in broadband access. *Telecommunications Policy, 31*, 660–674

Rogers, E. M. (1983). *Diffusion of innovations.* New York, NY: Free Press.

Schradie, J. (2011). The digital production gap: The digital divide and Web 2.0 collide. *Poetics, 39*(2), 145–168.

Seo, Y. (2001). 디지털 시대의 평등사회 구현을 위한 정보격차 해소방안 [A digital divide solution for an equitable digital society]. *Policy and Computers, 23*(1–33).

Van Dijk, J. A. G. M. (2012). The evolution of the digital divide: The digital divide turns to inequality of skills and usage. In J. Bus, M. Crompton, M. Hildebrandt, & G. Metakides (Eds.), *Digital enlightenment yearbook* (pp. 57–75). Amsterdam, Netherlands: IOS Press.

Warschauer, M. (2004). *Technology and social inclusion: Rethinking the digital divide.* Cambridge, MA: MIT Press.

World Internet Statistics. (2007). Internet usage and statistics: The big picture. World Internet Users and Population Stats. Retrieved from http://www.Internetworldstats.com/stats.htm

Yun, K., Lee, H., & Lim, S. (2002). Growth of broadband internet connections in South Korea: Contributing factors. Shorenstein Asia-Pacific Research Center. Retrieved from http://www.APARC.stanford.edu

CHAPTER 8

SOCIOCULTURAL ALIENATION OF FEMALE INTERNATIONAL STUDENTS AT A PREDOMINANTLY WHITE UNIVERSITY

Nastaran Karimi, Reiko Akiyama, and Yuwen Deng

ABSTRACT

An increasing number of international students are studying at U.S. universities. Often, research on international students generalizes their experiences, overlooking their great diversity. Some of the challenges that international students face include language barriers, culture shock, loneliness, discrimination, and alienation. In order to gain a more detailed and individualized perspective on the experiences of international students, the authors—three female students from different backgrounds—conducted autoethnographic research focusing on their experiences of alienation. They investigate their experiences in light of Seeman's (1959) framework of sociocultural alienation. Their stories reveal that they share a similar sense of sociocultural alienation. Nevertheless, this sense of alienation varies in form and degree. The findings of this study can assist institutions of higher education in promoting conversations that critically analyze cultural differences and encourage inter-

Internationalizing Teaching and Teacher Education for Equity, pages 125–141

cultural communication. Such findings can also provide teacher education programs with a framework that facilitates a more international outlook on cultural diversity.

INTRODUCTION

Globalization has transformed the form and nature of higher education on many levels. Global processes that continue to change the landscape of higher education are closely linked to the neoliberal economy, the latest trends in immigration, the development of international organizations, and an ongoing discourse on multiculturalism (Spring, 2008). Appudurai (1996) refers to this changing landscape as five interconnected scapes, which are constantly shifting in a global exchange of people, ideas, practices, and institutions. These five scapes—ethnoscape, or movement of people across borders; technoscape, or the digital World Wide Web; finanscape, or the interdependent economies of the world; mediascape, or the widespread influence of media; and ideoscape, or ideologies that drive local, national, and international interests—affect not only the institutional culture of higher education in the United States but also the cultural practices of both local and international students.

As an increasing number of international students pursue higher education in the United States, their experiences remain a relevant topic of research for host institutions seeking to attract and retain international students. According to an Open Door report (Institute of International Education, 2013), during the 2012–2013 academic year, 819,644 international students attended U.S. colleges and universities. Research on the experiences of international students in U.S. colleges and universities is based on two notions: globalization theory, which views full-fee paying international students as valuable sources of revenue, and internationalization theory, which values the diverse worldviews that international students bring to their host institutions (Lee & Rice, 2007). As international students attending a Midwestern university, in this autoethnographic study we collaboratively explore our own experiences of alienation within the sociocultural context of U.S. higher education. Our study sheds light on some factors that can contribute to the experience of alienation as a step toward bridging the gap between international students and their host universities.

LINGUISTIC AND CULTURAL CHALLENGES

Studies on international students' lives and educational experiences point to the variety of linguistic, social, and cultural challenges that these students, both graduate and undergraduate, encounter in their host countries. One of the most pressing challenges that some international students face in their new context is language, as their level of fluency in English affects their overall sociocultural experiences in higher education (Sherry, Thomas, & Chui, 2010). Language barriers may impede international students' interaction with native English speakers, resulting in their self-segregation (Rose-Redwood & Rose-Redwood, 2013) and may also influence international students' academic performance and achievement. International students with higher English language skills were less likely to consider academic settings to be stressful (Wan, Chapman, & Biggs, 1992). Sawir, Marginson, Forbes-Mewett, Nyland, and Ramia (2012) suggest that language proficiency is "a pervasive factor in the human security of the international students in all domains inside and outside the classroom" (p. 434). Language proficiency and communication skills affect the relationship between international and domestic students (Sawir et al., 2012). As a result, language fluency can be considered a major contributing or inhibiting factor to other difficulties that international students face.

Besides the language barrier, international students have reported experiencing culture shock upon arrival in their host country (Chapdelaine & Alexitch, 2004), as they are unfamiliar with the cultural norms and expectations of the host culture. Culture shock is defined as feelings of anxiety, stress, rejection, and isolation due to the loss of one's familiar symbols of social exchange and communication (Oberg, 1960). Sherry et al. (2010) have reported that international students encounter cultural barriers because most U.S. American students do not understand the cultural backgrounds of the international students. This lack of cross-cultural understanding on both sides affects the lives of both domestic and international students in various ways. For example, Spencer-Rodgers (2001) found that lack of cross-cultural knowledge led to stereotypical perceptions, overlooking the diversity among international students. Due to stereotypical perceptions, some international students report feelings of alienation and loneliness, while others report discrimination and unfairness (Lee & Rice, 2007).

The above review of literature suggests that language fluency and cultural understanding play a crucial role in international students' cross-cultural communication and adjustment in the host culture. These, in turn, can result in experiencing inclusion/exclusion from dominant social and cultural circles defining the experiences of international students in U.S. higher educational contexts.

SEEMEN'S CONCEPTUALIZATION OF ALIENATION

For the purpose of this collaborative autoethnography, we use Seeman's (1959) sociological examination of alienation as the frame of reference. Seeman first theorized alienation in 1959; however, his work is foundational to a historical understanding of social alienation and remains relevant to contemporary understandings of alienation in social and cultural contexts. Seeman delineates the factors of social alienation as powerlessness, meaninglessness, normlessness, isolation, and self-estrangement. *Powerlessness* refers to the discrepancy between what an individual would like to accomplish in a given context and what s/he is actually able to accomplish. *Meaninglessness* points to an individual's inability to control outcomes based on his/her own insight and understanding of matters. *Normlessness* occurs when the individual can no longer decipher social norms in a complex and foreign environment. *Isolation* refers to social alienation from the popular cultural standards of society, resulting in an inability to form relationships. *Self-estrangement,* or the sense of being alienated from one's own experiences, denotes being insecure in a social setting. Keeping in mind Seeman's multidimensional view of alienation, our collaborative autoethnography seeks to (1) explore sociocultural alienation as experienced by three international students at a U.S. university, and (2) analyze specific experiences of alienation as a first step toward addressing the sociocultural alienation of international students in U.S. higher education.

COLLABORATIVE AUTOETHNOGRAPHY

We engage in collaborative autoethnography in an attempt to gain an in-depth understanding of our similar and different experiences in the same cultural context (Chang, Ngunjiri, & Hernandez, 2013). Collaborative autoethnography enables researers to use personal stories to "gain understanding of society through the unique lens of self" (Chang et al., 2013, p. 18), in relation to broad educational, sociocultural, and political issues. An autoethnographic approach utilizes individual and subjective experiences to shed light on sociocultural issues (Ellis & Bochner, 2006; Young & McKibban, 2014)—in this case, the sociocultural alienation faced by minority students in a largely homogenous educational environment. According to Ellis, Adams, and Bochner (2011), "autoethnography expands and opens up a wider lens on the world, eschewing rigid definitions of what constitutes meaningful and useful research" (p. 275). Autoethnography is a form of self-reflective storytelling that goes beyond the researcher's personal experience, connecting autobiographical stories and narratives to broader social, cultural, and political issues.

Autoethnography recognizes subjectivity, emotionality (behavioral and physiological components of emotion), and the researcher's active participation, rather than claiming objectivity in research (Ellis et al., 2011). Each of us was born in a different country and grew up fully assimilated as a member of our home country's dominant society, which contrasted with the experience of being part of a minority cultural and ethnic group in the United States. Hence, autoethnography provides the space for understanding the complicated, multidimensional feelings and emotions of racial/ethnic, cultural, religious, and linguistic minority students, allowing the reader to be part of our vulnerable experiences (Ellis & Bochner, 2006).

WHO ARE WE?
WOMEN, INTERNATIONAL, GRADUATE STUDENTS

We are all PhD students studying in a college of education at a large, Midwestern university in the United States. The following autobiographies tell a small part of our stories.

Nastaran

I was born in Shiraz, a large city in the southern part of Iran. When I was young my family moved to Tehran, the capital of Iran, where I lived for most of my life. I was born in 1985, six years after the revolution of 1979 that led to the consolidation of the Islamic Republic of Iran by 1981. The revolution plays a significant role in the history of Iran as it dramatically influenced the relationship between Iran and the rest of the world, particularly the United States, thus influencing my experiences as an Iranian student studying in the U.S.

At the age of seven I moved to Australia with my family for my father's doctoral studies and completed my elementary school there. These four years play an influential role in my life. First, they laid the foundation for my enthusiasm to meet and learn about different cultures. Second, English became a second mother tongue to me as opposed to a second language that I struggled to speak and understand. In Australia we lived in Wollongong, a mid-sized city with a diverse population from around the world. Consequently, my elementary school consisted of a diverse student body; however, all of my teachers were White Australians, mainly females. Upon the completion of my father's PhD, my family returned to Iran and I continued my education there until the completion of my bachelor's degree in English language and literature. Because the years I had spent in Australia significantly enhanced my English proficiency, I started teaching English as a second language at the age of eighteen in a private English institute. During this period I was surrounded by friends, colleagues, students, and people from Iran.

After I finished my bachelor's degree, I moved to England to earn a master's degree in International studies in education at the University of Birmingham, where I met a variety of people from different backgrounds. After first moving back to Iran after graduating, I soon moved to the United States. At first, I hesitated to continue my education in the U.S. because of the political tension between Iran and the U.S., arising from events around the 1979 Iranian revolution. One of the reasons I hesitated to move was because student visas issued to Iranians studying in the United States are single-entry visas, meaning Iranians cannot travel back home—or leave the U.S. at all—during our period of study. This was a huge decision for me, as it necessitated being away from my family for a long time. Despite my initial hesitations, I moved to the U.S. in August 2010, and one year later I started my PhD, during which time I have also been teaching introductory courses in a teacher education program.

Reiko

I am in my mid-30s and a fifth-year doctoral student in a curriculum studies program. Born in a large city in Japan, I grew up in several different cities due to my father's job transfers. I grew up in a homogeneous society with little exposure to people from different backgrounds. When I was in 4th grade, my family moved to the city of Nirasaki in the Yamanashi prefecture, located in the central part of the Main Island (*Honshu*) and a two-hour drive from Tokyo. Nirasaki is categorized as a small rural area. I lived in Nirasaki for about 15 years and attended the local public elementary and middle schools and a private high school before attending the national university in the prefecture capital, Kōfu. I majored in English education and after completing my bachelor's degree I started working at an educational supplemental institution, or so-called "cram school," in Yamanashi. I taught English grammar, reading, and writing to upper-elementary and high school students for two years. At the age of 24, I continued my studies, this time abroad in Chico, California.

Chico's racial makeup was predominantly White (80%); Hispanics or Latinos were the second largest ethnic group (15%). During my stay in Chico, I mostly lived with a U.S. American host family (a White, Christian host mother and an Eastern Indian Sikh host father). The school at which I studied had a good number of Japanese students; therefore, I met many Japanese peers while I lived there. I first studied English at a language institute and then pursued a master's degree in teaching international languages. I taught introductory Japanese courses as a graduate assistant and worked as a Japanese instructor at a community college in California for a year after I graduated. Afterwards, I moved to Taichung, mid-sized urban city in Taiwan, where I worked as a Japanese instructor at a language school. While I lived in Taiwan, I mainly spoke English as I do not speak Mandarin Chinese. Although the city has a diverse population, I did not have the opportunity to meet people from different countries except for my foreign coworkers.

In the fall of 2010, I returned to the U.S. to pursue my doctoral degree at a Midwestern university. In addition to being a student, I also taught as a graduate instructor for a foundational education class and currently work as an instructor for Japanese language classes.

Yuwen

I am a Chinese woman in my late 20s, and a third-year PhD student in a curriculum studies program. I have been studying in the U.S. for three years. I was born in Nanning, an urban city in southern China with a large population of ethnic minorities. Each minority group has its own characteristics, dialect, customs, and traditions. The most common dialect in my hometown is Cantonese. At home we spoke Cantonese and also used Mandarin, the official language of China, particularly in public places. I went to elementary, middle, and high school in my hometown. After graduating from high school, I went to university in Wuhan in central China. I majored in education science at a normal university during my undergraduate years.

After graduation, I moved to Beijing, the capital city of China, to pursue my master's degree in curriculum and instruction at a normal university. I completed my master's degree and came to the United States to pursue my doctoral degree. Crossing national boundaries, I became a foreigner for the first time. I am now studying at a university located in a small city in a rural area of the Midwest. During my first year as a PhD student, I worked as a research assistant, participating in my advisor's study abroad research project. Since my second year, I have worked as a teaching assistant for an introductory course in the teacher education program.

UNCOVERING OUR STORIES

The data on which this chapter is based consist of autoethnographic narratives and open-ended dialogues. We started by writing individual autoethnographic narratives on a shared topic—our lived experiences as international graduate students interacting with a host culture. Individual narratives led us to discover distinctive experiences, which were not common to all participants. This provided opportunities for breaking away from "traditional generic constraints" of doing research (Ellingson, as cited in Geist-Martin et al., 2010, p. 9), while at the same time shedding light on sociocultural issues. After examining each narrative closely, we engaged in open-ended dialogue to delve deeper into our findings and understandings.

DISSECTING OUR STORIES

We analyzed our narratives by applying Chang et al.'s (2013) three steps: reviewing the data; coding, categorizing, and regrouping the data; and finding themes across data. This approach enabled us to examine our data closely and to create categories based on all of our perspectives. We began our analysis by reading each other's personal narratives multiple times to capture the focal points. Then, we extracted significant key words, phrases, and statements; identified their focal meanings; and categorized them thematically to write up the findings. In the next step, we connected our findings to the theoretical framework for understanding sociocultural alienation: powerlessness, meaninglessness, normlessness, isolation, and self-estrangement. We also analyzed specific experiences of alienation and connected those experiences to broader social, cultural, and political issues. Finally, as a step toward addressing the sociocultural alienation experienced by international students in U.S. higher education, we reflected critically on our own implication in contributing to the experience of sociocultural alienation.

POWERLESSNESS

Based on Seeman's (1959) definition, we analyzed our experiences of powerlessness. Powerlessness refers to the discrepancy between an individual's expectations of the outcome of his/her behavior and the actual outcomes. Nastaran's sense of powerlessness was reflected in her experience at the airport when she first arrived in the United States at the JFK airport in New York. When she responded to a question posed by a customs official inquiring about her country of origin, alarm bells seemed to go off for both Nastaran and the official:

> Iran and the United States have not got along since the Iranian revolution of 1979, so as an Iranian citizen I had to go through an extra set of security procedures in the airport. There were security guards around. Whoever passed the area where I was told to go and stand seemed to give me a questioning, suspicious glance. Since I didn't know what was going on, their in-

quiring looks seemed normal. As I tried to rationalize with myself about the procedure, never in my life had I felt so visible to every passerby's gaze. I felt simultaneously intimidated and frustrated but there was not much I could do about the legalities of immigration, so I had to wait. Never had I experienced this sense of frustration about who I am and where I am from.

Nastaran's experience highlights how an individual sense of powerlessness can relate to global politics—in this case the current hostility in diplomatic relations between Iran and the U.S.

Yuwen reflects on a sense of powerlessness that emerged from the sharp contrast in teaching and learning styles between her home country and the host institution.

As a newcomer to the U.S., I was a stranger in Western educational settings. I found that what I had learned in China did not seem applicable in the U.S. classroom. Students in China behave in accordance with the goals of the collective they belong to and comply with orders given by authority and seniors rather than overtly doubting or challenging leaders and seniors. By contrast, graduate students in U.S. classrooms are encouraged to critique academic authority, policies, and current affairs without deliberately avoiding some topics such as sex, religion, and political issues. However, most Chinese students and teachers think that these topics are sensitive and so never talk about them in class.

Because of the significant differences between the two types of classrooms, Yuwen felt powerless in her new environment. She often asked herself, "What should I do? In a U.S. classroom, should I still keep my Chinese silence or join the critique, as seems to be encouraged? Should I maintain my conservative Chinese habits or follow a progressive American trend?" She felt confused over what she should do or what she could achieve through her academic endeavors.

MEANINGLESSNESS

Seeman (1959) stated that individuals encounter a sense of meaninglessness when "the individual is unclear as to what [s]he ought to believe when the individual's minimal standards for clarity in decision-making are not met" (p. 786). That is, individuals—in this case, international students living in the U.S.—struggle to behave appropriately based on the standards of an unfamiliar society. Regarding this aspect of alienation, Nastaran's story reflects ethnic and cultural boundaries, while Yuwen and Reiko's narratives are associated with cultural and language barriers.

Regarding ethnic and cultural boundaries, Nastaran recalled her experience as a covering Muslim woman wearing the Iranian roosari[1] and teaching an undergraduate multicultural education course. On the first day of the class, she tried to incorporate all of her enthusiasm into her tone, body language, and class atmosphere.

> However, I was taken back by the same suspicious, questioning gaze I had experienced at the airport. I convinced myself that I was over-reading a simple look, but I felt the obligation to convince the students in my class, to a certain degree, of my capabilities. That is perhaps what most teachers feel the urge to do at the beginning of each class. So I started talking about my background, my teaching experience. I mentioned that I had lived and studied in Australia, England, and even Dubai. But the gaze did not seem to diminish.

As an international teaching assistant, Nastaran encountered many uneasy moments when she faced her students. Although she tried to minimize the sense of strangeness by introducing her various international experiences, she felt that the students did not change their attitudes towards her. Nastaran wondered what the reaction of students would be if a White North American teacher was running the class. Would they have the same reaction? Would she ever be accepted as a professional instructor in the classroom? What would be the best way of acting in this situation?

Yuwen also experienced cultural barriers as an international student. She grew up in China and received a teacher-centered education that emphasized collectivism. Hence, Yuwen felt herself a stranger in the U.S. classroom, which seemed to have the opposite norms and values. She faced an internal conflict in terms of how to behave in the new social setting.

> I felt like an in-betweener with one leg in Eastern territory, full of Chinese relatively conservative traditions, customs, and values, while the other leg was in Western territory, filled with U.S. ideology and practices of progressivism.

For Reiko, a language barrier became a significant element in her sense of meaninglessness. Reiko constantly negotiated her abilities as an international teaching assistant and was aware, even before she started teaching, that she would likely face language barriers. She sometimes had difficulty comprehending what students were saying, particularly when they spoke quickly or used colloquial expressions, and also struggled with giving on-the-spot oral feedback and directions to her students in class. She recalled as an English language learner:

> My accent, pronunciation, and incorrect grammar coming from my nervousness confused my students. Their blank looks expressed how hard it was to

understand me. On my student course evaluations, most of my students pointed out my insufficient language proficiency.

Reiko has taught the same course for six semesters and has been exposed to various opportunities to improve her English skills; nonetheless, she still feels a strong language barrier when she teaches. She concludes, *If I could speak English well, I wouldn't have to struggle that much. It feels as if my English proficiency is never sufficient.*

NORMLESSNESS

Normlessness is referred to as a sense of mismatch between the goals one has and the means at one's disposal to accomplish those goals. A sense of normlessness occurs when "there is a high expectancy that socially unapproved behaviors are required to achieve given goals" (Seeman, 1959, p. 788). This concept generally refers to an individual living in his/her local society. However, we focus on how our (international student) culturally prescribed norms do not yield the same outcomes we expected. We experienced feelings of normlessness during our studies and teaching in the United States.

Nastaran's first encounter with a sense of normlessness was when she started teaching at a Midwestern university. Despite her efforts to emulate the best teaching practices she had been exposed to during her five years of teaching experience, her students did not seem to accept her as a capable teacher. In her narrative, Nastaran wrote, "I faced a lot of resistance throughout the semester, which is perceived to be normal when teaching multicultural education classes." In the middle of the semester, she conducted an informal evaluation with her class to see how she could improve her lessons and how her students related to her. Reading students' anonymous comments, Nastaran encountered reactions from her students that she had not expected.

> What took me back at first was the tone students used in expressing these thoughts. I thought it very disrespectful, but I gave them the benefit of the doubt. In regard to their comments, on the other hand, I could not give them the benefit of the doubt. Their basic claim was "you don't understand our culture." Initially I had anticipated that this might happen so I had asked students to provide concrete examples. Most of the points that they brought up were related to the logistics of running the classroom, which were clearly stated in the syllabus. I could not help but wonder whether they would have the same reaction if I was a White American teaching the same course.

Reiko first encountered a sense of normlessness when she started her studies in the United States. The same behaviors that had cast her in the role of a "good student" in her schools in Japan now resulted in her being perceived as a silent, passive student. Reiko described school norms in Japan as follows:

> Good students are expected to receive instruction quietly while teachers are talking. If we want to give opinions, we should raise our hands and wait until the teacher points to us. Students who have questions should wait until the teacher provides time for asking questions or the end of the class. We share ideas in the classroom, but we rarely challenge our teachers or classmates. Active participation is not always accepted in a positive way; challenging peers is regarded as disruption rather than active participation.

However, Reiko noticed that the norms she had learned in Japan were not applicable in the U.S. classroom. She struggled with acclimating herself to the new norms.

> My classmates talk a lot! They love discussion. They aren't afraid of cutting in the conversation, even when the professor is talking. They suddenly jump into the conversation without raising hands or being called on. They admire others' opinions, but they aren't afraid of challenging peers. How can I participate in the U.S. class? That became my big problem at this university.

Reiko was at odds with the norms of a U.S. classroom setting and her struggle with socializing to these norms. This contributed to her sense of isolation and experience of alienation.

ISOLATION

According to Seeman (1959), a sense of isolation occurs when an individual experiences a disparity between their own goals and beliefs and what is typically valued by the society. In this self-study, we explored this aspect of alienation in relation to the disparity between what is valued in our home cultures and what we perceive as being valued in our host culture.

For Reiko, her most important encounter with alienation occurred with regard to religion. In Japan, religion does not play a significant role in people's lives. She found this to be in contrast with the value system of her new (U.S.) context, in which nonreligiosity is rare.

> Since coming to the U.S., one thing that I realized is that some people, especially in the Midwest, are very religious in comparison to people in my country. In my view, Japanese people are not very religious; religion or re-

ligious beliefs do not play a very significant role in my life. Midwestern university life impacted me greatly in terms of thinking about my nonreligiousness. I do respect what others believe—but I don't need to have the same religious views. Saying, "I'm not religious" is sometimes very challenging for me—I'm afraid people will misunderstand me as denying their views or values. Some people may accept my view, or they may think I'm a terrible person and that they should help to change my views. In my first year in the Midwest, two local students asked me if I attended any church in the area. I quickly answered that I didn't go to church. They asked me if I wanted to join their church. I said, "Uh . . . I'm actually not religious." The young students looked at me with pity and said, "Oh, I'm sorry to hear that. It's not too late, you can change your mind." Why is being not religious bad? Why did they feel sorry for me?

Reiko experienced a sense of alienation from the religious norms of the host culture and was discomforted by their inquiries about religion. Paradoxically, while the host students extended a welcome to Reiko and tried to be inclusive, Reiko felt more excluded and isolated as the encounter highlighted the sociocultural gaps that international students and host students must bridge in order to better understand each other.

SELF-ESTRANGEMENT

Self-estrangement happens when people feel they are aliens in a certain environment and they become isolated from themselves (Seeman, 1959). Self-estrangement can happen, on one hand, when international students realize their behavior and attitudes are perceived differently from people in the domestic culture; on the other hand, international students feel alienated from the self as they try to adjust into the host culture.

Nastaran: I am tired of convincing people that I went to school at the age of seven, like many other children throughout the world. I went to college at the age of eighteen. Yes, women ARE allowed to go to college in Iran. In actuality they comprise approximately 65% of college students. Neither my father nor anyone else objected to me continuing my education. In fact, he was so supportive of my education that he paid my entire tuition and expenses to do my master's degree in England. I am tired of explaining to almost everyone I meet that I used to work like many other adults my age. In fact, I think I was raised pretty normal. I don't think there was anything abnormal about my upbringing, neither in my family nor in my country. Beside the fact that I was brought up very privileged and not everyone else has the same experience, I would say I had a very normal life (the usual and ordinary life just as other people do).

In Nastaran's experience, her sense of self-estrangement stemmed from the stereotypical notion of what it means to be a Muslim woman. She found the host culture's perceptions of what it means to grow up as a Muslim woman to be in sharp contrast with her lived reality. While she considered her life to be "normal," her life seemed to be viewed by the host culture as bound by the norms of gender and religion symbolized in the roosari that she wore at all times.

While Reiko felt pressured by the religious norms of the host culture, the experience of alienation from the self was also compounded by her classroom experiences. She struggled with how to behave as graduate student, encountered a language barrier, and experienced cultural differences that were discomforting.

> I have no difficulties in face-to-face communication with others at the store, airport, or most public places. I usually don't feel nervous or need to stop to consider the meaning of something. When I speak to someone outside of my academic field, I am a talkative person. In contrast, I become very quiet in class. During the lecture or class discussion, I encounter various academic terms and expressions almost all at once. I try to understand what is being discussed but the conversation tends to move from topic to topic very quickly. When I am ready to join the conversation, the discussion has moved on to another topic. I am totally puzzled. Lacking the U.S. background knowledge—historical, political, and economical information—I feel I cannot catch up with the conversation.

In graduate courses, Reiko did not feel that she could fully participate because she could not always keep up with the fast-paced classroom conversation. As a graduate student, she understood that she needed to be involved in class discussions, but the pressure of "saying something sophisticated" made her quiet. Thus, Reiko's experience of alienation was not only caused by the pressures of communicating in English as a foreign language, lack of the host's knowledge of her cultural background, or the differences in classroom norms between Japan and the U.S., but it was also internalized as she isolated herself from the other students in the class. In addition, Reiko recognized a huge gap between the communicative person she wanted to be and her silence inside the classroom. In a complex configuration of emotions and reactions, in academic settings Reiko felt anxious and frustrated about her non-active attitude and contributed to her own experience of self-alienation.

WHAT DO OUR STORIES SAY?

From our lived experiences in the United States, we believe that other international students might share a similar sense of sociocultural alienation.

However, their sense of alienation varies in form and degree. For Reiko and Yuwen, a language barrier that hindered their active participation in class discussions and brought them a sense of powerlessness, meaninglessness, and normlessness was a major reason for their sense of alienation. The issue of language affected Reiko not only as a student, but also as a teaching assistant instructing predominantly White U.S. American students, creating a barrier between her and the class. Language as an integral component of culture, with its own set of nuanced regulating rules, created a sense of alienation beyond the boundaries of the language itself in all of our social and academic lives. Difference in teaching styles between our home countries and the host institute was another cause of sociocultural alienation. Since the teaching style in our home countries is top-down, with teachers giving instructions and students following, it was difficult for Reiko and Yuwen to find their voices in a more open, discussion-based environment. All of us struggled with how to be "good students" in our new host culture, and the discrepancy between expectations and actual outcomes elicited feelings of powerlessness and normlessness. This, combined with language and cultural differences, intensified the sense of alienation we experienced.

Religion was another aspect that contributed to feelings of alienation. Nastaran's cultural and religious background affected how she was perceived by the local population, most often in the light of negative stereotypes attached to Muslim women. Reiko found a significant contrast in the value system of her new context, in which religion is highly valued, and her home country, where religion does not play a crucial role.

Often university services view international students as a homogenous minority group with little diversity. Thus, the support services that universities provide are based on a generalized notion of international students' experiences studying abroad. In the process, universities tend to overlook the diversity within international students and their own institutional role in addressing the struggles international students may face. As our stories imply, international students are a diverse group in background and experiences. We recommend that universities provide international students with more individualized support based on their particular backgrounds and experiences to reduce their sense of sociocultural alienation inside and outside the classroom. This can result in individualized support programs for international students. Such programs can provide not only the support that international students require to transition into a new society, but can also provide them with insight into the culture of their new context.

In the current climate of immigration and human movement, many universities place great emphasis on cultural exchange and intercultural understanding (Knight, 2003). There are many attempts to bridge the gap between various cultures in order to create a sense of mutual understanding. However, this intercultural exchange often remains at the superficial level of merely learning basic facts about different cultures and nationalities, facts that could be learned through a simple internet search in a matter of minutes, such as a country's capital city, the languages spoken there, their religion, or their cuisine. Little is done to create an in-depth understanding of how different cultures and nations are related to one another, how they are implicated in larger dominant political and economic systems, and how individuals enact power dynamics in their daily interactions. Hence, institutions of higher education can focus on promoting conversations that critically analyze cultural differences, their historical roots, and how each individual plays a role. Such conversations encourage not only intercultural understanding, but also critical self-reflection for both domestic and international students to position themselves in a larger international discourse. This can be done through organizing critical cultural events, fairs, or shows that facilitate a critical interaction and communication between domestic and international students. There should be a mindful effort to encourage domestic students to take part in these events.

Research on international students and their experiences benefits teacher education programs in several ways. First, because teacher education programs in the United States are U.S.-centric (Gay & Howard, 2000), in conversations of multiculturalism and diversity, such studies can facilitate a more international outlook regarding cultural diversity. Second, with the diversification of U.S. classrooms (National Center for Education Statistics, 2015), it is necessary that teacher education programs prepare preservice teachers to teach a diverse student body in their future classrooms. Research about international student experiences can provide teacher education programs with insight into the experiences and emotions of diverse students, particularly immigrant students, English language learners, and religious minorities. In an ideal situation, this would result in better preparing future teachers for the reality of their classrooms and for creating a more socially just society for people from all backgrounds.

NOTE

1. Roosari is the headscarf worn by Iranian women, either by choice as a Muslim woman or because of a mandate based on the Islamic Republic of Iran's laws. The roosari is a form of hijab. Hijab is any form of covering that a Muslim woman may choose to wear for modesty and/or other reasons.

REFERENCES

Appadurai, A. (1996). *Modernity at large: Cultural dimensions of globalization.* Minneapolis, MN: University of Minnesota Press.

Chang, H., Ngunjiri, F. W., & Hernandez, K. C. (2013). *Collaborative autoethnography.* Walnut Creek, CA: Left Coast Press.

Chapdelaine, R. F., & Alexitch, L. R. (2004). Social skills difficulty: Model of culture shock for international graduate students. *Journal of College Student Development, 45*(2), 167–184.

Ellis, C., Adams, T., & Bochner, A. P. (2011). Autoethnography: An overview. *Historical Social Research, 36*(4), 273–290.

Ellis, C. S., & Bochner, A. P. (2006). Analyzing analytic autoethnography: An autopsy. *Journal of Contemporary Ethnography, 35*(4), 429–449.

Gay, G., & Howard, T. C. (2000). Multicultural teacher education for the 21st century. *Teacher Educator, 36*(1), 1–17.

Geist-Martin, P., Gates, L., Wiering, L., Kirby, E., Houston, R., Lilly, A., & Moreno, J. (2010). Exemplifying collaborative autoethnographic practice via shared stories of mothering. *Journal of Research Practice, 6*(1), 1–14.

Institute of International Education (IIE). (2013). Open Doors 2013: International students in the United States and study abroad by American students are at all-time high. Retrieved from http://www.iie.org/Who-We-Are/News-and-Events/Press-Center/Press-Releases/2013/2013-11-11-Open-Doors-Data

Knight, J. (2003). Updated internationalization definition. *International Higher Education, 33*(3), 2–3.

Lee. J. J., & Rice. C. (2007). Welcome to America? International student perceptions of discrimination. *Higher Education, 53,* 381–409.

National Center for Education Statistics. (2015). *Racial/Ethnic enrollment in public schools.* Retrieved from http://nces.ed.gov/programs/coe/indicator_cge.asp

Oberg, K. (1960). Culture shock: Adjustment to new cultural environments. *Practical Anthropology, 7,* 177–182.

Rose-Redwood, C. R., & Rose-Redwood, R. S. (2013). Self-segregation or global mixing? Social interactions and the international student experience. *Journal of College Student Development, 54*(4), 413–429.

Sawir, E., Marginson, S., Forbes-Mewett, H., Nyland, C., & Ramia, G. (2012). International student security and English language proficiency. *Journal of Studies in International Education, 16*(5), 434–454.

Seeman, M. (1959). On the meaning of alienation. *American Sociological Review, 24*(6), 783–791.

Sherry, M., Thomas, P., & Chui, W. H. (2010). International students: A vulnerable student population. *Higher Education, 60,* 33–46.

Spencer-Rodgers, J. (2001). Consensual and individual stereotypic beliefs about international students among American host nationals. *International Journal of Intercultural Relations, 25,* 639–657.

Spring, J. (2008). Research on globalization and education, *Review of Educational Research, 78*(2), 330–363.

Wan, T., Chapman, D. W., & Biggs, D. A. (1992). Academic stress of international students attending U.S. universities. *Research in Higher Education, 33*(5), 607–622.

Young, S. L., & McKibban, A. R. (2014). Creating safe places: A collaborative autoethnography on LGBT social activism. *Sexuality & Culture, 18*(2), 361–384.

CHAPTER 9

ETHNIC MINORITY STUDENTS IN HONG KONG

Betty C. Eng

ABSTRACT

Ethnic minorities from India, Pakistan, Nepal, Thailand, the Philippines, Sri Lanka, and Indonesia comprise approximately 5% of Hong Kong's total population, yet they have remained largely invisible in this predominately Chinese community. Until recently, ethnic minorities have not been recognized by the Hong Kong government, and little research and scholarship has been conducted about them. Among ethnic minority groups in Hong Kong, there are high unemployment rates, language barriers, and difficulties with integration and building social networks. Given this background of ethnic minorities in Hong Kong, the educational and counseling needs of ethnic minority students will be addressed in this chapter. Documents and archival materials from community groups, government records, and public policy organizations are examined, along with stories from selected members of ethnic communities. The chapter provides a brief history of ethnic minorities in Hong Kong and the way forward to addressing their social, economic, and political needs. In particular, the chapter examines and seeks to understand the mental health and counseling needs of ethnic minority students. The discussion invites educators to understand social justice with implications and recommendations for schools, educators, and policymakers.

Internationalizing Teaching and Teacher Education for Equity, pages 143–158
Copyright © 2016 by Information Age Publishing
All rights of reproduction in any form reserved.

PERSONAL RATIONALE: THE PERSONAL IS POLITICAL

I am Chinese and American, born in the People's Republic of China, raised and educated primarily in the United States. My home is Hong Kong, where I have lived and worked since the mid-1980s. My journey from China, the United States, and Hong Kong has been an expression of my search for understanding of identity, culture, and sense of belonging.

I was a student during the anti-Vietnam war and student movements of the late 1960s and 1970s in the United States. As a student activist, I became one of the founders of Asian American Studies and Ethnic Studies, creating and teaching some of the first courses taught in the program. It was from my participation in the Asian American movement and Asian American studies that I began the conscious and systematic narrative of recovery and reclamation of the stories of experience that had been invisible and lost to me. My personal experiences and narratives are political. My participation in the Asian American movement and Asian American studies provided the awakening of a new way of thinking about my identity, the power of students and the community, and a new understanding about the social and political structures and forces around me that determined my place in the future. Coming full circle, it would seem, I have crossed and crisscrossed the continents of North America and Asia over time and I have been a teacher and counselor in Hong Kong for over two decades.

The "Third World Strike" by students at San Francisco State College in the fall of 1968 remains an important and vivid event for me. Some Asian American commentators such as Omatsu (1994) have marked this year as the birth of the Asian American movement. The strike at San Francisco State College was an unprecedented militant strike by students composed of Blacks, Hispanics, Native Americans, and Asian Americans who called themselves "Third World Students" and went on strike, boycotting classes, and bringing the campus to a standstill with their protests and demands for educational equity at the college. According to Hirabayashi and Alquizola (1994), the results of the strike gave students, teachers, and community activists the power to create the curriculum for the new School of Ethnic Studies, as well as the power to hire and fire professors at San Francisco State College and the University of California at Berkeley.

The growing awareness and consciousness created by the social and political movements and Asian American studies of that epoch forcefully compelled me to reflect on my personal identity and culture. I came to view my growing ethnic awareness and self-redefinition as an act of defiance and recovery of power that had been denied to me and my community. I developed a growing realization of the systematic and purposeful ways that my community's voices had been excluded within the curriculum that gave me a deep sense of awareness, anger, and betrayal. My views found expression in the power of community organizing and education as constructive and meaningful ways for social change and social justice.

Reflecting on this experience over three decades later, I realize how the establishment of ethnic studies was a momentous and historical period in redefining the educational landscape across the country. Omatsu (1994) described the impact for Asian Americans in this way:

> For Asian Americans, these struggles profoundly changed our communities. They spawned numerous grassroots organizations. They created an extensive network of student organizations and Asian American Studies classes. They recovered buried cultural traditions as well as produced a new generation of writers, poets, and artists. But most importantly, the struggles deeply affected Asian American consciousness. They redefined racial and ethnic identity, promoted new ways of thinking about communities, and challenged prevailing notions of power and authority. (p. 20)

These experiences have become principles to live by that have been sustained and practiced in my personal and professional life in Hong Kong. My teaching, research, and scholarship, and my participation in community grassroots organizations, have centered on issues of diversity and creating a world that is just and fair for those who have been marginalized and discriminated against. Researching and writing about ethnic minority students in Hong Kong is a continuation and extension of my experiences as a student activist.

RATIONALE AND SIGNIFICANCE

The rationale and significance of this chapter has immediate and practical application to the Hong Kong context and to an increasingly diverse and complex global community. The significance of this chapter has a number of broad long-term contributions. Firstly, with race relations becoming a prominent and critical issue in Hong Kong (Equal Opportunity Commission, 2008), this study contributes to the goals of the Hong Kong government in creating a harmonious, inclusive, and diverse society. Secondly, with the emerging demands for democracy, social justice, and human rights at the end of British rule and return of sovereignty to the Peoples Republic of China in 1997, the voices of ethnic minorities in Hong Kong cannot be ignored. Thirdly, this chapter will contribute to the scholarship and understanding of a little-studied community. Finally, the academic discipline and field of counseling is relatively new in Hong Kong and has yet to become a recognized profession. Counselor education, training, and the scholarly body of academic research are just emerging in Hong Kong. Moreover, most of the established and studied counseling theories originate from

West. This discussion will contribute to the development of culturally relevant counseling theories and practices for ethnic minority students in Hong Kong and a contextualized Asian perspective of multicultural counseling with implications for communities internationally.

RESEARCH AND SCHOLARSHIP

There is a dearth of academic research and literature in Hong Kong addressing the mental health and counseling needs of ethnic minority students. Of the related studies conducted in Hong Kong, most are from community groups or organizations and address the general ethnic minority population. Considerably more academic scholarship is available internationally, particularly in countries where ethnic minorities constitute up to 50% of the population (Cuellar & Paniagua, 2000). This research project will conduct a more extensive search of literature related to the topic but the following are selected key references of work done by others internationally and in Hong Kong.

In the United States, psychologists and counselor educators Sue and Sue (1971) pioneered the concept of "culturally different" to acknowledge and honor cultural and ethnic differences in the field of mental health and counseling. The recognition that depression and mental health are constructed by culture was studied by psychiatrist Kleinman (1980). Multicultural competence has been considered a requirement for counselors of culturally diverse clients (Liu & Clay, 2002; Sue, Arredondo, & McDavis, 1992; Sue & Sue, 2013; Sue & Torino, 2005). The research of Fraga, Atkinson, and Wampold (2004) has indicated that ethnic groups preferred multicultural counseling; as counselors have more understanding in sociopolitical factors, they can use local helping practices and seek to achieve a nonracist identity. A study by Zhang and Dixon (2001) showed that Asians preferred multiculturally responsive counselors over multiculturally neutral counselors based on several dimensions, including expertness, attractiveness, and trustworthiness. Li, Kim, and O'Brien (2007) have suggested that consistency between counselors' and the clients' cultural value is positively related to perceived counselor credibility and multicultural counseling competence. Developing educational policies and school curricula that are inclusive and diverse is the focus of multicultural education in the research of Banks (1997).

In Hong Kong, Heung (2006), an educator in special education, has written of the special emotional and behavioral needs of ethnic minority students in Hong Kong. Using the perspective of pastoral needs, Hue (2010) raised challenges to making Hong Kong school guidance culturally responsive. According to research conducted by Hong Kong Unison

(2005), a charitable nongovernment organization, 85.8% of interviewees believed discrimination towards ethnic minorities exists in Hong Kong. And, since most ethnic minorities are not proficient in Chinese, one of their major difficulties is the language barrier (Hue, 2010; Yang Memorial Methodist Social Service, 2002).

Other studies have pointed to the difficulties encountered in the areas of employment, education, and social life. Caritas Community Centre (2010), a grassroots organization in Hong Kong, found that 70% of ethnic minorities surveyed experienced difficulty finding a job. Of those interviewed, 34% cited language as the main reason for not securing a job in Hong Kong. Moreover, ethnic minorities usually get lower salaries, less employees' welfare, and fewer promotion opportunities, but have longer working hours and more work load, and they are more likely to be laid off in comparison to local Chinese (Ku, Chan, & Sandhu, 2006).

BRIEF HISTORICAL BACKGROUND

The history of ethnic minorities in Hong Kong dates back to the 19th century (Lock & Detaramani, 2006; Pluss, 2005). Bilingual and international Hong Kong attracted ethnic minorities who sought employment and a better quality of life by working as merchants, traders, police officers, Gurkhas, and musicians (Oxfam, 2003). But with the end of British colonial rule and the handover of Hong Kong to the People's Republic of China in 1997, the Chinese language and culture have played a more critical role in determining educational access, employment opportunities, and access to social services. Because most ethnic minorities lack Chinese language proficiency and have limited social networks within the predominantly Chinese community in Hong Kong, they are restricted to jobs as laborers in such fields as construction and security, and they have difficulty obtaining adequate housing and healthcare, face language barriers, and encounter discrimination (Ku, Chan, Chan, & Lee, 2003; Working Group of Social Integration Project for Ethnic Minority People in Hong Kong & Unison Hong Kong, 2003).

With the handover of Hong Kong to China in 1997, the demographics of Hong Kong have shifted, with a growing number of ethnic minority students in Hong Kong schools (Education Commission, 2000, 2002). According to the Census and Statistics Department (2007), ethnic minorities comprise 5% of Hong Kong's total population. Ethnic minorities are identified as Filipinos (32.9%), Indonesians (25.7%), White (10.6%), Indians (6.0%), Mixed (5.3%), Nepalese (4.7%), Japanese (3.9%), Thais (3.5%), Pakistanis (3.2%), Other Asians (2.3%), Koreans (1.4%), and Others (0.6%). For the purpose of this chapter, the categories of ethnic minority are those from

South Asia and Southeast Asian (e.g., Indians, Pakistanis, Nepalese, Thais, Filipinos, Sri Lankans, and Indonesians). It is among these groups that there are high unemployment rates, language barriers, and difficulties with integration and building social networks (Working Group of Social Integration Project, 2003; Yang Memorial Methodist Social Service, 2002), which will be the focus of this chapter.

The British handover also resulted in a shift in the political landscape, which promoted a more democratic, diverse, and harmonious society and which, in turn, highlighted the needs of ethnic minorities in Hong Kong. The absence and neglect of ethnic minority issues were dramatically highlighted with the killing of Dil Bahadur Limbu, a Nepalese man, by a Hong Kong police officer, Hui Ka-ki, in March 2009. Hui had responded to a complaint by a resident that a man was seen loitering and behaving oddly in the neighborhood. In the attempt to obtain Limbu's identification, the officer was punched and hit with a wooden chair and subsequently shot Limbu twice, once in the head (Lo, 2009; Ng, 2010a). Accounts suggested that the death of Limbu might have resulted from a lack of communication since Hui issued warnings in Chinese, a language that Limbu may not have understood.

The jury found the actions of the police officer a lawful and justified killing, which implied that Hui had acted in self-defense. Members of ethnic minority communities were outraged and raised strong protests about the decision. They accused the police of neglecting the needs of ethnic minorities and being culturally insensitive. Community members raised questions such as: Did the officer consider the possibility of Limbu not understanding of Chinese when he issued his warning? Was shooting the only alternative? Were other courses of actions exhausted? Importantly, no recommendations were made to prevent such incidents from happening again in the future. Mr. Limbu's widow, Sony Rai, sought a judicial review to challenge the court's decision, but her petition for a review was rejected (Ng, 2010b).

ETHNIC MINORITY STUDENTS

After 1997, the demographics of Hong Kong shifted with a growing number of ethnic minority students in Hong Kong schools (Education Commission, 2000). Enrollment of school-aged ethnic students increased by 20% in 2006 with a total of 13,472 students. By 2007, this population had grown to 28,722 students (Census and Statistics Department, 2007). Ku, Chan, and Sandhu (2005) have reported that 56.5% of ethnic minority students do not believe they receive the same educational opportunities as local Chinese students. Students cited the following as discriminatory: There are fewer school choices and places open to them, they lack financial support to pay for tuition fees compared to the resources available to local Chinese students, and there is a language barrier of limited proficiency in Cantonese. Thirteen percent of the students reported being disliked by teachers, and 27% reported being punished more severely than local Chinese students. Loper (2004) found that access to information about schools was restricted, since much of the information is written only in Chinese.

Relatively few studies have addressed the social, personal, or emotional well-being of ethnic minorities. Studying the Pakistani community, Ku et al. (2003) found that their major social activities are staying at home, meeting friends, and going to worship. They are less likely to participate in social activities in the community, such as visiting public libraries, social service centers, or arts and cultural centers because these activities mainly cater to the Cantonese-speaking population. Of the participants in this study, 59.3 % of them stated that Hong Kong people are unfriendly, and 56.9% felt isolated because they did not know Chinese.

Because of systematic and perceived discrimination in Hong Kong, it would seem reasonable to expect that ethnic minorities would be more likely to experience high levels of stress, depression, less life satisfaction, and negative moods, as cited by Carter (2007) in the study of race-based trauma in the United States. Therefore, one of the main focuses of this discussion is how culturally relevant counseling can offer a proactive, effective, and healing response.

HONG KONG UNISON

Hong Kong Unison Limited (Unison) is a community-based, charitable nongovernment organization. Established in 2001 by volunteers composed of teachers, social workers, lawyers, and other community members, Unison's mission is to eliminate racial discrimination and promote racial harmony and strive for ethnic equality in the areas of education, employment, public service, and political and social participation (Hong Kong Unison, 2015a). To maintain its independence, Unison relies solely on private donations and currently has a staff of fewer than 10. Unison originally began by providing services such as employment, housing, and education to ethnic minority individuals. Recognizing the need for more long-term and sustainable measures, their services have expanded to advocacy for policy reforms. According to Margaret Ng, a legislator and supporter of Unison:

> The most fundamental challenge ethnic minorities face is the lack of proficiency in the Chinese language, which results in the difficulty in pursuing their studies and careers. The Chinese curriculum in mainstream schools

falsely assumes that all students are native Chinese speakers. Also, there is no effective support from the education system or the local community. Ethnic minority students are hence left alone in their daily struggle to learn Chinese and to integrate into society. (Hong Kong Unison, 2012)

As an advocacy group, Unison has been the primary force contesting and aggressively challenging the Hong Kong government to enact policies to protect and ensure the rights of ethnic minorities in Hong Kong. It has been through the efforts of Unison that research and surveys have been conducted that have revealed the systematic discrimination against ethnic minorities in Hong Kong in areas such as employment and education. It was found that in the 2011–2012 academic year, 1 out of every 38 students receiving basic education was an ethnic minority student. However, the ratio dramatically drops to 1 out of every 1,112 in universities and other post-secondary programs due to the lack of language proficiency in Chinese (Hong Kong Unison, 2012). According the 2001 Census and Statistics, the school attendance rate for ethnic minorities aged 19–24, was only 3.7%. This is much lower than the 26.4% of the majority population in the same age group (Census and Statistics, 2007).

With such findings, Unison organized educational forums and cultural sensitivity training for legislative council members, teachers, and policymakers; held demonstrations and protests; and developed proposals for the government, calling for the elimination of discrimination. In particular, Unison's challenge is to the Education Bureau for equal and fair inclusion of non-Chinese-speaking ethnic minorities in schools.

TELLING THE UNTOLD STORIES

Fermi Wong, the executive director of Unison, states that there are many untold and compelling stories of struggle and despair among ethnic minority students. Telling the stories of ethnic minority students make this community visible and educates the broader community. A few of the stories collected by Unison appear here along with accounts of intervention and support provided by Unison staff (Hong Kong Unison, 2015b):

Biju: *A Former Youth Drug Addict*

A second generation Nepalese immigrant, Biju moved to Hong Kong when he was seven years old. Due to the language barrier, and because his parents were too busy with their work to look after him, he became addicted to drugs at the age of 12. He was arrested by police at the "canteen" (where drug addicts get together to take drugs).

When I first met Biju's parents at the policy station, I could see their sense of helplessness and loss. Biju was terribly regretful and scared. Apart from giving support and comfort, I applied for child protection order immediately and arranged for Biju to undergo rehabilitation and continue his study. . . . He found his own interest and direction in life . . . and is now in his second year at a university in the United States and plans to come back to work upon graduation.

Over the years Unison has handled more than 200 drug addict cases. . . . Often when they needed help, all they found was apathy and discrimination. Our help and support bring them hope. We believe that most ethnic minority youths are willing to behave well and contribute to the society with more equal opportunities, care, and less discrimination. (Hong Kong Unison, 2015b)

Mohammand: *Dedicated Chinese Language Learner Who Wants to be a Fireman*

Mohammand, a Pakistani youth, is an easy-going, upright student who attended this year's HKCEE [exam required for university admission]. His dream is to be a fireman. Being a civil servant is mostly a dream to many ethnic minority youths with a poor grasp of the Chinese language. Mohammand is an exception. Through hard work, he cannot only speak fluent Cantonese but also read and write the language. He got an "A" in Chinese.

Ethnic minority youths used to have little chance of learning Chinese, but following the intense lobbying of Unison and the ethnic community, the government changed its policy in 2004 to allow ethnic minority students to attend mainstream schools using Chinese as the medium of instruction. Schools also offer Chinese courses for them to help prepare them for future employment and studies. Because of the policy change, Mohammand will have a different future from that of his brothers and sisters. Of course, there is still room for improvement in the new policy (e.g., the lack of teaching materials, uniform curriculum, and assessment criteria). Unison will continue to urge the government to enhance the quality of Chinese education so ethnic minority students will be proficient enough in the language. (Hong Kong Unison, 2015b)

Bilai: *Cherishing Further Study Opportunity*

When I met Bilai the first time, he looked lost and frustrated. He had finished secondary education (high school) for three years and yet could not further his study. Bilai is a Pakistani born and raised in Hong Kong capable of speaking fluent Cantonese. But because he did not have the chance to learn how to write and read Chinese in school, he faces much difficulty in finding jobs or furthering his study.

Before 2004, almost all ethnic minority students at public schools had to leave after completing Form Five [5th Grade]. Like other ethnic minority youths, Bilai wanted to further his study. We therefore looked hard for "Post-Form Five" studying opportunities for them. Finally in 2005, we raised enough funds to commission IVE (Haking Wang) for two consecutive years to run a one-year foundation diploma (hotel management) for 70 ethnic minority youths. Bilai finished the foundation programme with excellent results. He then moved on to a two-year diploma programme and is now doing community work for a non-governmental organization. His next goal is to get an associate degree in social work so as to contribute substantially to the society in the future. (Hong Kong Unison, 2015b)

Such compelling stories dramatically highlight the educational and social needs of these ethnic minority students. A review of the response from the Education Bureau of the Hong Kong government and an analysis of the policies for meeting the needs of non-Chinese speaking children as a result of the enactment of the Race Discrimination Ordinance.

RACE DISCRIMINATION ORDINANCE

Through the efforts of Unison and other community supporters, the Race Discrimination Ordinance (RDO) was enacted in July 2008. According to the Equal Opportunity Commission, an appointed body of the Hong Kong Government charged with investigating and conciliating complaints, the RDO is an antidiscrimination law aimed at protecting people "against discrimination, harassment and vilification on the ground of their race" (Equal Opportunity Commission, 2008, para. 1). The enactment of the RDO is certainly encouraging and a step in the right direction in eliminating discrimination and achieving social justice. The RDO has provided the basis for social and political reforms needed to pursue charges of discrimination. However, community organizations such as Unison and Oxfam are critical in monitoring and lobbying for sustained, equitable, and fair implementation of the RDO. This is the case with the challenge to the Education Bureau policies in addressing the needs of ethnic minority students in education and careers in Hong Kong.

The RDO has been contested and challenged for its limited authority, numerous loopholes, and lack of long-term vision. For instance, the RDO does not cover the government actions in carrying out its functions or its exercise of power. The RDO also exempts educational, employment, and training entities from language and other special requirements that pose barriers for entry by ethnic minorities. Moreover, there are no measures for an independent review and evaluation of the effectiveness of the RDO. The most encouraging development is that the RDO provides the basis and platform to which other government agencies must abide. This is the case with the Education Bureau (EDB) with its implementation of RDO to provide education for non-Chinese-speaking students.

SOCIAL JUSTICE:
A CURRICULUM FOR NON-CHINESE SPEAKING STUDENTS

The Education Bureau (EDB) of Hong Kong has attempted to address the needs of non-Chinese-speaking (NCS) children in schools. EDB (2008) encourages NCS children to integrate into the community through the study of the local curriculum. EDB promotes a government language policy to enable students to be proficient in Chinese and English with fluency in Cantonese, Putonghua (Mandarin), and English. In most primary and secondary schools, Chinese is the medium of instruction with English taught as a core subject. In response to the RDO, EDB has identified "designated schools" that have a high enrollment of ethnic minority students to qualify for grant subsidies. In the 2008–2009 academic year, six secondary schools and 16 primary schools were designated to receive such funds. Such measures by EDB are promising, but a closer examination and analysis of the EDB implementation of policies reveals some issues to address. A discussion of some of the limitations and recommendations are highlighted here.

Resources for schools are inadequate. Of the 533 primary and secondary schools that admit ethnic minority students, only 22 schools receive the government subsidies to support the teaching and learning of Chinese by NCS. Only designated schools receive subsidies, and other schools, which also have large enrollment of ethnic minority students, have not been able to receive the designated school status and its funds. It remains unclear what criteria and standards are required to qualify for this status. Some mainstream schools that have not received the designated school status have a student body composed of 56.6–83.1% ethnic minority students (Hong Kong Unison, 2011). No resources are allotted to educate and train teachers in how to work with ethnic minority students or non-Chinese-speaking students. Nor is there a curriculum that is designed to teach NCS. Generally, the EDB has shifted such responsibilities to the "front line teachers" and assumes that the current mainstream Chinese Language curriculum meets the needs of NCS. It is highly recommended that a long-range and comprehensive curriculum is developed that includes assessment tools and textbooks from primary to secondary school and that addresses the needs of NCS at each stage of their educational development.

Examinations for Chinese language are required at each stage of a student's progression and placement from primary school to secondary school and to university. As is often the case, NCS are disadvantaged when compared with native speakers, as evidenced by the scores of their Chinese language exams. The results of the Chinese language exams limit the school choices of NCS to gain admission to top schools with almost no chance of gaining admission to a local university. Many of these students are forced to study overseas for a university degree. Unison has recommended a review of the secondary school placement system and that NSC be assessed separately from local Chinese speaking students and given a comparable but fair standard to achieve common level of competiveness.

With limited proficiency in Chinese language and a disadvantage in receiving a higher quality of education and access to a university degree, the opportunities for employment and careers are highly restricted. Most of the job-training programs are designed for ethnic local Chinese speakers with Cantonese as the medium of instruction. Of the few programs that can accommodate ethnic minorities, they restrict the choices of jobs to the fields of business, catering, tourism, and nursery services, according to a survey conducted by Hong Kong Unison (2011). Unison has recommended that the government increase the number of job training bodies and expand the range of job types to include the arts, languages, and translation to address the needs of ethnic minority community.

CULTURALLY RELEVANT COUNSELING

With such a background of discrimination experienced by ethnic minorities in the Hong Kong community, and with the needs of ethnic minority students in particular in mind, the discussion now focuses on counseling. Ethnic minority students report suffering low self-esteem, bullying, and racist attitudes and discrimination not only from classmates but also the teaching staff. As discussed previously, ethnic students do not believe they receive the same educational opportunities as local Chinese students. Ethnic minority students also believe teachers dislike them and that they are punished more severely (Hue, 2010).

Counseling is the process of helping to promote self-understanding and understanding of others to attend to issues of living. Development of self-awareness, problem solving, and managing stress are some examples that can be addressed in counseling. Culturally relevant counseling takes the view that culture informs and shapes how we think, make decisions, behave, and understand our life experiences. Culturally relevant counseling seeks to use counseling theories and practices relevant to the experiences of a particular culture and their life experiences.

Training for teachers and administrators to be knowledgeable and sensitive to the needs of ethnic studies is needed. In Hong Kong, teachers have been identified as "front line" counselors, and their training should include basic counseling theories and practices. Attending to the personal and emotional needs of the students is as important as meeting their educational and academic needs. What may be viewed as normative in one cultural milieu may be seen as deficient or deviant in another (Eng, 2012). For instance, the belief that children are objects and possessions, particularly female children, under the control and authority of men is a pervasive belief in traditional Pakistani and other Southeast Asian families. Physical and emotional punishment can be viewed as a form of discipline and an acceptable practice of good parenting rather than child abuse (Ku et al., 2003). While child abuse is not condoned, understanding the beliefs of others demonstrates understanding and empathy.

Culturally relevant counseling includes awareness of one's own assumptions, values, and beliefs. Knowing oneself and confronting personal biases and acts of racism, sexism, and classism may be a sensitive and painful process, but it is critical to becoming a culturally relevant practitioner. Understanding the worldview of culturally diverse communities is another requirement for culturally competent counseling (Sue & Torino, 2005). This dimension requires the teacher to be knowledgeable about the worldviews of diverse communities in an accepting, nonjudgmental, and empathetic way. Some ways that can cultivate insights and understanding of indigenous groups are to seek out cultural informants such as community elders, mentors, and teachers. Engaging in cultural activities in their communities and reading materials related to their history, customs, and cultural practices is also helpful. Finally, developing culturally appropriate and comprehensive counseling programs designed for teachers is recommended (Watkins, 2001).

LOOKING FORWARD—WHERE DO WE GO FROM HERE?

For over a decade, the movement for social justice for ethnic minorities in Hong Kong has been rooted in the community of its people. It is the passion and commitment of grassroots organizations such as Unison to this invisible community that the efforts of social reforms, such as the Race Discrimination Ordinance and educational policies to create a curriculum for non-Chinese-speaking students, have been formulated. It has not been from governmental bodies or established political parties that this movement for social justice for ethnic minorities has been developed. Volunteers and charitable groups independent of the government have struggled to ensure that discrimination is eliminated and that all people have the same opportunities for basic human rights. Creating a just and fair society is an empowering principle that is personal, passionate, and participatory.

While the discussion of this chapter focuses on Hong Kong ethnic minority students, it invites an internationalizing of our understanding of the world that informs our pedagogy. Engaging in social and political transformation for the good of all people promotes new ways of thinking about who we are and who we are in the world. While the discussion here has centered on Hong Kong ethnic minorities, it is also relevant for other diverse communities worldwide.

REFERENCES

Banks, J. (1997). Multicultural education: Characteristics and goals. In J. Banks & C. A. M. Banks (Eds.), *Multicultural education: Issues and perspectives* (3rd ed., pp. 3–31). Boston, MA: Allyn & Bacon.

Caritas Community Centre. (2010). *Survey on working conditions of South Asians in Hong Kong.* Hong Kong: Author.

Carter, R. T. (2007). Racism and psychological and emotional injury: Recognizing and assessing race-based traumatic stress. *The Counseling Psychologist, 35,* 13–105.

Census and Statistics Department. (2007). *Hong Kong 2006 population by census thematic report: Ethnic minorities.* Hong Kong: Census and Statistics Department.

Cuellar, I., & Paniagua, F. A. (Eds.). (2000). *Handbook of multicultural mental health: Assessment and treatment of diverse populations.* San Diego, CA: Academic Press.

Education Commission. (2000). *Learning for life learning through life: Reform proposals for the education system in Hong Kong.* Hong Kong: Education Commission.

Education Commission (2002). *Progress report on the education reform: Learning for life, learning through life.* Hong Kong: Hong Kong Government.

Eng, B. C. (2012). Culturally responsive counseling, Hong Kong. In J. Banks (Ed.), *Encyclopedia of Diversity in Education* (pp. 543–546). Thousand Oaks, CA: Sage.

Equal Opportunity Commission. (2008). *Race discrimination ordinance.* Hong Kong: Author.

Fraga, E. D., Atkinson, D. R., & Wampold, B. E. (2004). Ethnic group preferences for multicultural counseling competencies. *Cultural Diversity and Ethnic Minority Psychology, 10*(1), 53–65.

Hirabayashi, L. R., & Alquizola, M. C. (1994). Asian American studies: Reevaluating for the 1990s. In K. Aguilar-San Juan (Ed.), *The state of Asian America activism and resistance in the 1990s* (pp. 351–364). Boston, MA: South End Press.

Heung, V. (2006). Recognizing the emotional and behavioral needs of ethnic minority students in Hong Kong. *Preventing School Failure, 50*(2), 29–36.

Hong Kong Unison. (2005). Report on Hong Kong citizens' perceptions and images toward Hong Kong ethnic minorities research. Retrieved from www.unison.org.hk

Hong Kong Unison. (2011). Hong Kong Unison—in response to the Tenth and Thirteenth Report of the Peoples Republic of China under the International Convention on the Elimination of All Forms of Racial Discrimination—Part two: Hong Kong Special Administrative Region. Retrieved from www.unison.org.hk

Hong Kong Unison. (2012, December). Message from Margaret Ng. Retrieved from www.unison.org.hk

Hong Kong Unison. (2015a). About Hong Kong Unison. Retrieved from http://www.unison.org.hk/aboutus.php

Hong Kong Unison. (2015b). Stories. Retrieved from http://www.unison.org.hk/stories.php

Hue, M. T. (2010). The challenges of making school guidance culturally responsive: Narratives of pastoral needs of ethnic minority students in Hong Kong secondary schools. *Educational Studies, 36*(4), 357–369.

Kleinman, A. (1980). *Patients and healers in the context of culture: An exploration of the borderland between anthropology, medicine, and psychiatry.* Berkley, CA: University of California Press.

Ku, H. B., Chan, K. W., Chan, W. L., & Lee, W. Y. (2003). *A research report on life experiences of Pakistanis in Hong Kong.* Hong Kong: Centre for Social Policy Studies, Department of Applied Social Sciences, The Hong Kong Polytechnic University and S. K. H. Lady MacLehose Centre.

Ku, H. B., Chan, K. W., & Sandhu, K. K. (2005). *A research report on the education of South Asian ethnic minority groups in Hong Kong.* Hong Kong: Centre for Social Policy Studies, The Hong Kong Polytechnic University.

Ku, H. B., Chan, K. W., & Sandhu, K. K. (2006). A research report on the employment of South Asian ethnic minority groups in Hong Kong. Hong Kong: Centre for Social Policy Studies, The Hong Kong Polytechnic University.

Li, C. L., Kim, B. S. K., & O'Brien, K. M. (2007). An analogue study of the effects of Asian cultural values and counselor multicultural competence on counseling process. *Psychotherapy: Theory, Research, Practice, Training, 44*(1), 90–95.

Liu, W. M., & Clay, D. L. (2002). Multicultural counseling competencies: Guidelines in working with children and adolescents. *Journal of Mental Health Counseling, 24*(2), 177–187.

Lo, C. (2009, March 22). Police chief promises fair inquiry into shooting of Nepali man. *South China Morning Post.* p. EDT4.

Lock, G., & Detaramani, C. (2006). Being Indian in post-colonial Hong Kong: Models of ethnicity, culture and language among Sindhis and Sikhs in Hong Kong. *Asian Ethnicity, 7*(3), 267–284.

Loper, K. (2004). *Race and equality: A study of ethnic minorities in Hong Kong's education system: Project report and analysis.* Hong Kong: Centre for Comparative and Public Law, Hong Kong University. Retrieved from http://www.law.hku.hk/ccpl/tc/pub/Documents/Occasional_Paper_12_KL.pdf

Ng, M. (2010a, May 25). Did officer use excessive force in shooting case? *South China Morning Post.* p. CITY2.

Ng, M. (2010b, May 26). Widow seeks review after shooting verdict. *South China Morning Post.* p. EDT1.

Omatsu, G. (1994). The "four prisons" and the movements of liberation. In K. Aguilar-San Juan (Ed.), *The state of Asian America activism and resistance in the 1990s* (pp. 19–69). Boston, MA: South End Press.

Oxfam. (2003). Ethnic minority and social exclusion. Retrieved from http://www.oxfam.org.hk/en/one_556.aspx

Pluss, C. (2005). Constructing globalized ethnicity: Migrants from India in Hong Kong. *International Sociology, 20*(2), 201–224.

Sue, D. W., Arredondo, P., & McDavis, R. J. (1992). Multicultural competencies/standards: A call to the profession. *Journal of Counseling and Development, 70*(4), 477–486.

Sue, S., & Sue, D. W. (1971). Chinese-American personality and mental health. *Amerasian Journal, 1*, 36–49.

Sue, D. W., & Sue, D. (2013). *Counseling the culturally diverse: Theory and practice* (6th ed.). Hoboken, NJ: Wiley.

Sue, D. W., & Torino, G. C. (2005). Racial-cultural competence: Awareness, knowledge and skills. In R. T. Carter (Ed.), *Handbook of racial-cultural psychology and counseling* (pp. 3–18). Hoboken, NJ: Wiley.

Watkins, C. (2001). Comprehensive guidance programs in an international context. *Professional School Counseling, 4,* 262–270.

Working Group of Social Integration Project for Ethnic Minority People in Hong Kong & Unison Hong Kong. (2003). *A research report on the employment situation of South Asian people in Hong Kong.* Hong Kong: City University of Hong Kong.

Yang Memorial Methodist Social Service, Yau Tsim Mong Integrated Centre for Youth Development (2002). *A study on outlets of the South Asian ethnic minority.* Hong Kong, China: Author.

Zhang, N., & Dixon, D. N. (2001). Multiculturally responsive counseling: Effects on Asian students' ratings of counselors. *Journal of Multicultural Counseling and Development, 29,* 253–262.

CHAPTER 10

PROFESSIONAL DEVELOPMENT FOR "PROFESSIONAL PEDAGOGUES"

Contradictions and Tensions in Reprofessionalizing Teachers in Cyprus

Stavroula Philippou, Stavroula Kontovourki,
and Eleni Theodorou

ABSTRACT

We explore contradictions and tensions that emerged in the ways in which elementary school teachers in the Republic of Cyprus perceived their (re) positioning as "autonomous professional pedagogues" by the Ministry of Education and Culture (MoEC, 2004) as part of the comprehensive reform of the Greek-Cypriot public educational system. This is examined by attending to the narrations of 66 teachers around the professional development (PD) they had experienced and that which they desired in the year 2010–2011, when new curriculum texts were published and related PD was

Internationalizing Teaching and Teacher Education for Equity, pages 159–179
159

organized by the MoEC. The analysis highlights the complexities of teachers' (re)positioning as a process that involved both openings and constrictions: teachers' critiques unveiled possibilities for their professionalization as decision makers and the democratization of the process of curriculum change. However, teachers' concurrent requests for direct guidance and support (re)confirmed their positioning as receivers of knowledge, which draws heavily on their historical experience as public servants in a centralized educational system.

INTRODUCTION

The purpose of this chapter is to explore the contradictions and tensions that emerged in the ways in which elementary school teachers in the Republic of Cyprus perceived their (re)positioning as "autonomous professional pedagogues" by the Ministry of Education and Culture (MoEC, 2004) as part of the comprehensive reform of the Greek-Cypriot public educational system. This is examined in relation to their notions of appropriate professional development (PD) during curriculum change in the year 2010–2011, when new curriculum texts were published and PD was organized by the MoEC to introduce these texts to teachers. Attending to teachers' narrations relating to the PD they had experienced and that which they desired, this analysis makes evident the complexities of teachers' (re)positioning as a process that involved both openings and constrictions. We thus argue that the teachers' critiques unveiled possibilities for teachers' professionalization as decision-makers, the democratization of the process of new curriculum introduction/implementation, and the establishment of more participatory forms of PD, which would facilitate their visibility as a professional group and destabilize existing institutional hierarchies. However, teachers' concurrent requests for direct guidance and support (re)confirmed their positioning as receivers of knowledge and as implementers of others' plans, which draws heavily on their historical experience as public servants in a centralized educational system wherein state-mandated official curricula and textbooks have been imposed by (more expert) others, usually ministry technocrats. It is this complexity that we illustrate through our analysis and raise questions about teacher professionalism, PD, and curriculum change, at a time when teachers' professionalism in the "successful implementation" of the new curriculum was discursively stressed at the policy level; yet at the same time, this official rhetoric worked towards their deprofessionalization, as subjection to existing institutional and social hierarchies remained largely unchallenged.

TEACHER PROFESSIONALISM AND PD FOR CURRICULUM CHANGE: AN UNEASY CONNECTION

Teacher professionalism in this study is perceived as a social construct that is constantly in flux and under negotiation within broader sociohistorical, political, and institutional structures (Hargreaves & Goodson, 1996; Mockler, 2005). Over the past few decades, there has been abundant agreement that in several countries teachers have been deprofessionalized and have had their professional autonomy, one of the key characteristics of their professionalism, constrained (Beck, 2008; Evans, 2008; Priestley, Edwards, Priestley, & Miller, 2012). However, researchers have also pointed to teachers as the agents of change and, thus, as potentially in a position to actively shape their work-lives, albeit within the limitations of their environments and structures (Hilferty, 2008; Vongalis-Macrow, 2007). This suggests that teachers' positioning during curriculum change should be seen as a contingently complex process that necessitates that both the context and the individual are simultaneously considered. As we intend to show, the concurrent consideration of an individual's freedom to act and the constraints or possibilities to do so, set by the institutional-systemic and broader sociohistorical context and incorporated by that same individual, requires that one is made sense of only in relation to the other. Hence, the analysis below will show that despite the constricting, hierarchical, and largely centralized PD practices that the state adopted to introduce new formal curriculum texts, teachers responded to these practices in diverse ways: at times resisting, yet at other times subjecting themselves and thus succumbing to these hierarchies of knowledge.

PD can take various forms. In terms of scale, Gaible and Burns (2005) divide teacher PD into three broad categories: standardized PD as the most centralized approach, used often to disseminate information and skills among large teacher populations through training sessions, and the cascade model of scaled delivery; site-based PD, which involves intensive learning by groups of teachers in a school or region, promoting profound and long-term changes in instructional methods; and self-directed PD, which refers to independent learning, sometimes initiated at the learner's discretion, using available resources. Discussions over forms of teacher PD note how different models or types of PD construct, envision, or assume a different kind of professional and of professionalism. In times of reform, this connection is rendered particularly visible in policy discourse (cf. Kontovourki, Theodorou, & Philippou, 2015), when PD is mobilized to "prepare," "train," and "develop" teachers towards certain directions. In terms of purpose, Kennedy (2014) outlines a spectrum of PD models that provide a means of transmission or facilitate transformative practice. At one end of the spectrum lies an understanding of PD as having the purpose of preparing teachers to implement reform prepared by others (transmission view), whereas at the opposite end lies an understanding of PD as supporting teachers in shaping education policy and practice (transformative view). Between these two ends lies a "transitional view" of PD (which includes the standards-based model, coaching/mentoring model, and the community of practice model), which refers to models that may support underlying agendas compatible with either of the purposes at the two ends of the spectrum. The increasing teacher autonomy implied from the one to the other end of the spectrum is not an easy task, even within the transformative view of PD. It seeks to challenge, yet occurs within the dominance of the constructed theory-practice divide that often threatens substantial transformation or teacher-researcher equitable collaboration (Bevins & Price, 2014). This occurs because traditionally theoretical knowledge (and academics/ researchers as its bearers) has been well established as of higher value and authority as opposed to the practical-contextual knowledge (and teachers/ practitioners as its bearers); this division, assuming (yet simultaneously reproducing) inequity, has thus fueled the "democratic" and "emancipatory" impulse of research under the knowledge-of-practice tradition discussed later in the chapter (Cochran-Smith & Lytle, 1999), from which a transformative view of PD largely stems.

Such tensions are ever-present, and it is of paramount importance, many authors conclude, to pay attention to the particular characteristics of the context before PD is developed/implemented. Day and Sachs (2004) suggest that all kinds of PD should take into account the teachers' needs, strongly criticizing PD practices that focus on transferring knowledge rather than building learning communities with a view of long-term prospects. "Professional learning communities" (PLC) have been defined as "a group of people sharing and critically interrogating their practice in an ongoing, reflective, collaborative, inclusive, learning oriented, growth promoting way, operating as a collective enterprise" (Stoll, Bolam, Wallace, & Thomas, 2006, p. 223). Thus, "collective learning" and "development in a professional community context" become crucial elements of PD that also ensure ongoing interaction among their members (Enthoven & de Bruijn, 2010; see also Moate, 2014), long-term commitment to sustain reflective dialogue (Ellis, 2007), voluntary participation and intrinsic motivation (Kimble, Hildreth, & Bourdon, 2007; Maloney & Konza, 2011).

Such PD values, acknowledges, and cultivates, teachers' "inner expertise" (Dadds, 2014) and promises to alter "the linear relationships through which information is handed down from those who discover the professional knowledge to those who provide and receive educational services" (Buysse, Sparkman, & Wesley, 2003, p. 265). Cochran-Smith and Lytle (1999) have distinguished between "knowledge-for-practice," which is produced by experts, "knowledge-in-practice," which is tacitly built by teachers at work, and "knowledge-of-practice," "the deliberate construction of knowledge by communities of teachers drawing on both outside experts and inquiry into daily practice" (as cited in Wood, 2007, p. 284). In the first case, teachers are constructed as "learners" or "consumers," whereas in the third case teachers are constructed as "knowers" or "producers" of knowledge (Wood, 2007; see also Bevins & Price, 2014; Dadds, 2014).

Since the state-mandated reform in Cyprus launched in 2004, the publication of new curriculum texts in 2010 and the ensuing PD in 2010–2011 conducted to introduce these texts to teachers, several of these approaches and concepts towards teacher professionalism, knowledge, and PD were mobilized in official texts and practices. These are presented below in order to enable us to later situate teachers' own perceptions thereof in the findings section of the chapter.

THE CONTEXT: PROFESSIONAL DEVELOPMENT FOR AUTONOMOUS PROFESSIONALS

The change of curricula was part of a comprehensive ongoing reform wherein teachers were re-envisioned as "autonomous or relatively autonomous professional-pedagogue[s]" (MoEC, 2004, p. 16). This supported a breakaway from the tradition of teachers as implementers of others' decisions, technocrat educators, and public servants (MoEC, 2004). The latter is a designation teachers received in 1929 (Persianis, 2010), when teachers earned state recognition for the profession by the then-British colonial government, which was reiterated after state independence through the 1959 Education Law and its subsequent revisions (Kontovourki et al., 2015). In the current reform, teacher autonomy was initially connected to an anticipation for increased teacher participation in decision making and "relative autonomy in curriculum development and teaching at the microlevel of the school unit and the classroom" (MoEC, 2004, p. 20). This was linked to the resignification of PD from a state-initiated, centralized practice to a matter of teachers' "self-education," "self-development," and "self-improvement" (MoEC, 2004, p. 114), as well as an issue to be handled both by the state and by/at the level of the school unit "with the utilization of capable and qualified school teachers" (MoEC, 2004, p. 177). As PD becomes teachers' and schools' responsibility, yet without the dismissal of the central position of the state, PD is conceptualized as simultaneously standardized, site-based, and self-directed, while the degree to which this constitutes a means of knowledge transmission and a scaffold for transformative practice is not addressed.

In 2008, with the appointment of a Curriculum Reform Committee by the Council of Ministers, the reform started taking shape with emphasis placed on the revision and development of new official curricula for all school subjects and grade levels. In line with the 2004 view of teachers as professionals with relative autonomy over curricular issues, the MoEC invited volunteer practicing teachers to collaborate with appointed academics and technocrats in 21 subject-area curriculum review committees that worked from March 2009 to March 2010 to produce draft curriculum texts and syllabi on each assigned subject area, which were then subject to public debate between March and April 2010. In September 2010, the temporarily "finalized" curriculum texts were sent to schools in print and were uploaded on the MoEC website.

During the year of the new curricula introduction (2010–2011), different PD practices were centrally organized by the MoEC. From a transmission point of view, the purpose was to inform and educate different actors in the institutional hierarchy. Such PD was differentiated between central and ongoing (as in standardized and site-based, respectively [Gaible & Burns, 2005]), with the former referring to seminars organized centrally by the MoEC and the latter adhering to the provision of support to teachers at the school level by ministry officers (seconded teachers, subject-area supporters/counselors, school inspectors) (MoEC & Pedagogical Institute, Αρ. Φακ. ΠΙ 7.7.09.16, 08.10.2010).

Adopting the goals of informing teachers and others of the general orientation and principles of the new curricula, facilitating their acquaintance with the content and methodology of new subject-area syllabi, and preparing teachers to engage in related practice, PD was organized in four phases based upon the groups of actors invited to participate in related practices (cf. MoEC, 2010). Phase 1 (September–October 2010) involved ministry officers, school principals, and subject-area supporters; Phase 2 (September–October 2010) targeted school inspectors and subject-area supporters. Teachers first appeared on the scene in Phase 3 (November 2010–February 2011), which was linked to the expectation that a small number of teachers would gain knowledge on given subject areas and transfer that to their teaching with the guidance of subject-area supporters (along a cascade model rationale). It thus involved the participation of one teacher per school, identified by the school principal on the basis of state-defined criteria, in a three-seminar series on selected subject areas that would help teachers "understand, embrace, and adopt" those new syllabi in their teaching (MoEC & Pedagogical Institute, Αρ. Φακ. ΠΙ 7.7.09.16, 08.10.2010).

Teachers who did not have the opportunity to participate in Phase 3 were targeted in Phase 4 (MoEC, 2010), which involved the compulsory participation of all public school teachers (MoEC & Pedagogical Institute, Αρ. Φακ. ΠΙ 7.7.09.16, 08.10.2010) in mass information seminars in December 2010 and January 2011. These seminars were led by school inspectors, academics, and subject-area supporters, who informed teachers of the general orientation of the new curricula and the content of key syllabi (math and Greek language arts, plus one among music, art, physical education, science, and home economics based upon teachers' selection). It was after teachers had experienced these forms of PD that the data analyzed in this chapter were collected, as detailed below.

METHOD OF DATA COLLECTION AND ANALYSIS

Drawing upon a broader project that examines teachers' positioning and sense of professionalism over the initial stages of curriculum change in Cyprus (2010–2014), the analysis presented in this chapter utilizes individual and focus group interviews conducted with 66 teachers between February and March 2011. We specifically investigated participants' perceptions regarding the purpose, process, and experience of participation in their PD, as well as their views of the curriculum change. Participants were identified through purposive and snowball sampling, and informed consent was given by all participants involved. In particular, interviewees were selected based on whether they had been teaching at elementary schools during data collection. Interviewees were able to nominate other participants, as long as the latter met the two criteria set for purposive sampling. Individual and group interviews were organized depending on teacher availability and convenience. Resulting from this, 7 focus group ($n = 19$ teachers) and 47 individual interviews were conducted.

Thematic analysis of teachers' perceptions on PD built on previous findings of the project that revealed (1) teachers' positioning on different points of a continuum, ranging from positions of none to full perceived agency (Philippou, Kontovourki, & Theodorou, 2014); and (2) a plethora of constructs and definitions of expertise mobilized by teachers (Theodorou, Kontovourki, & Philippou, 2012). Teachers' constructions of themselves as professionals and of knowledge (theirs' and others') were also central in teachers' perceptions of the process and their participation in PD, and these are addressed in this chapter as an example of teachers' uneasy positioning amidst a reform that requested/imposed their autonomy, extending it even to issues of PD, yet largely constricting the latter to plain transmission of information on the new curricula *to* them. As their general responses towards the PD were negative, these responses often came along with suggestions for alternative forms or characteristics of PD to that which they had experienced. The experienced and the desired PD thus became categories around which the analysis revolved and under which findings are structured below.

FINDINGS

Teachers reported diverse experiences of PD in the context of the curriculum change: collectively (as a professional body) in formal standardized PD; in groups (as site-based PD) and individually (as self-directed PD). Before we explore teachers' experiences of the formal PD organized by the MoEC, we first account for the additional PD that they pursued on a personal and mostly self-directed level in their effort to understand and prepare themselves in relation to the new curricula, mostly prior to their introduction. Such pursuits, teachers stressed, had required their personal commitment and investment of time and effort, with most of them occurring during their free, personal time. Doing so, teachers assumed responsibility for their PD in acknowledging the need to engage in PD so as to stand thoughtfully and knowledgeably opposite change, thereby positioning themselves as active and agentive in PD processes.

Assuming this responsibility was also seen as a means to counter or appease the stress related to a period of familiarization with something new. One of the teachers noted, "It is now more intense because it is something new, which will create stress, concern, it is not something tried out, tested. . . . It will be a period of transition, which I think will be stressful for the teacher" (Interview 23). Hence, learning of and about the new curricula prior to formal PD was a matter of personal effort for teachers who had to "run to some meetings, to some open discussions around the new curricula" on a voluntary basis (Interview 31); to participate in online forums; to read up on the reform in the press or from other sources; to visit and browse websites, including the MoEC website; to capitalize on personal and professional networks (including, for example, acquaintances who had participated in the curriculum review committees or held key positions at the state Pedagogical Institute or teachers' union); and to engage in conversations and interact with colleagues, inspectors, and subject-area counselors at school or in other settings (Interviews 2 [Teacher A], 13, 23, 31, 45, 50).

Experienced PD

Most of the examples of self-initiated and/or self-directed PD engaged in by teachers were contrasted to the formal, standardized MoEC Phase 4 seminars, which they characterized as "informative meetings" and not PD [επιμόρφωση] (e.g., Interviews 4, 12, 18, 29) since the new curricula were merely presented to them. For some teachers, such PD was unnecessary since they could have informed themselves, given that the new curricula had been available online for some time: "They might as well have told us [to] devote some personal time, study it, and then move on to practical applications [εφαρμογές]" (Interview 32). Teachers also made distinctions between Phase 4 (central, standardized, mass PD) and Phase 3 (smaller groups by subject-area along a cascade model) (e.g., Interviews 5, 30, 31, 8 [Teacher B]), finding the latter more meaningful. In general, however, the formal PD was criticized by teachers based on a number of criteria related to matters of (1) time (duration-frequency), (2) space (location in relation to size), (3) content and mode of delivery, and, finally, (4) the expertise of the PD leaders.

As far as time was concerned, the teachers thought that both Phases 3 and 4 were too short to go into any necessary depth or have any questions answered: "Every time I was informed [at a seminar] whereas I should have queries solved, new questions were born of course, which there was no time to answer" (Interview 29).

Other points of critique were that PD sessions were organized in the middle of the school year, and that they were held after rather than before the new curricula were introduced and before any teaching material production was complete. Teachers resented this particular sequence, which they actually perceived as disorderly (Interviews 31, 8 [Teacher A]). This thus conformed to and confirmed the MoEC construction of teachers as "in need" of (transmission-type) PD in order for the reform to be achieved. Some teachers expressed the need for more time to "digest" the new curricula through interacting with colleagues and trying things out "slowly and steadily" (Interviews 23, 29, 58), reasons for which Phase 3 was viewed more positively than Phase 4 in its being longer and more gradual (e.g., Interview 26).

As far as the criterion of space-size was concerned, the mass form of Phase 4 PD was severely criticized as it lacked "directness." In one teacher's words, "the fact that the number of participants was too big . . . [in groups of] 200, 250, and 300 people and it was difficult for a directness to be there" (Interview 31). Some teachers noted that even Phase 3 sessions were too large, with teachers coming from many different schools, for any real interaction to occur, thus largely missing the potential benefits of site-based over standardized PD. Though they could understand the MoEC's motive for "demographic coverage" of the teacher population, the fact that in some subject-area sessions schools were represented by only one teacher still jeopardized subject representation at the school the following year:[1]

> For example, when the new subjects were introduced, they told us English will be in. But in our school next year there might not be a teacher who has received PD, especially for the topic of English and so one of the existing teachers might have to teach the subject of English without any PD. (Interview 27)

Another issue that both Phases 3 and 4 PD seemed to overlook was that, eventually, all teachers would come into some contact with the new curricula, but only in certain subject areas; this was in contrast to teachers' self-understanding as teachers of an elementary school class and not of subjects:

> We had meetings for six teachers from each school for one subject area each. But every teacher wants to receive PD on all subject areas because he or she teaches them. . . . I mean, all teachers want to do all subject areas. It's something for which there has never been any provision. (Interview 23)

Teachers related these issues of space and size with the third criterion of "mode and content of delivery." As evident in teachers' accounts of these sessions, the large number of teachers in one room had "material" consequences in having teachers feeling silenced, bored (Interview 32), and rendered passive throughout the process of PD, at times without even an opportunity to pose questions (e.g., Interview 23). This setting led them to disbelieve that their questions and suggestions would be heard or considered, even when voiced:

> They themselves [the PD leaders] however, when we were discussing, had their reactions. I mean, both the inspectors and the committee members were wondering because they said, "Until now, many of our remarks have not been heard." And they had their doubts themselves if they would be heard. That's why I leave, I left with stress and I wonder what will happen next. (Interview 8 [Teacher C])

Despite this frustration over form, it should be noted that in terms of content, teachers generally agreed with the philosophy of the new curricula as presented during PD for pedagogical reasons: There was no overall disagreement with the ideal for a "humane and democratic school" (e.g., Interviews 49, 34, 55), or the change itself as education "should not be static" (Interview 23). However, they generally felt that the content of the Phase 3 PD was insufficient, being "vague," "theoretical" (Interviews 5, 29), "too general" (Interview 34), "confusing" (Interview 20), "hasty" (Interview 5), "superficial" (Interview 3 [Teacher B]), and not very convincing over the value of change (Interview 29) or what was really new (Interviews 24, 31).

Finally, critique over the content of the sessions was connected to who had delivered the seminars, the fourth criterion during this analysis. For instance, the teachers reported that school inspectors (mostly) had not been sufficiently aware and involved in the reform process to provide accurate information. They were seen by teachers as "just transferring some things" (Interview 34), as "not being persuaded, from what it seemed, on these new curricula" (Interview 31), as being inconsistent between them (Interview 23), and as not responding to questions adequately (Interview 34), if at all:

> A PowerPoint presentation by the responsible inspector was not appropriate.... I think we were not appropriately informed and any queries posed, the reactions we got were "we will note this and refer it further above." So, I think the PD was done just for the sake of being done. (Interview 35)

These encounters led to teacher disenchantment as the inspectors—traditionally authoritative figures ensuring the implementation of the official curriculum and textbooks—were delegitimized in their eyes and, by extension, so was the PD. Teachers were more satisfied with those they thought were "experts" on the new curricula, namely academics or members of the subject-area committees (e.g., Interviews 30, 8 [Teacher A]), which is why the Phase 3 PD and the third day of the Phase 4 mass seminars were viewed more positively. Relatedly, perhaps, these were also viewed as more practical (e.g., in "mapping" content and providing examples—Interviews 34, 8 [Teacher B]) in comparison to the first two days of Phase 3 PD led by inspectors. The practicality of suggestions was also used as a criterion of differentiating among PD in selected subject areas, recognizing as effective those suggestions that helped teachers "clear things in [their] minds" (Interview 8 [Teacher B]; Interviews 29, 31, 35).

Teachers also had positive experiences from the formal PD they received, which, combined with time, they viewed as necessary for change (Interviews 21, 29). Despite weaknesses, it was recognized as useful with applied (experiential) aspects being especially valued when they were present (Interviews 16, 32), even for the sake of self-directed, informal interaction with colleagues occurring during or after the sessions (Interview 23). Such positive experiences, along with their critique of negative aspects of PD during the year, fueled the teachers' constructions of desired forms of PD, which are addressed below. These are structured under the four criteria mobilized earlier in the analysis (i.e., time, space, content and mode of delivery, and PD leaders' expertise), before bringing these together in relation to identified tensions between PD as guidance and as/for autonomy.

Desired PD

When delineating desired PD along the criterion of time, teachers spoke of lasting and continuous, formal PD, planned for the entire year and generally for the long run, "not to stop with one or two years" (Interview 26), and provided during their personal time, as they thought it was unfair to the pupils that Phase 4 PD was organized on regular working days on which schools had been closed (e.g., Interviews 2, 15). This concurred with teachers' references to gradual, constructivist, and partial PD (in some subject areas and grades) (Interviews 2 [Teachers A & B], 15, 16), or at a regular pace to "keep up" with developments (e.g., once a month—Interview 3 [Teacher A]). Such suggestions seemed to be grounded in understandings of curriculum change as a long-term process requiring parallel long-term PD to support the effort:

> I want to believe that this is how it will be approached, that it will be a process which will be evaluated slowly and repeatedly, it will be corrected and move on, because, alas, let's say if we waited for the change of the curricula all these years, only to implement with the pressure of time and hastiness. (Interview 29)

Secondly, a number of suggestions were related to the use of space (and size/scale). Rather than having to attend mass seminars, teachers suggested participating in small(er) groups at the level of the school unit or school networks, echoing site-based forms of PD and the ministry's commitment to combining central with ongoing PD. Teachers moved further, suggesting that a more localized PD would render it more "situated" and personalized (Interviews 3, 8 [Teacher B]), more attuned to school and teacher needs, and thereby conducive to the emergence of bottom-up participatory processes in curriculum change (Interview 32), resonating with a transformative view of PD. In such requests, space intersected both with the first criterion of time and with the third criterion of content/mode of delivery, as PD conducted over a long period of time was viewed as working in parallel to continuous opportunities for interaction and curriculum development in stable small groups of teachers (Interviews 13, 32). The latter potentially read as an indirect plea for the creation of conditions for more participatory/collaborative models of PD, in groups of teachers the size of which would encourage, rather than hinder, interaction, a point that relates to the third criterion.

Suggestions based on the third criterion, content/topics and mode of delivery, to some extent reiterated how subject areas were hierarchized by the MoEC, since certain subjects, as opposed to others, were deemed important enough to reach all teachers (Interviews 23, 31). Teachers connected their critique of the limited number of teachers receiving PD on a limited number of subject areas to their desire for PD in all subjects because of not knowing which subjects they would be teaching in the future (Interview 23). They also saw PD as helping them to develop a more comprehensive picture of the new curriculum, of general pedagogical trends, and of the very concept of curriculum (Interviews 13, 21, 23, 29).

In addition, teachers requested more participatory forms of PD, allowing teachers' voices to be heard from the beginning of the reform and not just at the PD stage, in ways that acknowledged their expertise (Interviews 15, 16). They repeatedly emphasized the need for PD to move to the microlevel of the classroom and the meso-level of the school, speaking of PD as customized and personalized support to attend to a teacher's (or school's) needs through *mentoring* provided primarily by subject-area counselors (Interviews 29, 32), which would facilitate *learning by doing, collaborating, and experimenting*, as well as allow room for failure, so long as the latter was integrated in reflective practice and augmented by continuous practical advice and support (Interviews 13, 32).

Suggestions for more participatory forms of PD, however, coexisted with requests for forms of structured guidance that would give teachers "practical" tools to use in the classroom, thereby construing PD as guidance, as coaching with direct implications and relevance for their practice. In perceiving autonomy as something just now granted to them by the MoEC, teachers saw the need for them to be "guided" in how to enact it: "We want real help and I emphasize that. The autonomy they give us is great but if they don't educate us, our educational system will dissolve into chaos" (Interview 3 [Teacher B]). Examples of such support were requests for more "practical" PD with more "guidelines" (Interviews 25, 8 [Teacher C]), accompanied by constructions of "curriculum" as providing a more unitary mode/framework of working, and as a means to secure quality in teaching and progression from grade to grade (Interviews 16, 29). One particularly characteristic example of "practical" guidance requests were calls for *model lessons* taught by other teachers, subject-area counselors, or themselves, which teachers could observe in order to better understand what was expected of them, live (Interview 25) or through the use of video recordings (Interview 32) of such lessons. In effect, in conceptualizing PD as a form of practical training, teachers subscribed to traditional binaries of theory vs. practice, which conceive of the two as separate or even antithetical, rather than recognizing their complementarity. Yet, interestingly, at the same time they endorsed conceptualizations of knowledge as practical/empirical (Enthoven & de Bruijn, 2010) when emphasizing the complexity and dynamic nature of the classroom as a field from which and in which a different but equally valued type of classroom-based knowledge arises and is needed:

> What we felt very intensely was that we wanted more to see practically the implementation. I mean, the theory, anybody can take the curriculum and read it. And we know now, us educators, that theory is very far apart from practice. I mean it's different to say "it must, it must, it must," and it is very different to implement those things in a class, in Cyprus, in the specific school, at the given moment. (Interview 32)

As a result of such formulations, and in relation to the fourth criterion, teachers suggested different "experts" to provide the various forms of PD they requested but envisioned one among them as the "ideal." In doing so, teachers acknowledged and hierarchized a multiplicity of knowledges and expertise: academic, managerial, and classroom-based (Theodorou et al.,

2012), using the latter as leverage to render their own expertise visible and challenge that of academics (Interview 32). For instance, teachers saw academics or subject-area counselors as the more suitable PD leaders for "in-depth" subject-focused PD, as opposed to inspectors who, although seen as holders of managerial expertise, were reported by teachers as often not being in a position to answer their queries in a knowledgeable manner (Interviews 29, 30, 31, 8 [Teacher A]) at the more general "superficial-theoretical" mass seminars. Reversely, teachers saw other teachers or subject-area counselors as more suitable than inspectors and even academics for "practical" or experiential forms of PD (such as model lessons or workshops), those who could relate PD directly to their teaching practice in the sense that they would "train" or "coach" them on the use of specific teaching materials or books, regarded as particularly useful or even necessary in the absence of school textbooks. In this sense, subject-area counselors were deemed to be the ideal PD providers, as the embodiment of both academic and classroom-based expertise, giving teachers the best of both worlds: just enough theoretical background to keep them versed in the language of the reform and plenty of the much-desired examples of practical implementation.

DISCUSSION

From Autonomy to Guidance and Back

The professionalization of teachers—mainly through (relative) autonomy over curricular matters and teaching, participation in decision-making processes, and through continuous professional (self-)development—constituted a rhetorical and discursive opening at the moment of its introduction in 2004, when the reform of the Greek-Cypriot educational system was launched. As teacher educators in this context, involved in initial and in-service teacher education, we hoped that this opening would create more possibilities for teacher repositioning in more socially just ways as an example of how schooling could be reimagined as democratic. These hopes were anchored in different meanings of professionalism, where teachers' self-regulation and autonomy in practice are central (e.g., extended professionality [Evans, 2008]), as well as classical and complex professionalism (Hargreaves & Goodson, 1996). Yet the circumstances under which such discursive openings appeared, changed, and materialized as the reform moved from policy rhetoric to implementation objectivized teachers as professionals with PD holding a central and crucial position in this process of teacher subjection and subjectivation (Kontovourki et al., 2015).

Against this background, and located as researchers in a theoretical and epistemological space wherein teacher voice and experience is of value, we simultaneously sought teachers' perceptions of such PD to explore how these discursive openings at the policy level were taken up, negotiated, and resignified by teachers themselves. Looking at teachers' critiques of the PD that they experienced at the introduction of new curricula, their suggestions over desired forms of PD, and the discursive rifts created by the envisioning of "professional autonomous pedagogues" at a policy level, one distinguishes the potential all of these held for creating openings for resignifying teachers as professional pedagogues and reconstituting them as agentive participants in the PD and broader reform process in more equitable ways than prior to the reform. However, the ways in which teachers were cast by the MoEC as passive receivers of knowledge through the provided standardized and centralized PD, and also the ways in which teachers positioned themselves as curriculum implementers in relation to their PD experience, significantly diverted from the official proclamation for (re) positioning teachers. Hence, the "briefing" nature of the seminars that focused on informing and familiarizing teachers with the new curricula turned out to be incompatible with the notion of professional autonomy, which was presented as a paradigm shift during PD in the given context of the reform: a point of incompatibility that was accentuated as teachers, in turn, expected more over *what to do with* the new curricula within this new paradigm of autonomy. Such responses are telling of the tensions and contradictions created when "granting" autonomy to professionals who have been historically subjected to control without concurrently altering the structures or practices in which relationships are immersed, and without attending to the skills, values, and sensibilities that teachers need in order to engage in transformative professional development.

These contradictions eventually resulted in teachers regressing to requests for state guidance, which undermined their professional autonomy, and in the state falling short of fulfilling its promise for democratization of/through the reform. In a sense, both the ministry—in opting to provide the kind of content-focused, informative seminars, mass or small-scale, that it did—and the teachers themselves—in jettisoning theory over an emphasis on the practical—were, in fact, undercutting the repositioning of teachers as professionals. The former by stripping the reform of the vision, values, and aims it wished to promote and reducing it to a matter of curriculum content change, which was communicated through teacher PD that positioned teachers not as autonomous pedagogues but as policy executers. The latter did so in constricting the meaning of teacher professionalism by positioning themselves through their persistent requests for recipe-like guidance/PD—especially in the form of teaching material—not as professional pedagogues but as curriculum implementers.

Furthering the argument that teachers' (re)positioning as professionals during curriculum change is a process involving both openings and constrictions set by both contextual realities and teachers themselves, we identify three issues regarding PD in which these were instantiated, as those emerged from the findings presented above: constructions of PD (mostly in terms of form and scale), of worthwhile knowledge, and of guidance as the primary goal of teacher PD. Setting them up front as closely interlinked and interdependent, we discuss each point attending both to openings and constrictions, by the state and the teachers.

In terms of the PD form, the analysis indicates that teachers were critical of the provided mass PD because of a perceived lack of expertise of the teacher trainers, the large participant size and traditional physical layout of the sessions, the long duration and limited frequency of the sessions, and the focus on the presentation of the new official curricula with little opportunity for interaction and negotiation. With the PD construed merely as "informative," the MoEC positioned teachers as in need of information to be "transmitted" from external "upper/expert" to "lower/non-expert" levels in the hierarchy, thus adopting standardized transmission forms of PD (e.g., Dadds, 2014; Gaible & Burns, 2005). Located by the MoEC as being at the bottom of this hierarchy (as reflected in PD phases), teachers seemed to resent and resist such positioning, often noting that it was in tension with the tenets of the "autonomous professional pedagogue" and the "democratic and humane school," which were the quintessential values of the reform and of which teachers were reminded during the PD. As Dadds (2014) noted, "it is antithetical to democracy and the educative enterprise" to "assume that those who work closest to children should have their thinking about the nature of 'good practice' arranged for them by those outside schools" (p. 10).

Teachers thus envisioned different forms of PD, which they thought would be more effective on the conditions that: (1) they valued their or others' expertise as experienced practitioners and, (2) they allowed time for interaction and participatory, reflective, iterative, and collaborative processes that would enable them to have their voices heard, the latter condition also connecting with claims for having their practical (i.e., classroom) expertise recognized (see also Theodorou et al., 2012). These requests indeed opened up the field of PD to transformative learning experiences that resonated with the notions of "continuing" professional learning and professional learning communities (PLC), which converge in construing PD as a long-term process to be pursued at the workplace with colleagues (e.g., Ellis, 2007; Stoll et al., 2006). However, the feasibility of such PD (and possibility for openings) should be considered vis-à-vis characteristics of the context and, especially, the fact identified by teacher-interviewees that school staff in Greek-Cypriot schools changes every school year. This, along with the imposition of mass PD seminars as compulsory for all teachers (Phase 4) and the participation of selected teachers in more intense

PD based upon state-defined criteria and others' (principals') decision (Phase 3), subvert the possibility that PD could be organized around PLCs based on voluntary participation, intrinsic motivation, and commitment.

Such PD forms are widely seen as serving both teacher PD *and* the production of knowledge, even though the latter has been weaker in comparison to the PD aim (McIntyre, 2008). Such knowledge is usually "practical," which is more relevant to teacher contexts (e.g., Gibbons, Limoges, Nowotny, Schwartzman, Scott, & Trow, 1994; Hargreaves, 1996; Tam, 2014), as participation in these learning and working communities aims at "explicating the locally existing tacit professional knowledge...and, sometimes, at creating new relevant, practical knowledge that is also recognized as a legitimate knowledge source" (Enthoven & de Bruijn, 2010, p. 289). Practical knowledge is dependent upon context and use, and often contrasted to formal, academic-scientific knowledge that has value in reference to requirements for codification, and as generic knowledge that can eventually derive from the former (Bevins & Price, 2014; Enthoven & de Bruijin, 2010; Gibbons et al., 1994). However, when teachers in this study mistrusted the value of "theory" as "pure" academic knowledge and criticized the provided PD seminars for offering "knowledge-for-practice," or rather knowledge-without-practice, they did not demand to co-determine curriculum, nor did they argue for their practical knowledge to be acknowledged and employed. Rather, just as they were carving openings through their claims for transformative PD, they were simultaneously closing them down by reiterating the theory vs. practice binary in ways that eventually undervalued their professed expertise. This was evidenced in their incongruous desire for long-term, small-size, collaborative forms of PD by the person presumed to ideally combine theoretical and practical knowledge (subject-area counselor) and their insistence on the provision of guidance/training on how to deliver the (given) new curriculum, mainly through ready-made materials or exemplary lessons. And even though the latter bear the potential of challenging the binary of practice-theory and creating contextual cues for discussions in communities (Marsh & Mitchell, 2014; Wise, Padmanabhan, & Duffy, 2009), teachers in this case repeatedly conceived of them as models to follow rather than examples to reflect on.

Teachers thus requested forms of PD with strong elements of guidance and transmission, which further widened the division between theoretical/academic knowledge and tacit/practical knowledge by construing the two as separate entities. Such PD undermines notions of complex professionalism and threatens teacher autonomy by leading to knowledge-in-practice rather than knowledge-of-practice. As Villegas-Reimers (2003) warned,

> [E]ven when teachers and their societies have the intention of promoting the role of teachers as researchers, the long-existing perception of teachers as being mere interpreters of the knowledge handed down to them by experts is a

tough barrier to overcome before it is possible to revolutionize the expectations and practices related to teachers and teaching. (p. 111)

In the historicized present of teachers in Cyprus, the transmission PD approach adopted for the introduction of the new curricula was not very different from the traditional PD provision that prevailed in the past and has taken the form of "experts" delivering information at "off-site" meetings (Karagiorgi & Lymbouridou, 2009). Though there have been previous calls for transformative forms of PD such as action research (e.g., Karagiorgi, Kalogirou, Theodosiou, Theophanous, & Kendeou, 2008; Koutselini, 2007), systemic support for reflection, self-study, and feedback on teaching these has been rather weak (Karagiorgi & Nicolaidou, 2009).

As argued in this chapter, at this point in time, PD for teachers in Cyprus stands as a moment riddled with contradiction: It is both an exertion of centralized state power that has undermined its own attempts to (re)position teachers as "autonomous professional pedagogues," and a forum in which and with which teachers have concurrently created and confined intentions to (re)signify their sense of professionalism through the voicing of their concerns and desires over PD. The questioning of mass, standardized/centralized PD alongside teachers' demands for more localized and collaborative PD to cater to their individual and school needs with the aim of better implementing the (given) new curricula (rather than creating their own) reminds us that antinomies and tensions are produced when curriculum change becomes a top-down policy mandate that is unaccompanied by destabilizations and reconfigurations of hierarchies of/ in structures, and structures in hierarchies. Thus, neither teachers' desired PD nor the state's ongoing, school-based PD (through the subject counselor, in this case) could ever serve as a guarantee against practices and mentalities that end up deskilling and deprofessionalizing teachers and are often masked under the guise of promoting teacher "autonomy," "professionalization," and "reform."

NOTE

1. Teachers are traditionally centrally appointed to different schools at the beginning of each school year regardless of who might have received PD for the new curricula.

ACKNOWLEDGMENTS

This research was partially funded by the European University Cyprus Internal Research Grant Award and by funds from the University of Cyprus. We would like to acknowledge the contribution of the students enrolled in EDG 402 "Curriculum development" and EDG216 "Greek Language

Teaching for the Primary School" during the Spring Semester 2011 at the European University Cyprus for their help in collecting the data.

REFERENCES

Beck, J. (2008). Governmental professionalism: Professionalising or deprofessionalising teachers in England? *British Journal of Educational Studies, 56*(2), 119–143.

Bevins, S., & Price, G. (2014). Collaboration between academics and teachers: A complex relationship. *Educational Action Research, 22*(2), 270–284.

Buysse, V., Sparkman, K. L., & Wesley, P. W. (2003). Communities of practice: Connecting what we know with what we do. *Exceptional Children, 69*(3), 263–277.

Cochran-Smith, M., & Lytle, S. L. (1999). Relationships of knowledge and practice: Teacher learning in communities. *Review of Research in Education,* 24, 249–305.

Dadds, M. (2014). Continuing professional development: Nurturing the expert within. *Professional Development in Education, 40*(1), 9–16.

Day, C., & Sachs, J. (2004). Professionalism, performativity and empowerment: Discourses in the politics, policies and purposes of continuing professional development. In C. Day & J. Sachs (Eds.), *International handbook on the continuing professional development of teachers* (pp. 3–32). Berkshire, UK: Open University Press.

Ellis, V. (2007). Taking subject knowledge seriously: From professional knowledge recipes to complex conceptualizations of teacher development. *Curriculum Journal, 18*(4), 447–462.

Enthoven, M., & de Bruijn, E. (2010). Beyond locality: The creation of public practice-based knowledge through practitioner research in professional learning communities and communities of practice. A review of three books on practitioner research and professional communities. *Educational Action Research, 18*(2), 289–298.

Evans, L. (2008). Professionalism, professionality and the development of education professionals. *British Journal of Educational Studies, 56*(1), 20–38.

Gaible, E., & Burns, M. (2005). *Using technology to train teachers: Appropriate uses of ICT for teacher professional development in developing countries.* Washington, DC: World Bank. Retrieved from http://www.infodev.org/articles/using-technology-train-teachers

Gibbons, M., Limoges, C., Nowotny, H., Schwartzman, S., Scott, P., & Trow, M. (1994). *The new production of knowledge: The dynamics of science and research in contemporary societies.* London, UK: Sage.

Hargreaves, D. H. (1996). *Teaching as a research-based profession: Possibilities and prospects.* London, UK: Teacher Training Agency.

Hargreaves, A., & Goodson, I. (1996). Teachers' professional lives: Aspirations and actualities. In I. Goodson & A. Hargreaves (Eds.), *Teachers' professional lives* (pp. 1–27). London, UK: Falmer Press.

Hilferty, F. (2008). Theorising teacher professionalism as enacted discourse of power. *British Journal of Sociology of Education, 29*(2), 161–173.

Karagiorgi, Y., Kalogirou, C., Theodosiou, V., Theophanous, M., & Kendeou, P. (2008). Underpinnings of adult learning in formal teacher professional development in Cyprus. *Journal of In-Service Education, 34*(2), 125–146.

Karagiorgi, Y., & Lymbouridou, C. (2009). The story of an online teacher community in Cyprus. *Professional Development in Education, 35*(1), 119–138.

Karagiorgi, Y., & Nicolaidou, M. (2009). Elementary school leaders' approaches towards staff development in Cyprus schools. *International Studies in Educational Administration, 37*(3), 71–83.

Kennedy, A. (2014). Models of continuing professional development: A framework for analysis. *Professional Development in Education, 40*(3), 336–351.

Kimble, C., Hildreth, P., & Bourdon, I. (Eds.). (2007). *Communities of practice: Creating learning environments for educators.* Charlotte, NC: Information Age Publishing.

Kontovourki, S., Theodorou, E., & Philippou, S. (2015). Governing teachers through curriculum reform in Cyprus: Subjects or subjects? In H.-G. Kothoff & E. Klerides (Eds.), *Governing educational spaces: Knowledge, teaching, and learning in transition* (pp. 107–126). Rotterdam, Netherlands: Sense Publishers.

Koutselini, M. (2007). Participatory teacher development at schools: Processes and issues. *Action Research, 5*(4), 443–462.

Maloney, C., & Konza, D. (2011). A case study of teachers' professional learning: Becoming a community of professional learning or not? *Issues in Educational Research, 21*(1), 75–87.

Marsh, B., & Mitchell, N. (2014). The role of video in teacher professional development. *Teacher Development: An International Journal of Teachers' Professional Development, 18*(3), 403–417.

McIntyre, D. (2008). Researching schools. In C. McLaughlin, K. Black-Hawkins, D. McIntyre, & A. Townsend (Eds.), *Networking practitioner research* (pp. 13–41). London, UK: Routledge.

Ministry of Education and Culture (MoEC), Educational Reform Committee. (2004). *Democratic and humane paideia in the Eurocypriot polity.* Nicosia, Cyprus: Author.

Ministry of Education and Culture. (2010). *Νέα Αναλυτικά Προγράμματα 2010–2011: Ενημερωτικό Δελτίο* [New curricula, 2010–2011: Information bulletin]. Nicosia, Cyprus: Cyprus Pedagogical Institute.

Ministry of Education and Culture & Pedagogical Institute, (2010, August 10). Αρ. Φακ.: ΠΙ 7.7.09.16. Προσφορά προγράμματος επιμόρφωσης στο πλαίσιο εισαγωγής των νέων Αναλυτικών Προγραμμάτων [Professional development seminars for practicing educators in the context of the introduction of the New Curricula]. Nicosia, Cyprus: Cyprus Pedagogical Institute.

Moate, J. (2014). A narrative account of a teacher community. *Teacher Development: An International Journal of Teachers' Professional Development, 18*(3), 384–402.

Mockler, N. (2005). Trans/forming teachers: New professional learning and transformative teacher professionalism. *Journal of In-Service Education, 31*(4), 733–746.

Persianis, P. K. (2010). *Τα πολιτικά της εκπαίδευσης στην Κύπρο κατά τους δύο τελευταίους αιώνες (1812–2009)* [The politics of education in Cyprus over the last two centuries (1812–2009)]. Nicosia, Cyrus: University of Nicosia Publications.

Philippou, S., Kontovourki, S. & Theodorou, E. (2014). Can autonomy be imposed? Examining teacher (re)positioning during the ongoing curriculum change in Cyprus. *Journal of Curriculum Studies, 46*(5), 611–633.

Priestley, M., Edwards, R., Priestley, A., & Miller, K. (2012). Teacher agency in curriculum making: Agents of change and spaces for manoeuvre. *Curriculum Inquiry, 42*(2), 191–214.

Stoll, L., Bolam, R., Wallace, M., & Thomas, S. (2006). Professional learning communities: A review of literature. *Journal of Educational Change, 7*(4), 221–258.

Tam, A. (2015). The role of a professional learning community in teacher change: A perspective from beliefs and practices. *Teachers and teaching: Theory and practice, 21*(1), 22–43.

Theodorou, E., Kontovourki, S., & Philippou, S. (2012, July). *Whose knowledge counts? Teachers' discourses on expertise during curriculum change in Cyprus.* Paper presented at the 13th annual Conference of the International Society for the Study of European Ideas (ISSEI), Nicosia, Cyprus.

Villegas-Reimers, E. (2003). *Teacher professional development: An international review of the* literature. Paris, France: International Institute for Educational Planning. Retrieved from http://www.unesco.org/iiep

Vongalis-Macrow, A. (2007). I, teacher: Re-territorialization of teachers' multi-faceted agency in globalized education. *British Journal of Sociology of Education, 28*(4), 425–439.

Wise, A. F., Padmanabhana, P., & Duffy, T. M. (2009). Connecting online learners with diverse local practices: The design of effective common reference points for conversation. *Distance Education, 30*(3), 317–338.

Wood, D. R. (2007). Professional learning communities: Teachers, knowledge, and knowing. *Theory into Practice, 46*(4), 281–290.

CHAPTER 11

ACROSS CULTURAL BOUNDARIES

Immigrant Teachers As Potential for Dialoguing

Inna Abramova

ABSTRACT

As a part of a larger study, I explored how the beliefs of Russian-speaking immigrant teachers about the role of a teacher were shaped by their prior experiences of living in the Soviet Union. I acted as a participant and not as an authority in the research process (Phillion & He, 2008). In this chapter, I reflect on our often overlapping collective memories and make connections between the past and the present to bring our experiences with the curriculum in diverse contexts and perspectives on teaching to the forefront. I argue that immigrant teachers' voices, which are still marginalized in teacher education, have to sound loudly, as they create spaces for thinking in transformative ways about what teaching and learning in multicultural contexts entails. Among the themes is understanding of teaching as emotional, sociocultural, and professional enterprise, as well as the work for social justice.

Internationalizing Teaching and Teacher Education for Equity, pages 181–200
Copyright © 2016 by Information Age Publishing
181

INTRODUCTION

Immigrant teachers' stories have been the focus of educational research in recent years. They have become the milieu through which researchers learn about teachers' lives, careers, and teaching. Many narratives have revealed that in the process of becoming teachers, immigrant teachers encountered problems. These problems were related to their differences in race (Beynon, Ilieva, & Dichupa, 2004), social class (Cruickshank, 2004), immigrant status (Michael, 2006), gender (Walsh, 2007), and language (Braine, 2010). Research has also indicated, however, that immigrant teachers bring their cultural, social, and linguistic capital to schooling and actively use these assets in teaching. They develop a sense of belonging in students (Elbaz, 2005) and use students' languages as resources for learning; they instill in them pride in their culture (Monzo & Rueda, 2001) and help them learn about other cultures (Ng, 2006). Immigrant teachers become cultural brokers in their communication with parents (Kamhi-Stein, 2004); they see language as a potential for dialoguing and as a way to empower students to acquire new content knowledge (Maum, 2003). Moreover, they involve community members in school activities and become advocates for students (Bascia & Hargreaves, 2000).

There is a lack of research, however, that explores the role of context and how it shapes immigrant teachers' beliefs about teaching. Such contextual factors as immigrant teachers' past and present situations, socioeconomic conditions of the family, educational background, and the influences of educational institutions, among others, are important because they shed light on values, perceptions of teaching, and practice that immigrant teachers bring to schooling. These beliefs and practices are also shaped by their prior experiences of living and teaching in different sociocultural and political contexts (Goodson, 1994).

At the same time, it is important to understand the immigrant experience from the perspective of the immigrant; immigrant stories reveal a sense of the complexity of the immigrant experience in the multicultural landscape (Abramova, 2012). Each story represents a voice that is distinct, and each story holds meaning that is important for a person who has lived it. Some scholars have emphasized the need to attend to voices. Bakhtin (1981) referred to the concept of language and argued that language was associated with the multiplicity of voices that could represent the language of the lawyer, the doctor, the businessman, the politician, and the public education teacher, among others (Bakhtin, 1981). According to Bakhtin, each language is symbolic of specific points of view on the world, various ideas and philosophies that could supplement or contradict and conflict with each other. At the same time, they all are in relation to one another. However, little attention has been paid to the concept of multivoicedness in relation to the experiences of immigrant teachers and the efforts they have made to claim a voice in a particular social, historic, and cultural setting (Elbaz, 2005). In this chapter, I reflect on the immigrant experiences of teachers from the Soviet-Russian context and illuminate their multiple voices and their collective memories. I believe that this study will contribute to the understanding of positive effects of internationalization of teacher education.

THE STARTING POINT FOR THE INQUIRY

Little research has been done on immigrant teachers from the former Soviet Union who now live and work in the United States. One study was aimed at identifying factors that prevented teachers from Russia from continuing their teaching careers in the United States (McFadden, 2002). Among the factors given were a language barrier, the complicated application process, the lack of information about resources, differences in pedagogical practices, and family issues. Another study explored the lived experiences of bilingual paraeducators (Carrison, 2007). The findings demonstrated that the teachers in the study exhibited leadership skills and used culturally relevant pedagogy in their teaching. None of the studies on Russian-speaking immigrant teachers have explored how contextual factors have shaped their beliefs.

This research is based on the gaps in the literature, and it adheres to the major ideas and principles of multicultural education. These principles acknowledge that cultural difference has to be recognized; these principles criticize assimilative practices and repressive institutions (Duarte & Smith, 2000). Moreover, this research is based on the ideas of multicultural education for social justice. The underlying goals of multicultural education for social justice are to create conditions that support diverse individuals and communities, explore issues that have political and social importance, and invite educators to become agents for social change by participating actively in the transformation of society (Kincheloe & Steinberg, 1997).

The purpose of this inquiry was to explore how immigrant teachers' beliefs about teaching and learning were shaped by their personal histories within a broader context, and how they understood their roles as teachers in a new cultural setting. In this narrative, I acted as a participant and observer. I start the narration with vignettes from my life and elaborate on how critical incidents influenced my beliefs. I place my narrative in the context of sociocultural and political events. Then, I introduce the theoretical framework and methodology, and present the findings from my participants' vignettes from their narratives. I identify themes that often overlap the narratives and discuss them in the context of educational policies and events.

DISCOVERING SOCIAL JUSTICE IN EDUCATION

When . . . a writer knows he or she has something to say and feels the power of voice,
that writer must find a way of saying what he or she wishes to speak.
—Clandinin & Connelly, 2000, p. 147

In this section, I illuminate key points that have influenced my understanding of my role as a teacher and directed my understanding of the importance of multiculturalism in education. During my graduate studies, as I was taking a course in multicultural education, I wrote a cultural autobiography paper in which I shared my experiences with different cultures and languages. There, I shared my early memories from age seven to nine years old. In the late 1960s, I lived in Tallinn, the capital of Estonia, which was a part of the Soviet Union at that time. My family lived in an apartment complex in the center of Tallinn. Children of my age used to play in the backyard for hours after school. Usually, a group of six or eight boys and girls gathered together and spent hours playing imaginary games. Russian and Estonian children rarely played together because of the language barrier. Often, however, I heard the words that the children said to each other, "We do not want to play with you Russians," and "We do not want to play with you Estonians." Although these episodes took place long ago, I still remember them. There was something offensive in the words that were said on both sides; moreover, there was some emerging conflict. As a graduate student, I began to value the power of reflective practice, which helped me realize that children have to develop multicultural understanding and learn how to appreciate and value differences at an early age (Paley, 1989). I also came to realize how critically important it was to develop cultural knowledge, skills, and respectful attitudes towards people from different ethnic, racial, and cultural groups in order to be able to understand them and communicate with them effectively.

When describing the next stage of my pedagogical development, I bring my personal experience to the inquiry and connect the personal with political (Phillion & He, 2008). After graduation from a pedagogical institute in the Soviet Union in 1979, I began to look for a job. At that time, my ambition was to become a translator of the English language and I was looking for a job in one of the research institutes. Incidentally, all of the places where I applied had security constraints. Imagine my surprise when officials returned my passport to me with the words, "Sorry, we cannot hire you." I was frustrated and needed explanations. Eventually, I received a reply from an authoritative figure: "Sorry, your husband is a Jew." This episode played a dramatic role in my personal life because I had to change my children's last names to prevent them from experiencing similar problems in the future. In fact, from 1934 until the mid-1990s, all Soviet citizens were equipped with an internal passport in which nationality was stated in "the fifth graph" (Simonsen, 1996). This "graph" was discriminatory because it deprived many ethnic minorities of work and other opportunities and, in extreme cases, some members of minority groups were deported solely on basis of their ethnicity, which was stated on the fifth line in their internal passport, or in their so-called "fifth point" entry (Simonsen, 2005). Consequently, my personal experience of discrimination led me to thoughts of social justice. I began to think about the existing injustices in the society, and how different groups of people were not provided with equal access to opportunities because of their culture, ethnicity, or race.

When I was teaching English as a foreign language in a secondary school in the late 1990s I had another incident, which was my first recognition of the concept of race in my educational experience. My students had to read a text in English about New York City. They learned from this text that Harlem was "the ghetto where Negroes lived." At this time, neither teachers nor students in the school knew that the word "Negro" was not acceptable anymore in a global educational community. A PhD student from the U.S. told the school teachers about the issue of political correctness, which in this case referred to language that addressed racial discrimination against a particular group of people. The school community participated in the discussion, which led to a conversation about the importance of cultural sensitivity. That incident opened my eyes to the cultural aspects of education. Overall, these experiences became starting points for my adherence to the principles of multicultural education as a move toward internationalizing teacher education for social justice.

As a graduate student, I was inspired by the ideas of scholars who raised critical questions regarding educational equity and social justice. Among them were Joe Kincheloe, bell hooks, Jonathan Kozol, Christine Sleeter, and many others. I was fascinated by the concepts of critical thinking and encouraged my students to explore educational issues from multiple perspectives (hooks, 2010). I agreed with the view of multiculturalism that emphasized the power of difference when it was conceptualized within a larger concern for social justice (Kincheloe & Steinberg, 1997). When I taught courses for undergraduate and graduate students in teacher education at the university, I focused on controversial topics such as "achievement gaps," "stereotyping," and "educational equity," and I believed that debates would make my students think more deeply about these issues. In class, we discussed the difference between the subject-oriented curriculum and the social justice curriculum, and how schools could prepare students to create a more equitable society. The students participated in the inquiry process and problem-solving activities and shared their views on how they could personally participate in making their local communities, schools, and classrooms a better place. They interviewed principals and teachers and wrote letters to the editor with the purpose of sharing their concerns about existing problems. I also asked my students to share their experiences with diversity and believed that they would develop cultural awareness, cultural sensitivity, and empathetic attitudes by critically examining who they were in relation to others (He & Phillion, 2008). In open conversations, I emphasized the role of culture, language, ethnicity, race, and other categories of diversity. I wanted to develop cultural competence and critical thinking skills in them, and I encouraged them to actively participate in the life of school, community, and society in order to make the world a better place. One of the topics on which we focused was immigration. While teaching, I used to share my experiences of living in the Soviet Union and discuss my immigrant experiences. Consequently, the experiences of immigrant teachers in the United States became the focus of my dissertation research. Based on my own experiences as an immigrant teacher, I began to wonder what beliefs about education and experiences immigrant teachers from the Soviet-Russian contexts brought to the Unites States, and how they implemented these beliefs in practice. I was also interested to know how they adjusted to a new cultural environment and how they felt about their roles as teachers in a new cultural situation.

BUILDING CONCEPTUAL UNDERSTANDING

The conceptual framework for my inquiry was developed based on the ideas of multicultural education and curriculum theory. Multicultural education was chosen because it emphasized the importance of culture including language, ethnicity, social class, and gender in understanding beliefs. Curriculum theory was selected because it emphasized the importance of experience, which was critical for understanding beliefs of immigrant teachers. Mikhail Bakhtin's theory of language (1981) provided insight for understanding beliefs from the perspective of language used by the participants. As beliefs are constructs shaped by language, I had to pay attention to specific cultural meanings embedded in the language use. The conceptual framework, which illuminated such concepts as experience, context, and culture in understanding beliefs and experiences of immigrant teachers, provided a working theory for my inquiry. I emphasized the idea that language was an interpretive lens through which teachers conceptualized their teaching worlds (Abramova, 2011). I believe that context—including family heritage, ethnic background, socioeconomic conditions, educational background, and the influences of educational institutions, political conditions, and other factors (Cole & Knowles, 2001)—was important for understanding beliefs. Culture was defined as aspects of human experience including customs, rituals, habits, attitudes, beliefs, values, and norms (Duarte &

Smith, 2000). I assumed that language had social and cultural meanings that reflected an individual's experience and the contexts in which the individual lived (Bakhtin, 1981).

WALKING IN THE FIELD

The collection of data was an ongoing process in the inquiry. The data were collected in different ways. Five immigrant teachers were interviewed twice, before and after observations of their teaching. Between the interviews, the teachers were observed in various settings such as the school, home, church, and other places. After teaching they were asked to comment on their teaching practice. Other methods of data collection included gathering demographic information from researcher-developed questionnaires, my field notes, and my reflective journals. The data were analyzed on two levels. On the first level of analysis, I illuminated the beliefs of each individual participant and placed them in context of their prior and current experiences. On the second level, I asked myself questions about the meanings and social importance of the findings, which constituted the interpretive analytic process in the research (Clandinin & Connelly, 2000). In the inquiry, I became the researcher and collaborator. I developed relationships of trust with my participants when I shared my personal story while I was listening to the stories of others (Conle, 1996).

In this narrative, I refer to the vignettes of my participants: Dina, Lena, Sasha, Rita, and Nina. Four of them are females and one is a male (Sasha). All teachers, including myself, were raised and educated in the former Soviet Union and immigrated to the United States during or soon after the collapse of the Soviet Union in 1991, which means that we were exposed to similar sociocultural and educational environments. Two of the five participants were people whom I knew well. Each successive participant was named by a preceding individual. The "snowball sampling" strategy (McMillan & Schumacher, 2001) allowed me to find participants scattered throughout the population of a Midwestern state in the United States.

Dina immigrated to the United States following her husband, who was a U.S. citizen. Upon arrival, she worked in a school where she taught Russian to immigrants and after her diploma was evaluated, she was hired as a teacher's assistant in a kindergarten class. Lena graduated from a social studies institute and had seven years of teaching experience in high school and teaching literature in a Soviet school. She moved to the United States with her family and worked in an elementary school as a teaching assistant for one year and in a school for immigrant children where she taught Russian, literature, and history. Sasha, the only male teacher in the study, had a master's degree in music education. Before his immigration, he had worked in a musical college.

Upon his arrival in the United States with his family, he worked as an accompanist to a public school choir and did some tutoring. Nina graduated from a musical college with a master's degree and had worked in a music school for gifted children for thirteen years. In the United States, she volunteered to work in a public school as a teacher's assistant. After seven years, she was hired to teach music to undergraduate students in teacher education. She had a private practice giving music lessons to children of all ages. Rita graduated from one of the pedagogical institutions and, after graduation, worked in a public school for ten years. In the United States, she worked in a Russian school for immigrant children school for ten years. Three years ago, she was temporarily hired to teach Russian to undergraduate students at a college. She quit her job sometime during the research process. I am the researcher and narrator in this study. I graduated from a pedagogical institution in the former Soviet Union and worked in a public school for twenty years teaching English. I was a graduate student in the United States for nine years and graduated with a doctoral degree.

VIGNETTES FROM LIVED AND TOLD STORIES

*Over the years, teachers develop a store of practical knowledge that is personal
and unique, yet in part held in common with other teachers. It is shaped
by the particular biography and life experience of an individual teacher
and the way that she undergoes and interprets her work as a teacher.*

—Elbaz, 2005, p. xi

Here, I present vignettes from my participants' narratives. I illuminate their voices and my own and identify the themes that unite our narratives; these themes often overlap. I attempt to understand the influences that shape my participants' beliefs and present their beliefs in the context of their "lived and told" stories (Clandinin & Connelly, 2000, p. 20). I encourage the reader to explore the contextual factors in participants' narratives, such as the role of family, schooling and teaching experiences, and ideological aspects of education in the former Soviet Union, and think about the perspectives that immigrant teachers brought to the United States. The following themes emerged: Teaching is nurturing, teaching is developing imagination and creativity, and teacher agency is emotional, sociocultural, and professional.

TEACHING IS NURTURING

The theme of nurturing pervaded the narratives during the interviews and observational times. My participants were concerned about their students whom they worked with in the United States and cared about them. Dina emphasized that she wanted to find an individual approach to every child in the preschool and regretted that it was not always possible. She said:

> We have a girl in class. She does not understand a word in English.... I want to help her. But how can I help? It is not my language.... But I want to spend more time with her. I try to involve her. I want her to feel comfortable.

During my class observations, I noticed that Dina came up to children and asked if they needed help. When children stayed outside in cold weather, she asked them to put on warm jackets and calmed those children who were crying. I wrote in my journal:

> Parents continue bringing children. The boy is crying, he does not want to stay. Dina takes the boy by the hand and says, "Do not cry. Come with me. I will help you to find a friend." The girls are not wearing jackets although it is very cold. Dina gives them their jackets and tells them to put them on.

Lena emphasized that it order to know the child, teachers had to work with parents. She said, "I need to know what is going on in their families in order to understand my students better. If I do not know what is going on in their families, it is hard to work."

In the vignettes, my participants discussed the role of parents in their education. Dina's parents were teachers, and she used to observe her mother's lessons. Dina believed that "finding a contact with the child" was the most important attribute of a teacher. "I probably felt like a mother sometimes," she said. Lena's parents could not provide her with "additional help" for financial reasons, but they tried to develop in her a love for Russian literature by reading stories to her. It was one of the reasons she decided to become a teacher. My own parents insisted that I know at least one foreign language, and at the age of 7, they sent me to an English specialized school where I learned English from the second grade. In the Soviet Union, many teachers stayed with us for years, and this allowed us to develop a bond with favorite teachers. Lena elaborated, "My mother still meets my teacher. She knows about my life here. She knows everything about her students . . . we send her postcards and congratulate her on holidays, and even now, she remains a part of our family."

All the participants told me that their parents were willing to give them the best education possible. In the Soviet family, parents provided children with substantial emotional support to ensure the best results in education (Bronfenbrenner, 1970). Education was considered a priority; usually, parents devoted all necessary financial and psychological resources to their children, often at the expense of their own needs (Savina, 2008). Moreover, parents were supposed to participate in the harmonious all-round development and upbringing of the children, and they worked together with educational institutions to achieve this goal (Dunstan, 1983). We grew up in an environment where teachers often stayed with the same group of students for years. Teachers were responsible for their students' learning; they had to know their interests and moral qualities, family influences, and conditions (Dmitriyev, 1985). Teachers who supervised large classes usually functioned as an additional parent, and their relations with students often continued after students' graduation (Post, 2005).

TEACHING AS DEVELOPING IMAGINATION AND CREATIVITY

The theme of teaching as developing imagination and creativity in children was suggested by my observation of Rita, who participated in a "gala event" at the university to which I was invited. Rita organized this event for her 18-year-old students, who had to demonstrate their knowledge of Russian language skills learned in class. Based on this observation, I made notes in my journal:

> Students participated in various activities. They were showing a puppet theatre, reciting Russian poems and repeating tongue twisters; they were standing in a circle and playing games to revise Russian verbs; they were competing in writing activities and were receiving prizes for the best performance.

Rita told me that her love of fairy tales and creative games stemmed from her childhood and from what she learned in her teacher education program. Rita graduated from a pedagogical institute in the late 1980s. It was a time of political changes in the Soviet Union. The country became more open to the world, which affected education. In teacher education programs, more attention was paid to pedagogical studies; future teachers were taught how to integrate courses that incorporated music and art (Holmes, Read, & Voskresenskaya, 1995). Rita opened her own educational center where she taught nature studies, biology, and anatomy. She incorporated fairy tales in teaching and used role play, which she considered an effective teaching strategy. Rita incorporated role plays in teaching and told stories about nature:

> I told stories about nature, about animals, and told the students that they were a part of nature . . . and how beautiful nature was, and how important it was for humans, and that they had to love it. We had classes in the building but we often went outside.

Dina's teaching practices were somewhat similar. She brought puppets of Russian fairy tales to class, made toys of clay herself, and told stories about them. Dina shared with me that once she brought a Russian samovar and made tea for all the children. She explained, "I am trying to teach the Russian language through culture." Dina told me that she always wanted to be creative. When she worked with children in a kindergarten class in Russia, she had to follow a standardized educational program. She felt that she needed more freedom to develop the curriculum.

The themes discussed above were reflected in other teachers' narratives as well. Each of us wanted to attain a professional status in the new setting, which was not an easy process. Creativity was a way for us to express ourselves. At the same time, it embodied our struggle for voice and our desire to be recognized among students and teachers. We wanted to reveal ourselves and speak our words to show how we were different from the existing discourses (Bakhtin, 1981).

TEACHER AGENCY:
EMOTIONAL, SOCIOCULTURAL, AND PROFESSIONAL

We believed that being emotional and passionate motivated students' learning and helped to create an atmosphere of openness in the classroom. We also believed in the students' respect for the teacher's authority. Finally, we brought our cultural beliefs and cultural practices into teaching.

Emotional

During the interviews, each of my participants used the words "love" and "understanding" many times in various contexts. Sasha said, "Children feel when the teacher treats them with love. What does this mean? The teacher has to be patient. It is not the child's fault if the teachers cannot explain the material in an accessible way." Rita explicitly stated in the interviews that developing emotions in students was a part of the teacher's work. Being emotional helped her to overcome the language barrier. She reflected:

> When my students see that I am passionate, they become more interested. Emotions help me to create an open classroom atmosphere, in which my students feel comfortable to express their feelings. They help me find contact with my students and alleviate my language problems.

My experiences of teaching "resonated" with my participants' views on teaching (Conle, 1996). I used to start teaching a class in teacher education with an excerpt from the piece "How is Education Possible When There is a Body in the Middle of the Room?" (Elbaz, 2005). In this piece, the author, an immigrant teacher herself, raised a controversial question—to what extent could students share emotions across different cultures in a multicultural classroom? Instead of creating a space in which political events were left out, and in which the focus was on some "neutral" course content (p. 160), I allowed my students to openly share thoughts and feelings regarding controversial issues and discussed with them how to deal with conflict. This approach allowed me to listen to my students' voices and develop multicultural understanding in them.

We believed in the power of emotions, but the reason why we believed in that power was different for each of us. For Sasha, it was the result of his former teachers' influence. His teachers who were "patient and loving" never gave up on the student. For Rita, it was a part of her teaching philosophy shaped by her experiences of teaching in the former Soviet Union. Rita was confident that the role of a teacher was to develop a harmonious personality in the child. To achieve this goal, the teacher had to "give a child proper knowledge together with the proper attitude, and this will touch the soul."

Sociocultural

Teacher authority and respect were important subthemes that recurred in various ways in the teachers' accounts. Sasha was shocked by the "the lack of distance between the teacher and the student" in the U.S. schools, while Rita was disappointed when "the boys did not take off their hats when entering the classroom." She compared her current experiences with the time when she was a teacher in the Soviet school:

> When the teacher entered the classroom, we stood up. When the teacher left, we stood up too. We were respectful. But here...there is definitely less respect. I teach them to respect the teacher in a different way. I tell them about the Russian culture and what is expected from students.

Similarly, Lena remembered how on Teacher's Day students brought her many flowers, and how students showed respect to the teacher in Soviet schools:

> In our Soviet educational system, the teacher was supposed to teach children how to behave, and I believe this teacher's role was amazing. The teacher had much authority and could teach morals in the same way as parents did. A teacher could take an action and punish the student and had much power. I remember a situation when a boy pushed me, and I fell and hit my knee.

The teacher invited [his] parents and he apologized before me in his parents' presence. Well, teachers actively participated in upbringing.

Although Nina agreed that the teacher had more authority in Soviet schools than in United States' schools, she reflected on the change of her beliefs: "When I began teaching here, I considered myself something big. Now, I am more interested in my students. I respect them more....I am interested in them as individuals."

Nina believed that organizing extracurricular activities was an important part of teachers' work. I took notes during the class observation:

As Nina presented the syllabus for her undergraduate college students, she said, "I will give you the list of all concerts available in the area. I want you to get some experience with classical music. Please, go to the concert once a semester and write the report about it. I will give you the form."

At her school in the Soviet Union, Nina spent additional time with her students. She often invited them to take additional lessons or took them to the philharmonic on Saturday evenings.

She remarked, "Out-of-school activities were a usual practice in Soviet schools. I believe the administration expected teachers to behave that way. You would be considered a good teacher if you did these things."

Likewise, Rita participated in cultural events in the university setting, and Lena organized them in the Russian school. Lena invited her students to watch movies about the history of Russia in the evenings, and Dina volunteered to teach Russian in the preschool where she prepared concerts for parents in which her students participated. Nina shared her experiences of teaching music:

We always talk about different cultures. I always encourage them to bring to class some musical pieces from their countries. I encourage this because they, future teachers, need to know how to integrate various cultures in the curriculum and tell their students about their own country, the music of this country.

Our beliefs were shaped by our personal experiences and the context of schooling in the former Soviet Union and later in Russia. The authoritarian Soviet school influenced our beliefs about the role of a teacher. We continued to subconsciously mix the terms *authoritarian* and *authority* and assigned them cultural meanings. For example, we believed that a cultural tradition to "take hats off" when the teacher entered the classroom or the celebration of Teacher's Day symbolized respect for the teacher's authority; we did not realize, however, that such behavior might indicate the authoritarian school culture and superficial respect for the teacher and that the teacher could exhibit authority in a different way, for example, by listening to students' voices and opinions (Abramova, 2011).

In the Soviet Union, teachers were supposed to organize social activities and participate in extracurricular work. These activities included organization of class meetings, participation in various clubs where teachers developed students' interests in arts and crafts, and field trips. Often, these activities went beyond teachers' professional interests and participation in them was "the exhaustive use of the teachers' time ... the full exploitation of this trained resource ... which the state has determined are socially useful" (Rosen, 1971, p. 111). However, some teachers resisted. As Sasha noted, "I tried to organize current events in a different way ... not by focusing on political moments but by telling my students interesting facts about other countries and life in these countries, and also about historical events that took place in our country."

Professional

We believed in the necessity of professional development and in creating possibilities for English language learning in the United States. Upon arrival, each of us continued learning English in different ways. Four teachers attended English language courses, and everyone continued to learn English independently. Lena thought that immigrant teachers needed courses for professional development because there were "so many various teaching methods, various didactic materials that can help the teacher. I think it will be very useful if somebody could share these ... prepare some conferences, meetings so that teachers could improve their qualifications." It was critical for her "to work on the language all the time, to improve it, and to try to get rid of the accent." Nina liked participating in conferences and became a member of professional organizations. She said, "I feel the need to interact with my colleagues. I feel the need to participate in conferences, in workshops, and seminars. I think the teacher should never stop learning." Sasha, however, was skeptical and indicated that it was hard for him to find time for self-education. He related his "minority" status to the lack of English language skills, which he considered a "cultural difference that will not disappear throughout my life," he said.

From our country, we brought a thirst for new knowledge and the desire to learn and grow professionally. Our family members encouraged us to get good educations. Moreover, each of us had between five and fourteen years of experience in English language learning in our native country. In the Soviet schools, students began to learn English in the second or the fifth grade; bilingual or multilingual education was focused on learning another language in order to understand another culture and its historical heritage (Sinagatullin, 2001).

While we were striving to become successful in the new country, we found that it was not an easy task. Few immigrant teachers in this narrative achieved their educational goals and regained the professional status they had before they arrived. It took many years for some of them to establish themselves in their new settings. Dina, who had 10 years of teaching experience in the Soviet Union and Russia, continued to work as a teacher's assistant in a preschool. Sasha, who graduated from a musical college, worked in school guiding the orchestra and also did some tutoring. It took Nina several years to find a job at a university and Rita did not have a permanent position for 10 years and was hired only temporarily. After working in food services for several years and as a substitute teacher for a year, Lena became a graduate student at a university. Lena said that in order to find a job related to teaching, she had to continue her studies in the United States:

> You cannot do anything else but to get education here. It does not matter how long you have studied already and what education you have received. When I tried to find a job, nobody took my previous education into account. They said, "You have to get education here too."

Lena's words symbolize the dilemmas that the immigrant teachers faced. Many researchers have emphasized that barriers to the professional integration of immigrant teachers include their inability to prove previous education (Phillion, 2003). In addition, many studies have demonstrated that immigrant teachers occupy secondary positions in schools and are not promoted to senior positions (Michael, 2006). Moreover, immigrant teachers struggle with the English language and believe that their lack of English language skills is the major reason for the problems they face (Cruickshank, 2004). It is critical to raise awareness about the needs of teachers from diverse cultural backgrounds and provide them with equal access to educational opportunities, resources, and the emotional support that they need.

COUNTER NARRATIVES AS POSSIBILITIES

> *Good teachers are not just well-oiled machines. They are emotional, passionate beings who connect with their students and fill their work and their classes with pleasure, creativity, challenge and joy.*
> —Hargreaves, 1998, p. 835

In this narrative, I have presented vignettes from the life histories of six immigrant teachers from the Soviet-Russian context, including myself. I have identified the themes that unified our stories and articulated our multiple voices and views on teaching. In each case, our stories were shaped by personal histories, critical incidents in our lives, and broader discourses. The four themes that emerged were: understanding of teaching as nurturing; emotional, sociocultural, and professional work; and work for social justice. In the narratives, we talked about love and understanding, human relations, creative and imaginative work, and schooling beyond the classroom doors. We believed that parents could help us educate their children, and we spent extra time with students outside of the classroom. We were open to new perspectives and were passionate about learning. In this respect, our narratives serve as counternarratives to the commonly accepted discussions of teachers' work and educational themes in the context of teacher effectiveness and accountability and technical aspects of teaching (Abramova, 2012). The orientation presented in this narrative presents a somewhat different perspective from the mainstream and opens up a transformative way of looking at the work of teaching and asking questions about what teaching entails.

ENVISIONING THE FUTURE

In present times, U.S. society is becoming more and more diverse. In 2007, the U.S. immigrant population was 37.9 million people. Immigrants accounted for one in eight U.S. residents, the highest level in 80 years (Camarota, 2007). It is estimated that by 2050, the foreign-born population will account for about 15% of the total U.S. population (Capps, Passel, Perez-Lopez, & Fix, 2003). These demographic changes affect education in various ways. It is possible that more immigrant teachers from diverse backgrounds will work in schools. Learning about these teachers' experiences is important because this knowledge can enrich the mainstream culture. At the same time, it is one of the ways to better understand one's own culture. On the other hand, it is possible to assume that when there are more immigrant teachers in schools and more mainstream teachers are aware of their experiences, discussions of such concepts as social justice, sociocultural, and emotional aspects of the teaching profession will become more welcoming and open. As immigrant teachers bring the complexity of their cultural autobiographies and language experiences in the classroom, they contribute to discussions of diversity and how to bridge the gap between cultural differences in education.

MAKING CONNECTIONS TO TEACHER EDUCATION

Although researchers have explored the experiences of immigrant teachers in the United States, the majority of these studies have focused on the experiences of minority immigrant teachers. This narrative attempts to fill a gap in the research and presents a view on teaching from the vantage point of the immigrant teachers from the Soviet-Russian contexts. By illuminating the voices of these immigrant teachers, this narrative makes its contribution to teacher education. In preservice teacher education and multicultural education courses, teacher educators should involve their students in conversations about immigration and, among other issues, discuss international perspectives on teaching and learning. Teacher educators need to invite immigrant teachers to their classrooms so that they can share their experiences of teaching in diverse contexts with the purpose of engaging students in a dialogue around issues of social justice, language, culture, educational policies, and the overall role of a teacher in a multicultural society. These conversations provide opportunities for critical self-reflection, as students start questioning their own attitudes and beliefs towards diversity and develop multicultural competences (Sharma, Phillion, & Malewski, 2011).

On the other hand, collaboration between teacher educators and immigrant teachers in schools has to become a common practice, as it provides possibilities for transformative experience allowing integration of international practices and perspectives. Consequently, students will have more opportunities to develop critical thinking skills by listening to and learning from multiple viewpoints, which, in turn, will help them to develop knowledge, skills, and attitudes necessary to live and make informative decisions in a multicultural world.

In order to fulfill their potential, the voices of immigrant teachers have to be heard. By presenting the stories of teachers whose experiences were previously marginalized in education, I have attempted to engage in social justice-oriented work, the goal of which is to use stories to tell hidden and silenced narratives as counter narratives of underrepresented groups (Phillion & He, 2008). At the same time, I hope that learning about the experiences of immigrant teachers in this narrative will create opportunities for educators to think collectively across cultural boundaries about new possibilities in the world of teaching. In that respect, this piece contributes to internationalizing teacher education for social justice.

REFERENCES

Abramova, I. (2011). *Russian-speaking immigrant teachers in the United States: Arts-informed inquiry into experiences and beliefs.* Saarbrucken, Germany: VDM Verlag.

Abramova, I. (2012). Through the eyes of immigrant teachers who "tend to go against the grain." *Multicultural Education, 19*(3), 34–37.

Bakhtin, M. M. (1981). *The dialogic imagination: Four essays by M. M. Bakhtin.* (M. Holquest, Trans.). Austin, TX: University of Texas Press.

Bascia, N., & Hargreaves, D. (2000). Teaching and leading on the sharp edge of change. In N. Bascia & D. Hargreaves (Eds.), *The sharp edge of educational change: Teaching, leading and the realities of reform* (pp. 3–26). New York, NY: Routledge.

Beynon, J., Ilieva, R., & Dichupa, M. (2004). Re-credentialing experiences of immigrant teachers: Negotiating institutional structures, professional identities and pedagogy. *Teachers and Teaching: Theory and Practice, 10*(4), 429–444.

Braine, G. (2010). *Nonnative speaker English teachers: Research, pedagogy, and professional growth.* New York, NY: Routledge.

Bronfenbrenner, U. (1970). *Two worlds of childhood: U.S. and U.S.S.R.* New York, NY: Russell Sage.

Camarota, S. A. (2007). Immigrants in the United States, 2007: A profile of America's foreign born population. Washington, DC: Center for Immigration Studies. Retrieved from http://www.cis.org/sites/cis.org/files/articles/2007/back1007.pdf

Capps, R., Passel, J. S., Perez-Lopez, D., & Fix, M. (2003). *The new neighbors: A user's guide to data on immigrants in US communities.* Baltimore, MD: Annie E. Casey Foundation.

Carrison, C. (2007). *Learning from lived experiences: Strength and insights of bilingual immigrant teachers* (Unpublished doctoral dissertation). Washington State University, Pullman, WA.

Clandinin, D. J., & Connelly, F. M. (2000). *Narrative inquiry: Experience and story in qualitative research.* San Francisco, CA: Jossey-Bass.

Cole, A. C., & Knowles, J. G. (2001). *Lives in context: The art of history research.* New York, NY: Rowman & Littlefield.

Conle, C. (1996). Resonance in pre-service teacher inquiry. *American Educational Research Journal, 33*(2), 297–325.

Cruickshank, K. (2004). Towards diversity in teacher education: Teacher preparation of immigrant teachers. *European Journal of Teacher Education, 27*(2), 125–138.

Dmitriyev, A. E. (1985). *A reading book for pedagogical colleges. Xrestomatiya dlya pedagogicheskix uchilish'.* Moskva, Russia: Prosvesheniye.

Duarte, E. M., & Smith, S. (2000). *Foundational perspectives in multiculturalism.* New York, NY: Addison Wesley Longman.

Dunstan, J. (1983). Now they are six: Soviet primary education in transition. In J. J. Tomiak (Ed.), *Soviet education in the 1980s* (pp. 50–84). New York, NY: St. Martin's Press.

Elbaz, F. (2005). *Teachers' voices: Storytelling and possibility.* Greenwich, CT: Information Age Publishing.

Goodson, I. F. (1994, April). *"The story so far": Personal knowledge and the political.* Paper presented at the annual meeting of the American Educational Research Association (AERA), Atlanta, GA.

Hargreaves, A. (1998). The emotional practice of teaching. *Teaching and Teacher Education, 14*(8), 835–854.

He, M. F., & Phillion, J. (2008). *Personal–passionate–participatory inquiry into social justice education.* Charlotte, NC: Information Age Publishing.

Holmes, B., Read, G., & Voskresenskaya, N. (1995). *Russian education: Tradition and transition*. New York, NY: Garland.

hooks, b. (2010). *Teaching critical thinking: Practical wisdom.* New York, NY: Routledge.

Kamhi-Stein, L. D. (Ed.). (2004). *Learning and teaching from experience: Perspectives on nonnative English-speaking professionals*. Ann Arbor, MI: University of Michigan Press.

Kincheloe, J. L., & Steinberg, S. R. (1997). *Changing multiculturalism*. Philadelphia, PA: Open University Press.

Maum, R. (2003). *A comparison of native-and nonnative-English-speaking teachers' beliefs about teaching English as a second language to adult English language learners* (Unpublished doctoral dissertation). University of Louisville, Louisville, KY.

McFadden, C. (2002). *Identifying factors preventing Russian immigrant teachers from filling vacancies in New York City public schools* (Unpublished doctoral dissertation). Capella University, Minneapolis, MN.

McMillan, J. H., & Schumacher, S. (2001). *Research in education: A conceptual introduction* (5th ed.). New York, NY: Longman.

Michael, O. (2006). Multiculturalism in schools: The absorption of immigrant teachers from the former Soviet Union into the educational system in Israel. *Teaching and Teacher Education, 22*, 164–178.

Monzo, L. D., & Rueda, R. S. (2001). *Sociocultural factors in social relationships: Examining Latino teachers' and paraeducators' interactions with Latino students*. (Research Report No. 9). University of California, Santa Cruz: Center for Research on Education, Diversity, and Excellence.

Ng, O. M. (2006). *Narrative beyond teaching: Inquiry into shifting identity, culture and professional practice of five visible minority immigrant teachers in a diverse landscape* (Unpublished doctoral dissertation). University of Toronto, Toronto, ON.

Paley, V. (1989). *White teacher*. Cambridge, MA: Harvard University Press.

Phillion, J. (2003). Obstacles to accessing the teaching profession. *Multicultural Education, 11*(1), 41–45.

Phillion, J., & He, M. F. (2008). Conclusion. In M. F. He & J. Phillion (Eds.), *Personal–passionate–participatory inquiry into social justice education* (pp. 267–273). Charlotte, NC: Information Age Publishing.

Post, B. (2005). What we can learn from Russian schools. *Phi Delta Kappan, 86*(8), 627–629.

Rosen, S. M. (1971). *Education and modernization in the USSR*. Reading, MA: Addison-Wesley.

Savina, E. (2008). The application of the fairy tale in Russia. In C. Coulacoglou (Ed.), *Exploring the child's personality* (pp. 119–138). Springfield, IL: Charles C. Thomas.

Sharma, S., Phillion J., & Malewski, E. (2011). Examining the practice of critical reflection for developing pre-service teachers' multicultural competencies: Findings from a study abroad program in Honduras. *Issues in Teacher Education, 20*(2), 9–22.

Simonsen, S. G. (1996). Raising 'the Russian question': Ethnicity and statehood—Russkie and Rossiya. *Nationalism and Ethnic Politics, 2*(1), 91–110.

Simonsen, S. G. (2005). Between minority rights and civil liberties: Russia's discourse over "nationality" registration and the internal passport. *Nationalities Papers, 33*(2), 211–229.

Sinagatullin, I. M. (2001). In Russia: Multicultural strategies of an elementary school teacher. *Multicultural Perspectives, 3*(4), 26–32.

Walsh, B. (2007). Internationally educated female teachers who have immigrated to Nova Scotia: A research/performance text. *International Journal of Qualitative Methods, 6*(3), 1–28.

ABOUT THE EDITORS

Jubin Rahatzad is a curriculum studies doctoral candidate at Purdue University, and holds an M.A. in political science from Purdue University. Research interests are postglobal topics in education, critical curricular theories, and international teacher education. Teaching experiences include a foundational multicultural education course for preservice teachers, international education courses through a study abroad program in Honduras, and preparatory courses for international student teaching. Professional activities include serving as an assistant director for a study abroad program in Honduras, and as a council member of the Curriculum and Pedagogy Group.

Hannah Dockrill is a doctoral student in curriculum studies at Purdue University and has a Masters of Education in school counseling, also from Purdue University. She teaches undergraduate courses in multicultural education and preservice teacher development. Her research interests include study abroad in teacher education, postcolonial theory, and decolonial pedagogy.

Suniti Sharma is an associate professor in the department of teacher education at Saint Joseph's University, Philadelphia. She teaches literacy across the curriculum, instructional techniques for ELA and Social Studies, and ESL pedagogy. Her research focuses on the education of at-risk youth, ending the school-to-prison pipeline, and preparing multicultural teachers. Her scholarship includes an authored book, *Girls Behind Bars: Reclaiming Education in Transformative Spaces*; a co-edited book, *Internationalizing*

Internationalizing Teaching and Teacher Education for Equity, pages 201–202
Copyright © 2016 by Information Age Publishing
201

Teacher Education: Theory, Research and Practice, and articles published in peer-reviewed educational journals such as *Race, Ethnicity and Education*; *Teachers College Record*; and *Journal of Curriculum Theorizing*.

JoAnn Phillion is professor of curriculum and instruction, Purdue University. She teaches graduate courses in curriculum theory and multicultural education and an undergraduate course in preservice teacher development. Her research interests are in immigrant student education, multicultural education, and teacher education in international contexts. She has directed a teacher education summer immersion study abroad program in Honduras since 2002. She is also involved in teacher education and research in Hong Kong and Chiner professional identities, mainly investigated through qualitative research methodologies.

ABOUT THE CONTRIBUTORS

Inna Abramova worked in St. Petersburg, Russia, for 20 years teaching English to elementary, middle, and high school students. She received a master's degree in literacy and language education and a PhD in curriculum studies from Purdue University, Indiana. Currently, she is a lecturer in the College of Education at Purdue University. She teaches courses in literacy and language and multicultural education and supervises student teachers. Her major research and teaching interests include immigrant education, critical multicultural teacher education, culturally relevant pedagogy, and the education of English language learners. Her work appears in *Multicultural Education* and *Multicultural Perspectives*.

Reiko Akiyama is a PhD candidate in curriculum studies at Purdue University and has taught educational courses and Japanese language as a teaching assistant. As a non-native English-speaking instructor who is also an international student, her teaching experiences at Purdue University influence her research endeavors and give her a unique lens through which she instructs future teachers about working with diverse populations. Her areas of research interest are social justice, multicultural education, and teacher education. Her dissertation topic focuses on the learning experiences in culturally and linguistically diverse educational environments for adolescent Japanese sojourner students in the U.S. Midwest.

Sandro Barros is an assistant professor in the College of Education, Michigan State University. His research interests focus on broad issues connected

Internationalizing Teaching and Teacher Education for Equity, pages 203–207
Copyright © 2016 by Information Age Publishing
All rights of reproduction in any form reserved.

with multilingual development, culture, and language politics in K–16 curricula. His work analyzes the connections between ideologies of language learning and how public debates on languages other than English influence multilingual pedagogy discourse. Barros asks: How do intellectuals and policymakers exercise their institutional power to influence public thought in the name of the common good? How do second language pedagogy discourses reinforce monolingual ideologies and how do they assist us in cultivating linguistic diversity?

Yuwen Deng is a PhD student in curriculum studies at Purdue University. Her research interests include narrative approaches to multicultural education, immigrant student education, teacher education, and bilingual/bicultural education for English language learners. Her current research focuses on the educational experiences of Chinese immigrant students in the United States.

Kadriye El-Atwani has a BS in elementary mathematics education from Middle East Technical University in Turkey and an MS and a PhD in curriculum studies from Purdue University. Her dissertation, *Cultivating Multicultural Education in Islamic Schools in the U.S.: Teachers' Perspectives about Diversity in Islamic Schools,* explored the ways in which Islamic school teachers experience multicultural education as internal diversity of Muslim culture is considered. Kadriye has worked as a mathematics teacher in private and public schools and taught an undergraduate foundational education course. Her research interests broadly include teacher education, multicultural education, and social justice.

Betty C. Eng has been an educator and counselor with the University of California–Davis and California State Universities where she was one of the founders of Ethnic Studies. Working and living in Hong Kong for over 20 years, she taught at the Hong Kong Institute of Education (HKIEd), a teacher education institute, and City University of Hong Kong. The focus of her research and scholarship are narrative inquiry, social justice, multiculturalism, gender, and class. She is currently a research fellow with HKIEd researching a book on women in Hong Kong.

Nastaran Karimi is a PhD student in curriculum studies at Purdue University. She teaches preservice teachers in an exploring teaching course and has also taught a multicultural education course. At Purdue, she has also worked with international students and scholars through the Afghan Junior Faculty Development Program and Benjamin Franklin Transatlantic Fellowship Program. Her research interests include Islamophobia, postcolonial theory, and international education. She focuses on the intersectionalities between gender, religion, and nationality, and how these relate to the lived experiences of international students, particularly Muslim females studying in the United States. Through her research she attempts to address equity issues that diverse populations face in an attempt to create a more socially just environment for all minorities.

Stavroula Kontovourki is a lecturer in literacy and language arts education in the department of education, University of Cyprus. She holds a BEd (Hons) in primary education from the University of Cyprus, an Ed.M. in Curriculum and Teaching, and an EdD with a concentration in literacy education, both from Teachers College Columbia University. Her research interests cover literacy and language arts education, the performance of literate identities in and out of school, multimodality (textual and embodied), the realization of literacy curricula in elementary classrooms, literacy teachers' professional identities, and literacy policy and educational change.

Helen A. Marx is an associate professor in the School of Education at Southern Connecticut State University in New Haven, CT. She coordinates the undergraduate elementary education programs and co-directs the Urban Education Fellows. Marx has worked on a number of initiatives with NAFSA: Association of International Educators on efforts to internationalize teacher education. With Dr. David M. Moss, she has developed the My Cultural Awareness Profile (myCAP), an instructional tool designed to support preservice teaches' intercultural development. Her current research interests are in the areas of urban teacher education, intercultural development, and study abroad program design.

Stavroula Philippou is a lecturer in curriculum and teaching in the department of education, University of Cyprus. Her studies include a BEd (Hons) in primary education (University of Cyprus), an MEd in curriculum studies (University of Sydney), and a PhD in education (University of Cambridge, England). She has worked in a variety of educational contexts and as a consultant for UNESCO and the Council of Europe. Her research draws upon the theoretical, historical, and sociological study of curriculum and teaching, focusing on teacher professionalism and curriculum change, curriculum inquiry and teacher education, genealogies of curriculum studies, European education policy, and social studies education.

Anatoli Rapoport is an associate professor of curriculum and instruction at Purdue University. Before he received his PhD in social studies education, he had worked as a classroom teacher and school administrator. Since 1999 he has actively participated in international programs for educators. Dr. Rapoport is the past chair of Citizenship and Democratic Education

Special Interest Group (CANDE SIG) of the Comparative and International Education Society. His research interests include global and international perspectives in citizenship education, comparative education, and the influence of culture and ideology on education. He is the author of two books: *Fields Unknown* and *Civic Education in Contemporary Global Society* (with A. Borshevsky) and more than 40 book chapters and journal articles.

Eloisa Rodriguez obtained a bachelor's degree in pedagogy from the National University of Honduras and a master's degree and a PhD in curriculum and instruction from Purdue University. Her research focuses on community schooling. She is currently an assistant professor in the department of graduate studies at UNITEC University in Honduras. Since 2003 she has coordinated Purdue University's College of Education's Study Abroad Program in Honduras. Eloisa began her teaching career in 1993 and is also the curriculum and teacher development director of a private K–12 bilingual school in Honduras.

Eleni Theodorou is an assistant professor in social foundations of education at the European University Cyprus where she teaches courses in the social and cultural foundations of education. She earned her doctorate from the University of Virginia with a focus on anthropology of education. Her research interests include sociological and anthropological constructions of childhood, children's identities, multicultural education politics and policy, family involvement, and sociological understandings of teacher professional identities, mainly investigated through qualitative research methodologies.

Sunnie Lee Watson is an assistant professor of learning design and technology in the department of curriculum and instruction at Purdue University. She received her PhD in educational leadership and policy studies (with a focus on comparative and international education studies) and instructional systems technology at Indiana University–Bloomington. Sunnie teaches and conducts scholarly work in the field of information age, learner-centered education. Her areas of research focus on attitude change instruction, information-age educational technology such as MOOCs and PIES, and Critical Systems Theory for qualitative educational research and school change.

Diane P. Watt is a postdoctoral scholar in the Werklund School of Education at the University of Calgary. Her current participatory video project engages the DIY media making and sense of identity of three Somali-Canadian Muslim female YouTubers as a critical digital literacy practice. This research considers the significance of new literacy practices that minority youth are engaged in outside of school as media activism. Diane and her research collaborators are producing a documentary to tell their unique story, bringing seldom heard youth voices to community, youth, and teacher education audiences. Visit the project website at www.muslimfemaleyoutubersspeakback.com

CPSIA information can be obtained
at www.ICGtesting.com
Printed in the USA
BVOW06s0946291016

465903BV00025B/4/P